The Conservative Century

CRITICAL ISSUES IN AMERICAN HISTORY

The Unfinished Struggle: Turning Points in American Labor History, 1877–Present
by Steven Babson
Conceived in Liberty: The Struggle to Define the New Republic, 1789–1793
by Lance Banning
The Evolutionists: American Thinkers Confront Charles Darwin, 1860–1920
by J. David Hoeveler
America's Great War: World War I and the American Experience
by Robert H. Zieger
American Evangelicals: A Contemporary History of a Mainstream Religious Movement
by Barry Hankins
The Conservative Century: From Reaction to Revolution
by Gregory L. Schneider

CRITICAL ISSUES IN WORLD AND INTERNATIONAL HISTORY

The Vikings: Wolves of War
by Martin Arnold
Magic and Superstition in Europe: A Concise History from Antiquity to the Present
by Michael D. Bailey
Peter the Great
by Paul Bushkovitch
A Concise History of Hong Kong
by John M. Carroll
Remaking Italy in the Twentieth Century
by Roy Palmer Domenico
A Concise History of Euthanasia: Life, Death, God, and Medicine
by Ian Dowbiggin
The Idea of Capitalism before the Industrial Revolution
by Richard Grassby
The New Concise History of the Crusades
by Thomas F. Madden
The Great Encounter of China and the West, 1500–1800, Second Edition
by D. E. Mungello
The British Imperial Century, 1815–1914: A World History Perspective
by Timothy H. Parsons
Europe's Reformations, 1450–1650: Doctrine, Politics, and Community, Second Edition
by James D. Tracy
War and Genocide: A Concise History of the Holocaust, Second Edition
by Doris L. Bergen
The Work of France: Labor and Culture in Early Modern Times, 1350–1800
by James R. Farr

The Conservative Century

From Reaction to Revolution

Gregory L. Schneider

ROWMAN & LITTLEFIELD PUBLISHERS, INC.
Lanham • Boulder • New York • Toronto • Plymouth, UK

ROWMAN & LITTLEFIELD PUBLISHERS, INC.

Published in the United States of America
by Rowman & Littlefield Publishers, Inc.
A wholly owned subsidiary of The Rowman & Littlefield Publishing Group, Inc.
4501 Forbes Boulevard, Suite 200, Lanham, Maryland 20706
www.rowmanlittlefield.com

Estover Road
Plymouth PL6 7PY
United Kingdom

British Library Cataloguing in Publication Information Available

Library of Congress Cataloging-in-Publication Data:

Schneider, Gregory L., 1965–
  The conservative century : from reaction to revolution / Gregory L. Schneider.
    p. cm. — (Critical issues in history)
  Includes bibliographical references and index.
  ISBN-13: 978-0-7425-4284-6 (cloth : alk. paper)
  ISBN-10: 0-7425-4284-X (cloth : alk. paper)
  ISBN-13: 978-0-7425-6394-0 (electronic)
  ISBN-10: 0-7425-6394-4 (electronic)

  1. Conservatism—United States—History—20th century. 2. Conservatism—United
States. 3. United States—Politics and government—20th century. 4. United States—
Politics and government—2001– I. Title.
  JC573.2.U6S352 2009
  320.520973—dc22   2008025837

Printed in the United States of America

⊗™ The paper used in this publication meets the minimum requirements of American
National Standard for Information Sciences—Permanence of Paper for Printed Library
Materials, ANSI/NISO Z39.48-1992.

For Petra

Contents

Acknowledgments

Finishing a book is always a joyful experience, and for the author, one which allows expressions of gratitude to those individuals who brought him to the endpoint. My wife Petra, my most valuable colleague, is owed the greatest debt. She has fulfilled every duty given her by marrying an increasingly busy and burdened academic, raising the kids while "Daddy worked." She has been incredibly supportive of my career and our children. I owe her everything and it is to her that I dedicate this book.

My two young children, Bailey and Balin, are developing into remarkable human beings who have a deep and abiding interest in the past. It is my hope that they one day read this book (and many others) and remember how much they helped inspire me to finish it by getting me out of the house every now and then to pull wagons, play jump rope, shoot baskets, and go to plays.

This book started out as a history of the Old Right and morphed into something else completely (as books are wont to do). For assistance, I owe a tremendous debt to the Earhart Foundation, which provided two grants that allowed me extensive time to do the research for this book. I also owe thanks to Emporia State University, which provided a sabbatical leave for one semester during which most of the book was written. I am grateful to the archivists and librarians at the Hoover Institution at Stanford, the Herbert Hoover Presidential Library, the University of Oregon, the Chicago Historical Society, the Library of Congress, Yale University Sterling Library and Beinecke Library, the Hagley Library, and the University of Virginia.

I like to keep things close to the vest when I work on a book but I have benefited from conversations on history, conservatism, and politics with many colleagues, including Don Critchlow, whose own work on conservatism continues to inspire me. George Nash, John Earl Haynes, Dan Harden, John Sacher,

Clay Arnold, Chris Phillips, and the many people with whom it has been a delight to meet and to speak at academic conferences, where much of this work was at one time or another presented, have also been extraordinarily helpful in the completion of this book. I am also grateful to the editors and staff at Rowman and Littlefield for their faith in the project and their assistance in its completion. Two anonymous reviewers for the press helped immensely with their comments on the manuscript.

I would also like to thank George Pearson, Sarah McIntosh, and the trustees and staff of the Flint Hills Center for Public Policy in Kansas, who embody the spirited dedication of those conservatives (they would prefer the word *libertarian*) who work to reform the climate in which Kansans live.

Finally, I owe a special note of thanks to Senator Sam Brownback, a good friend who has helped in this book as well by allowing me to stay at his Washington apartment on numerous occasions while doing research, using his Senate office for downtime (and by chance meeting and having discussions with some interesting people), and taking me to western Kansas to meet the people he represents: good, solid people who are the basis of conservative electoral victories over the past two decades. The lesson he has given me in retail politics has been invaluable in helping me understand how politics really works as opposed to the academic theorizing in which those of us in the ivory tower often engage.

To those whom I have inadvertently left out, my apologies (and thanks).

Introduction

One hears quite frequent claims made by television commentators, radio hosts, presidents, politicians, voters, and even a few bold academics, that their views are conservative. The label is in frequent use and has come to stand for certain ideas and principles in the public sphere, most notably a skepticism, even at times an outright hostility, toward government social policies; a muscular foreign policy combined with a patriotic nationalism; a defense of traditional Christian religious values; and support for the free market economic system. Not all conservatives believe in these goals equally and within the conservative disposition in America there are inherent contradictions between supporters of social order and tradition and supporters of individual freedom. With conservatism as a dominant political force in recent years it is high time to explain the shifting sands upon which American conservatism developed over the last century.

This is a good time to be writing the history of American conservatism. There are a number of recently published narratives focusing on the history of conservatism in the twentieth century and more are soon to be published.[1] In 1994 Columbia University historian Alan Brinkley labeled the history of conservatism "an orphan in historical scholarship."[2] No longer; the history of conservatism in America is a major subfield in the study of twentieth-century American history.

What differentiates this book from others on the market is the focus on conservatism over the course of the twentieth century. The book explores how conservatism developed from a set of ideas focused on individualism and laissez-faire, the maintenance of the cultural traditions of Western society, and a hostility to mass democracy—what one could easily label a reactionary set of ideas—into a revolutionary, democratic political movement capable of winning and holding on to political power. This is a remarkable development and the story of how this happened is the main focus of the book.

The book also examines how conservatives have made this transition over the course of the century. I am particularly interested in examining the threads of what passed for conservatism in the first half of the century and how they changed or were altered in the second half of the century. The focus on factionalism demonstrates that American conservatism possesses a protean character and that self-definition has been an elusive, and fascinating, conservative quest for a century. Combining analysis with synthesis, the book attempts to historicize conservatism in America, examining what passed for conservatism at various stages in the twentieth century.[3] It is not the complete history of the twentieth century; rather it is a history of conservatism's travails in the twentieth century.

Scholars, academics, pundits, and politicians have tried to define conservatism, without much success, for decades. It might be time to move beyond such efforts. That conservatism represents the defense of tradition there can be little doubt. Yet what tradition do conservatives want to defend in America, a nation possessed with no established church, no aristocracy, and no feudal system? In America, as numerous scholars have all recognized, conservatives defended ordered liberty, embodied in the revolutionary era's founding principles. Such principles achieved their greatest exposition with the national Constitution. It is a defense of constitutional order to which most conservatives have subscribed throughout American history.

Conservatives have also sought to preserve the rule of law and the Christian religion. In the twentieth century they have defended Western civilization from the challenges of modernist culture and totalitarian governments. Conservatives have involved themselves throughout the twentieth century in battles over culture. The so-called culture wars, over issues like abortion, are reflections of wider conflicts between defenders of religious order and apostles of liberation. They have been ongoing. While some see the culture wars as a product of the battles between radicals and conservatives since the 1960s, culture wars have been a mainstay of twentieth-century America. Conservatives have been deeply involved in such conflicts from the beginning, sometimes in surprising ways.

Finally, conservatives have sought to uphold the principles of liberty by fighting against the encroachment of state power, supporting the free market economic system, and protecting individual liberties from encroachment by the state. Free market–oriented conservatives, labeling themselves libertarians, have defended the precepts of individual rights and the application of reason to solve social problems. They were opposed equally to liberals, who favored state planning, as well as to traditional conservatives who believed in religious authority, a threat, libertarians believed, to individual liberty. Obviously, none of the above strands represent any consistent ideological creed. My contention that conservatism possesses a protean character allows for a place at the proverbial table for all conservatives who come close to fitting the label. The protean character is necessarily latitudinarian and it will unduly alarm those individuals who believe they are the true heirs of American conservatism. Conservatives could well adapt the title of historian Carl Becker's 1931 address before the American Historical Association, "Everyman His Own Historian," changing it to "Everyman His Own Conservative." The tremendous variety within conservative thought and politics explains why conservatism has stayed alive over the course of a century so ruinous to many other political ideologies and beliefs. Conservatives have had the capacity to change.

I contend that the twentieth century could easily be labeled the conservative century. Within this century the ideologies of communism and fascism were vanquished by American military power, the mobilization of the capitalist economy, and especially, ideas. Modern liberalism developed as a political creed, but then declined, seemingly exhausted by its failure to adjust to new realities in American politics. Only conservatism, which late in this short century became a political movement, has survived. It was the dominant political idea in America at the end of the century. Such a development is, to put it mildly, the most unlikely of outcomes.

How could this be the case? How could ideas allegedly resistant to progress, hostile to the increase of governmental power, defensive of tradition and supportive of free market capitalism, have survived a tumultuous century when ideologies so better disposed to being the vanguard of progress, from fascism to communism to liberalism, all collapsed around it? How could such an affectation wind up being one of the true survivors of the twentieth-century war of ideas, and indeed, come to stand for policies and prescriptions so revolutionary in their consequences? It is toward an explanation of such developments that this book now turns.

NOTES

1. See George H. Nash, *The Conservative Intellectual Movement in America: Since 1945*, 3rd ed. (Wilmington, Del.: Intercollegiate Studies Institute, 2006); Donald T. Critchlow, *The Conservative Ascendancy: How the GOP Right Made Political History* (Cambridge, Mass.: Harvard University Press, 2007); Alfred S. Regnery, *Upstream: The Ascendance of American Conservatism* (New York: Threshold, 2008); Gregory L. Schneider, ed., *Conservatism in America since 1930: A Reader* (New

York: New York University Press, 2003); and Paul Gottfried, *Conservatism in America: Making Sense of the American Right* (New York: Palgrave Macmillan, 2007). There are many histories of specific organizations, issues, biographies, and other interesting work focused on conservatism, which are highlighted in the notes and bibliography.

2. Alan Brinkley, "The Problem of American Conservatism," *American Historical Review* 99, no. 2 (April 1994): 409–29.

3. For an earlier (and controversial) attempt to explain the prevalence of Hegelian historicist thinking on the Right, see Paul Edward Gottfried, *The Search for Historical Meaning: Hegel and the Postwar American Right* (DeKalb: Northern Illinois University Press, 1986).

Chapter One

The Nemesis of Democracy

Fighting a whole generation is not exactly a happy task.

—Irving Babbitt

Garet Garrett is not a name well remembered, if at all, in the pantheon of American journalism. Born in 1878 in Illinois, Garrett's family migrated westward to Iowa and the young man grew up on a farm experiencing the difficulties of agricultural life during the tumultuous depression of the 1890s. At age twenty Garrett left for points east, working as a printer's apprentice in Chicago and Cleveland before securing work as a financial reporter for a variety of eastern newspapers, among them the *New York Post*, the *New York Times*, *The Wall Street Journal*, and *The Evening Post*. He published books and novels and his writing appeared in popular magazines and newspapers throughout the 1920s. He was an advocate of laissez-faire, believing strongly in the idea of individualism long propagated as the American ideal. "There is no evidence that men want to be equal," Garrett wrote in one of his books. "Here, if a man says the state owes him liberty, protection, and equality of opportunity that is already acknowledged. These are political beliefs. But if he says the state owes him a living, he is ridiculed."[1]

Given these sentiments it was not surprising that Garrett was an opponent of Franklin Roosevelt's New Deal, which drew his harshest criticism throughout the 1930s. Employed by the popular weekly *The Saturday Evening Post*, Garrett wrote extensively on how government was taking over the direction of the economy. He feared inflation and a dependent class of individuals living on what government provided. When Social Security passed Congress in 1935, Garrett wrote, "No government can provide social security. It is not in the nature of government to be able to provide anything. Government itself is

1

not self-supporting. It lives by taxation. Therefore, since it cannot provide anything for itself but by taking toll of what other people produce, how can it provide social security for the people?" In *The Revolution Was*, a pamphlet published in 1938, Garrett depicted the true nature of the New Deal: "with the coming of the New Deal the ultimate power of initiative did pass from the hands of private enterprise to government. There it is and there it will remain until, if ever, it shall be reconquered. Certainly government will never surrender it without a struggle."[2]

Garrett argued that the New Deal was revolutionary, brought about not through violence or bloodshed but rather by intellectuals who employed symbolic language to attack capitalism, free enterprise, and the Constitution. "Capitalism was the one enemy, the one object to be hated," Garrett wrote. "But never was it directly attacked or named; always it was the *old order* that was named." Garrett examined Roosevelt's rhetoric and his use of language to undermine the Constitutional basis of government and the free enterprise system. "Like the hagfish, the New Deal entered the old form and devoured its meaning from within." "A government that had been supported by the people and so controlled by the people became one that supported the people and so controlled them."[3] "Where was the New Deal going?" Garrett wondered. "The answer to that question is too obvious to be debated. Every choice it made, whether it was one that moved recovery or not, was a choice unerringly true to the design of totalitarian government."

Describing the New Deal as totalitarian and revolutionary became a staple criticism for a group of individuals collectively labeled the Old Right. Garrett was one of many journalists and writers who referred to Roosevelt and the New Deal in less than favorable terms; one, Albert Jay Nock, actually spoke of Roosevelt's staggering electoral victory in 1932, in which he won 58 percent of the popular vote, as a "coup d'etat."[4] To make such claims about the New Deal in the depths of the Depression fell on deaf ears with most Americans. Roosevelt's revolution was political, leading to the creation of an administrative state and a programmatic liberalism which bound a variety of constituent groups to the Democratic Party until the late 1960s. It was spawned from the crisis of economic collapse and lacked any overarching ideological framework. It had the support of the American people in a desperate time.

The Old Right lacked the institutions necessary to confront the New Deal political revolution. While there were plenty of newspapers and magazines willing to publish their opinions, they did not control a political party—the Republican Party was not a vehicle for them as it would be for conservatives later. Old Rightists lacked the popular touch and were willing to castigate "the people" as willing dupes of Roosevelt and other Left-wing influences in America such as labor union leaders and the communist party. Mass democracy particularly alarmed conservatives; combined with the development of a managerial state, they increasingly interpreted the historical situation as a revolutionary one, in which the old Republic and constitutional government would be undermined.[5] The Old Rightists never were effective in addressing the central tendencies of liberalism and remained, as historian George H. Nash described them, "scattered voices of protest, profoundly pessimistic about the future of the country."[6]

Yet it was out of these scattered voices of protest that modern American conservatism was born. Historians have been too quick to dismiss the early twentieth-century "conservatives"—no one really defined themselves as such in any meaningful or consistent way—as an aberration, as a collection of eccentrics without much to tell us about contemporary conservative concerns.[7] Conservatism developed instead, according to most chronicles of the conservative movement, from the concerns of intellectuals, politicians, and grassroots activists in the 1950s and 1960s.[8] Few histories have looked at the continuities and discontinuities within conservatism over the course of the twentieth century. Before conservatives could organize effectively and achieve political power, they would have to abandon certain roads in order to find their chosen path. For the first half of the twentieth century they would do just that.

LAISSEZ-FAIRE CONSERVATISM[9]

"The new world which dawned after Appomattox," historian Robert McCloskey wrote, "ushered in not only a radical alteration in the economic and social structure of American life, but a fundamental revision of the democratic tradition. Post-bellum political thought was distinguished by two salient and related characteristics—its materialist premises and its conservative conclusions."[10] The dominant creed of conservatives in the late nineteenth century was laissez-faire. Believers in laissez-faire sought to uphold the primacy of the individual property holder against the power of the state. But the doctrine, as English writer Herbert Spencer argued, went well beyond simply being a justification for private property. Laissez-faire was "not simply a politico-economical principle" but also "a principle of letting all citizens take the benefits and evils of their own acts; not only such as are consequent on their industrial conduct, but such are consequent on their conduct in general."[11]

Private property, individualism, the primacy of commerce and hostility toward state power—this became the basis for the dominant ethos of late nineteenth-century capitalists. Layered on top of laissez-faire was the doctrine of social Darwinism. Created by Spencer in England it was imported to the United States and defended here by prominent intellectuals and businessmen, foremost among them Yale University professor William Graham Sumner. A former minister, Sumner advocated natural distinctions between the fit and unfit, "fitness [being] defined in terms of material success." "Let it be understood," Sumner wrote, "that we cannot go outside of this alternative: liberty, inequality, survival of the fittest; not—liberty, equality, survival of the unfittest. The former carries society forward and favors all its best members; the latter carries society downwards and favors all its worst members."[12]

This was a harsh code but it was one adhered to among the capitalists who believed it justified their immense fortunes. When efforts were made to reform society Sumner strongly objected. In one of his most famous essays, "The Forgotten Man," Sumner argued about how reform always produced an unintended victim and that, therefore, reform was harmful. "As soon as A observes something which seems to him to be wrong, from which X is suffering, A talks it over with B, and then A and B propose to get a law passed to remedy the evil to help X. Their law always proposes to determine . . . what A, B, and C shall do for X." But C is never asked his opinion even though he winds up paying the way to help X. C is the forgotten man, Sumner claimed. "He works, he votes, generally he prays—but he always pays—yes, above all, he pays." What was responsible for this trend? Sumner blamed the rise of mass democracy: "no fallacies in politics are more pernicious than those which transfer to a popular majority all the old claims of the king by divine right. The legislative machinery can be set in motion too readily and too frequently; it is too easy for the irresponsible hands of the ignorant to seize the machinery."[13]

Social Darwinists instead looked to the judicial branch as the true preserve of constitutional authority. Not only was the judiciary immune from the emotionalism and irresponsibility of mass democracy but it was a privileged elite; Alexis de Tocqueville once remarked that legal training tended to leave lawyers and judges "eminently conservative and anti-democratic." This may have been a bit of an overstatement by the French aristocrat but there is little doubt that the courts reflected the values of the elites in Gilded Age America. Through the use of "substantive due process," an interpretation of the Fourteenth Amendment which gave judges the power to restrict or expand on the substance of legislation, the Court routinely used its power to uphold business rights. Supreme Court Justice Stephen Field read the Declaration of Independence into the Constitution in many of his opinions in a manner which allowed the natural rights philosophy asserted in that document to become a basis for the defense of individual rights, private property, and entrepreneurialism.[14]

Advocates of both laissez-faire and social Darwinism stressed a particular doctrine of progress. For them progress came from the natural laws of the marketplace shepherded by elites. It was this belief in progress which dominated the age. Authors like Horatio Alger in his many stories of down-and-out young boys struggling to make it in American life, clinging to Victorian habits of propriety, hard work, and religious belief in the face of tremendous odds, helped enshrine this particular idea of progress on a whole generation who believed that they too could rise and become wealthy in America. "Failure to advance," wrote Christopher Lasch, "according to the mythology of opportunity, argues moral incapacity on the part of individuals." Similar sentiments had been expressed by Standard Oil founder John D. Rockefeller: "failures which a man makes in his life are due almost always to some defect in his personality, some weakness of body, or mind, or character, will, or temperament." Immorality, weakness, deficiencies in body and mind—this made the individualist ethos so attractive to many intellectuals and yet so difficult to sustain in an era when the social forces of industrialization helped undermine the individualism necessary to long sustain the social Darwinist doctrine.[15]

The populists were the first to sound the tocsin against the laissez-faire idea. A collection of Midwestern and Southern farmers, the Populist Party demanded a more democratic political system and economic reforms that would strengthen the regulatory power of government to protect "the people's interests." Farmers particularly complained about rising indebtedness to eastern banks and high shipping prices charged by railroads. The populists believed men were victimized by social forces, by a sinister conspiracy of capital. The depression of the 1890s galvanized their call for reform. Instead of reform, the populists fell prey to conspiracies linking foreign banks with the low prices for commodities at the root of their discontent. The solution to this economic problem became the "free coinage of silver." In 1896 they embraced the Democrat presidential candidate William Jennings Bryan, who stumped across the nation speaking out in favor of free silver, a panacea that would bring recovery and restore the prominence of democracy in American life. The better organized and pro-gold standard GOP won the argument in the election and William McKinley won the presidency ushering in not an era of easy money based on silver, but stable money based on gold.[16]

The progressive movement followed on the heels of populism. Middle class, professional, and urban, some progressives emphasized Christian moral exhortations concerning the duty to care for others, dubbed the Social Gospel, while others practiced the new disciplines of social science advocating reforms based on the use of rationalism and science to solve the complex problems facing society. This often made for a combustible mix with religious reformers insisting on social and moral reforms, such as Prohibition of alcohol, and social scientists advocating economic and political goals.

What all the progressives shared in common was their belief that the state had a role to play in refereeing unregulated capitalism. Republicans were the first to respond, with Midwesterners like Wisconsin Governor Robert LaFollette using expertise from the university to advance reforms in the state. Progressive reformers altered institutions, attacked social conventions, and changed laws in a manner heretofore unachieved in American history. Reformers regulated and brought under control vital areas of economic, social, and political life in America, ensuring that the provinces of health, environment, labor, democracy, and education were no longer left to the whims of the capitalists.

There were fewer individuals by that time who continued to espouse unabashedly the doctrine of laissez-faire and who resisted the trend toward a welfare state. Sterling Morton of Nebraska, a gold Democrat and former Agriculture Secretary during the second presidential administration of Grover Cleveland, dedicated himself to defending laissez-faire in the remaining years of his life. Morton founded the *Conservative*, a weekly published from 1899 until his death in 1902. He wished the magazine to be "useful as a truth-teller, and influential as a militant exponent of everything . . . which the experience of one hundred and twenty-two years of national independence has proved to be worth conserving." The *Conservative* was dedicated to the principles of laissez-faire and of Jeffersonian individualism. His defense of small-town and rural America was distinctly at odds with that of the populists and especially of Bryan, whose monetary views Morton labeled "Bryanarchy."[17]

With the exception of the *Conservative* there was no other concerted effort to defend laissez-faire. The political parties had been converted to the progressive cause; after McKinley's assassination in 1901, Theodore Roosevelt helped in the creation of the modern presidency by expanding the role of executive power and establishing an administrative state conducive to the goals of reformers. He was constrained in going further during his presidency by the powerful influence of pro-business conservative legislators in Congress. After Roosevelt left office in 1909 he became more vocal in his calls for reform and joined the progressive "insurgency" within the GOP seeking to wrest power from the hands of businessmen. He broke with his handpicked successor William Howard Taft and challenged him for the GOP nomination in 1912 on a platform called the New Nationalism.

Roosevelt's New Nationalism borrowed heavily from *The New Republic* founder Herbert Croly's book *The Promise of American Life* (1909). Roosevelt sought "to use government as an efficient agency for the practical betterment of social and economic conditions throughout the land." During the first decade of the twentieth century the concentration of power in the hands of ever larger corporations, exemplified by the creation of U.S. Steel in 1901, had made laissez-faire no longer a practical possibility. He had experimented with antitrust during his presidency but this was cumbersome and ineffective. "The way out lies," Roosevelt urged, "not in attempting to prevent such combinations, but in completely controlling them in the interest of the public welfare."[18] Who would control corporations and how that power would be exercised were interesting possibilities Roosevelt never got to test. He lost the election to Democrat Woodrow Wilson.

The biggest problem for laissez-faire conservatives during Wilson's presidency was not the domestic programs he had enacted—those continued the drift toward an administrative state begun by Roosevelt. The drumbeat for war which began when World War I broke out in Europe in 1914 proved more troublesome and contributed to a growing split among conservatives. Laissez-faire conservatives had long opposed imperialism and the quest for empire in the late nineteenth century. Sumner had opposed expansion believing "our system is unfit for the government of subject provinces."[19] He had also opposed the Spanish-American War along with businessmen, including steel magnate Andrew Carnegie. Both men participated in the Anti-Imperialist League which lobbied for the independence of the Philippines taken from Spain in that war; Carnegie even offered to pay for their freedom.[20]

Most progressives endorsed expansion. Roosevelt was an ardent imperialist and when war broke out in Europe, he urged America to enter the conflict on the side of Great Britain. Wilson invoked neutrality in the conflict. Roosevelt and others advocated preparedness and this issue became an important one, especially in the 1916 election year. Wilson's aides sold him as the peace candidate that year on a slogan which was interesting for its use of the past tense—"He Kept Us Out of War." The GOP ran Charles Evans Hughes, who emphasized the connections between Britain and the United States and preparedness to assist the Allied cause. Wilson prevailed, narrowly winning reelection. Events proved the tenuous nature of his promise to keep the United States out of war. Germany resumed submarine warfare in February 1917; that same month the United States received an intercepted telegram from the German foreign minister asking Mexico to attack the U.S. with the promise of regaining lost territories. Finally, in March 1917 the Russian tsar abdicated and a provisional government took power. Wilson now could enter the war fighting against autocracy and extremism—he took the plunge, declaring war on Germany and arguing that the war would "make the world safe for democracy."[21]

Wilson mobilized the economy to produce war material. He also backed policies designed to gain support for the war effort from a heterogeneous ethnic population. This involved the denial of freedoms granted in the Bill of Rights. The Sedition Act forbade the publication and dissemination of material deemed harmful to the war effort. Extended beyond its purview it even made criticism of Wilson's policies seditious—Socialist leader Eugene V. Debs was arrested and convicted of sedition when he criticized the president's war policies. The Espionage Act allowed officials in the Justice Department and the Post Office Department the power to eradicate dissent. Hundreds of magazines and newspapers were shut down owing to their political perspectives and beliefs. Wilson also sponsored the creation of a wartime propaganda board, the Committee on Public Information, headed by progressive advertising man George Creel. Creel wished to create what he called a "war will . . . a passionate belief in the justice of America's cause that would meld the people of the United States into one white hot mass instinct with fraternity, devotion, courage and deathless determination."[22]

The war split progressives. Many supported the war effort hoping to use the conflict to promote a "laboratory of reform" at home. They also supported Wilson's desire—expressed best in his January 1919 Fourteen Points speech—to spread democracy and to support free trade, national self-determination, an end to empire, and collective security through international organization. Many more radical progressives saw Wilson's war policies in problematic terms. Antiwar critic Randolph Bourne summarized his views about Wilson's wartime leadership when he wrote, "war is the health of the state."

Less noticed by historians has been the impact war had on conservatism. Before the war conservative nationalists and patriots had been emphasizing America's close connections with Great Britain and had urged Wilson to go to war. Organizations such as the National Security League and other patriotic groups, many of them composed of northeastern pro-business Republicans, had been emphasizing the idea of "100% Americanism," a slogan George Creel readily employed to sell the war to Americans. Men such as Roosevelt, retired Army General Leonard Wood, and others looked suspiciously on dissenters, the ethnic population, and immigrants. The Bolshevik Revolution in Russia in November 1917 solidified this view and made nationalist conservatives hostile to further immigration. Immigrants might bring with them not only strange religions, cultures, and languages, but revolutionary doctrines as well.[23]

Few laissez-faire conservatives remained to challenge the statism of the progressives and the conservative nationalism of 100% Americanism. While the laissez-faire intellectual movement briefly rebounded with the founding of the journal *The Freeman,* published from 1920 to 1924 and edited by Albert Jay Nock, most conservatives supported the postwar Red Scare and fought efforts to limit immigration and support investigations into Bolshevik influence in America.[24]

As one of the founders of *The Freeman*, Nock himself imbibed the radical spirit he propagated at the journal—what could best be called "radical individualism"—throughout his life. Born in 1876 in Scranton, Pennsylvania, Nock became an adept baseball player, turning down professional offers to play in order to attend St. Stephen's College. He was an Episcopal minister, had married with two sons, but left his family in pursuit of a career as a journalist. He had been a backer of progressive reform, especially the local urban scale reforms of Cleveland Mayor Tom Johnson. He had written for several publications including the *American* magazine and *The Nation*. But he was never comfortable with the reformist drive to remake the world and also dubious and hostile to the idea of using state power to coerce individuals to do anything. As he wrote, "God's interest is in the individual and he puts the individual up above every socialist creed or dogma in the world."[25]

The Freeman gave him a platform in which to articulate his growing indebtedness to the Jeffersonian-individualist philosophy he espoused throughout the 1920s. His five-part series "The State," running in 1924, became the basis for his later book critical of the New Deal, *Our Enemy, the State* (1935). In the essays Nock distinguished between social power and state power, focusing on how the former preserved liberty since it was employed with the consent of the individual; the latter accumulated power only through force and at the expense of society.

Nock borrowed heavily in his articles on state power from the work of Austrian economist Fritz Oppenheimer, whose 1913 book *The State* informed much of his distinction between social and state power. The Austrian school of economics was growing in importance in America during the 1920s and *The Freeman*'s editors were aware of works by that school of thought. Ludwig Van Mises would become a prominent advocate in America of the Austrian approach, taking a teaching position at New York University during World War II. His 1927 book *Liberalism* described the view of classical liberalism put forth by that school of thought. *The Freeman* popularized such academic work. Yet in spite of a decent circulation, the journal lost money and it ended publication in 1924. Managing editor Suzanne LaFollette would resume publication briefly in 1930 before giving up the fight. While a short-lived publication, it had an immense influence on the reawakening of laissez-faire conservatism, which would have to wait until after World War II to experience a true revival.[26]

CULTURAL CONSERVATISM

In 1895 French sociologist and psychologist Gustav Le Bon, a principal figure in the development of the field of crowd psychology, wrote: "the memorable events of history are the visible effects of the invisible changes of human thought. . . . The present epoch is one of those critical moments in which the thought of mankind is undergoing a process of transformation." "The ideas of the past," he continued, "although half-destroyed, being still very powerful, and the ideas which are to replace them being still in the process of formation, [our] age represents a period of transition and anarchy."[27] Le Bon explained presciently the cultural changes right around the corner in Western society: the modern period ushered in new conceptions of form, time, and even space. Modernism in art, literature, music, drama, psychology, and physics represented "the lure of heresy" as moderns attempted to shatter social conventions.[28]

Modernity threatened the old genteel tradition and made defenders of Western civilization profoundly pessimistic about preserving what Matthew Arnold had labeled "the knowledge of the best that has been thought and said in the world." Henry Adams was one intellectual who captured this best. In *The Education of Henry Adams* (1918), Adams wrote about the modern age and its transformative effect, about how the worship of materialism and democracy had undermined the best virtues of America's founding. "The progress of evolution from President Washington to President Grant was alone enough to upset Darwin," he wrote, including his grandfather and great-grandfather on the descending scale. Adams looked with awe at the products of machine civilization and the immense physical power of the "Dynamo" but wondered about its spiritual effect. Conservative author Russell Kirk captured this quite well when he wrote, "for centuries society has frenziedly sought centralization and cheapness and incalculable physical power; now all these things are near to attainment; and they mean the end of civilized life. Once man turned from the ideal of spiritual power, the Virgin, to the ideal of physical power, the Dynamo, his doom was sure."[29]

Henry's brother Brooks Adams also insisted that America was in decline away from the founding generation. He believed that the powerful businessmen were not suitable replacements for the men who had gone before. They were not a new aristocracy as some had called them; rather, Adams wrote, "the modern capitalist looks upon life as a financial combat of a very specialized kind. . . . He is not responsible for he is not a trustee for the public. . . . He is, in essence, a revolutionist without being aware of it."[30]

Many cultural conservatives picked up on this theme. "A few more Harrimans and we are undone," wrote Irving Babbitt, a professor of French and comparative languages at Harvard University, about the chairman of the Union Pacific Railroad. Babbitt was a distinguished professor and one of the more important cultural conservatives in early twentieth-century America. He was born in 1865 in Dayton, Ohio, had studied Sanskrit and Eastern languages at Harvard, and in 1893 joined the faculty there, where he stayed until his death in 1933. Along with his former classmate and Princeton University professor Paul Elmer More, Babbitt founded the new humanism, a critical literary movement that emphasized the search for standards in literature. New humanists were to be an antidote to "literary avant-gardists, naturalistic psychologists, uncritical traditionalists, liberals, collectivists, progressivists and pragmatists." Put more succinctly, "the new humanism sprang from a profound dissatisfaction with the modern age."[31]

The new humanists believed that "it was necessary to create standards" in literature and that the best place to search for such standards was in the ancient world. Eighteenth-century French *philosophe* Jean-Jacques Rousseau drew criticism from the new humanists. Babbitt labeled Rousseau "the first among the theorists of radical democracy" and "most eminent of those who attacked civilization." Rousseau was guilty of elevating mass man to the highest point of civilization when instead, according to Babbitt, this humanitarianism led to barbarism not liberation.[32]

What the new humanists postulated instead was a way to control man's appetites, to allow individuals to develop an "inner check" on impulse and behavior. "The humanist," Babbitt wrote, "as opposed to the humanitarian, is interested in the perfecting of the individual rather than in the schemes for the elevation of mankind as a whole; and although he allows largely for sympathy, he insists that it be tempered by judgment." The inner check was the necessary instrument to allow the intelligent self-control crucial for the individual human person. Babbitt and More were not pushing a Christian morality; the problem, as Social Gospel advocates showed, was that Christianity all too often succumbed to a Rousseau-like humanitarianism as well. For both Babbitt and More, Eastern religions and philosophies such as Buddhism and Confucianism came closest to the idea of the inner check necessary for human development.[33]

Babbitt's most widely noticed work, *Democracy and Leadership* (1924), was a study of how leadership had declined in the modern age. Babbitt argued that democracy, no less than literature, had been impacted by the decline of standards. "The basis upon which the whole structure of the new ethics has been reared is, as we have seen, the assumption that the significant struggle between good and evil is not in the individual but in society." National leaders reflected this view, damaging the basis for democratic government and substituting in its place a fuzzy humanitarianism. "Let one consider again Mr. Woodrow Wilson," Babbitt wrote, "who more than any other recent American, sought to extend our idealism beyond our national frontiers. In pursuit of his scheme for world service, he was led to make light of constitutional checks on his authority and to reach out automatically for unlimited power."[34]

Ralph Adams Cram was another critic of mass democracy writing on the subject in the post–World War I era. An architect and designer of Gothic cathedrals, churches, libraries, and universities—the campus of West Point is entirely a Cram design—Cram viewed himself as a reactionary proudly defending the Middle Ages as the high point of civilized life. He was born in 1862 in New England into a Unitarian religious environment. On a trip to Europe as a twenty-six-year-old he became enamored of the Gothic architecture, classical art, and statuary he saw everywhere displayed. He also became quite fond of the music of German Romantic composer Richard Wagner, after attending the Wagner festival in Bayreuth. Upon his return to America he converted to Episcopalianism and dedicated his career in architecture to the Gothic revival.[35]

Cram turned toward social criticism, writing several books and dozens of articles focusing on the problem of mass democracy and the modern era. In *The Nemesis of Mediocrity* (1918), Cram wrote, "the soul of man demands leadership and in spite of academic aphorisms about equality, a dim consciousness survives of the fundamental truth that without strong leadership democracy is a menace; without strong leadership, culture and civilization will pass away." A few years earlier than Babbitt, Cram had diagnosed the same problem with leadership. "It is perhaps not so much that men now reject all leadership as it is that they blindly accept the inferior type; the specious demagogue, the unscrupulous mastery of effrontery."[36] What was responsible for this development? Cram pointed to the Bolshevik Revolution in Russia as the prime cause. Many other conservatives agreed.

Cram saw nothing to love about mass democracy. "Democracy has achieved its perfect work and has now reduced mankind to a dead level of incapacity where great leaders are no longer either wanted or brought into existence, while society itself is unable, of its own power as a whole, to lift itself from the nadir of its own uniformity." Cram never accepted the tenets of either the populists or the progressives when it came to empowering the people and defending the people's interests. He was equally indignant at the leaders of Western democracies in the early century, writing, "in the year before the war the government of the great democracies . . . was profoundly cursed by the incubus of little men in great office, by chaotic, selfish and unintelligent legislation, dull, stupid and frequently venal administration and by partial, unscrupulous and pettifogging judicial procedure." Only in the Middle Ages, Cram concluded, did "the ideal of democracy [reach] its highest point."[37]

Cram's eccentricities made him attractive to many journals on the Right. Cram often was published in *The American Mercury*, including the acerbic "Why We Do Not Behave like Human Beings" in 1932. Cram rejected Darwinian evolution as a basis for development and as a way of understanding human development. Instead he argued that most people "do not fall within the classification as we have determined it for ourselves, since we do not measure up to the standard." If most people were not even capable of being labeled human, then what were they? "Millennium after millennium this endless flood of basic raw material sweeps on. It is the everlasting Neolithic man. . . . It is the matrix of the human being, the stuff of which he is made." Cram pointed out the fallacy of progressive efforts to raise human standards to a higher level. All of the reforms they advanced, "free and compulsory education, democratic government and universal suffrage, and the unlimited opportunities of industrial civilization have clothed [man] with the deceptive garments of equality, but underneath he is forever the same."

Nothing could prevent this, Cram argued. Political and social democracy, "with their plausible devices and panaceas; popular sovereignty, the Protestant religion of the masses; the technological triumphs that were to emancipate labor and redeem the world; all the multiple manifestations of a free and democratic society fail of their predicted issue. . . . I suggest that the cause of comprehensive failure and the bar to recovery is the persistence of the everlasting Neolithic Man and his assumption of universal control."[38] Such a diagnosis left little hope for ever reaching the mass man; Cram ultimately decided that only a small remnant could preserve Western civilization from destruction and decay.

Cram was sui generis, remembered better for his architecture than for his social commentary. Few conservatives went so far as Cram to deny the humanity of the masses. Yet one celebrity journalist came awfully close in his satirical descriptions of democracy. That person was Henry Louis Mencken. Born in Baltimore in 1880, in the German milieu of Union Square, where he lived the remainder of his life, Mencken became one of the most famous journalists of the twentieth century, writing for Baltimore newspapers and coming to fame as a columnist for the *Baltimore Sun*. He was an avid collector of American language and traced its roots and origins and wrote many books on the subject. He came to some literary fame as well, helping found and edit prominent journals like *The Smart Set* and *The American Mercury*.

It was this latter journal where his celebrity really took off. Mencken is impossible to classify as conservative, liberal, or laissez-faire; he has best been described as "a lifelong skeptic, constitutionally unable to believe in anything absolutely."[39] *The American Mercury* would give him the purpose "to explore this great complex of inspirations, to isolate the individual prophets from the herd and to examine their proposals, to follow the ponderous revolutions of the mass mind—in brief, to attempt a realistic presentation of the whole gaudy, gorgeous American scene."[40]

His most famous description of that gaudy and gorgeous scene came in his coverage of the famous Scopes Monkey Trial in Dayton, Tennessee, during the summer of 1925. John Scopes was arrested for violating a Tennessee law prohibiting the teaching of evolution in public schools. A group of Dayton boosters who were looking to gain publicity for their town used the opportunity provided by Scopes's arrest to secure the newly established American Civil Liberties Union (ACLU) to defend the teacher in court. Renowned trial lawyer and admitted atheist Clarence Darrow agreed to act as the defense; better still for the town, William Jennings Bryan, who had spent the previous decade writing editorials for a syndicated column attacking Darwinian evolution, agreed to act as the prosecution. It was a classic show trial and there was little doubt at all, given the evangelical fervor surrounding the town of Dayton, that Scopes would be convicted.[41]

Mencken spent about a week in Dayton writing dispatches before the trial on the town and the evangelical religious culture everywhere on display. In "The Hills of Zion," Mencken described a tent meeting and the itinerant preacher he witnessed: "words spurted from his lips like bullets from a machine gun—appeals to God to pull the penitent back out of Hell. . . . Suddenly he rose to his feet, threw back his head and began to speak in tongues—blub-blub-blub, gurgle-gurgle-gurgle. His voice rose to a higher register. The climax was a shrill, inarticulate squawk, like that of a man throttled. He fell headlong across the pyramid of supplicants." He routinely labeled the people of Dayton in his dispatches as "half-wits," "yokels," and "hillbillies." He described the religious pageantry on display as "the political and theological pathology of the Bible country."[42]

Mencken left Dayton before the trial had ended. The verdict was preordained—Scopes was guilty. Two days after the trial ended Bryan died in the small burg. Mencken wrote one of the most caustic obituaries in American journalism: "It was hard to believe, watching him at Dayton, that he had traveled, that he had been received in civilized societies, that he had been a high officer of state. He seemed only a poor clod, like those around him, deluded by a childish theology, full of an almost pathological hatred of all learning, all human dignity, all beauty, all fine and noble things. . . . What animated him from end to end of his grotesque career was simply ambition—the ambition of a common man to get his hand upon the collar of his superiors, or failing that, to get his thumb into their eyes."[43]

Mencken wrote a critical exposé of democracy after the Scopes Trial, in part his attempt to do what Babbitt had done before him—explain why mass democracy elevated the worst in society at the expense of the best. Published in 1926 as *Notes on Democracy* it proved to be an entertaining examination consistent with Mencken's desire to expose the gaudy and glorious in American life. "I enjoy democracy immensely," Mencken wrote. "It is comparably idiotic, and hence incomparably amusing. Does it exalt dunderheads, cowards, trimmers, frauds, cads? Then the pain of seeing them go up is balanced and obliterated by the joy of seeing them come down." Mencken discussed a Southern congressman who "until he got to Washington . . . never met a single intelligent human being." This particular congressman was, in Mencken's estimation, "a knavish and preposterous nonentity, half-way between a kleagle of the Ku Klux Klan and a grand worthy bow-wow of the Knights of Zoroaster. It is such vermin who make the laws of the United States."[44] Mencken offered nothing more than his typical bromides against mass man. "It is a crime for any man to hold himself out as better than other men and, above all, a most heinous offense for him to prove it."

By the end of the 1920s hostility to mass democracy was a key part of the makeup of what constituted intellectual conservatism in America. The onset of the Great Depression in the 1930s would intensify this hostility even more. The rise of fascism in Italy and of National Socialism in Germany—combined with the dangers conservatives saw from the spread of communism—convinced conservatives at home and abroad of the disastrous consequences of the rise of mass man to power. Spanish political philosopher Jose Ortega y Gasset captured this best in his book *The Revolt of the Masses* (1930). "The characteristic of the hour," Ortega wrote, "is that the commonplace mind, knowing itself to be commonplace, has the assurance to proclaim the rights of the commonplace and to impose them wherever it will." This left Europe devoid of a moral code and an aristocracy willing to define it when Bolshevism threatened its societies, providing an easy mechanism for the rise of fascist dictatorships to substitute for the natural aristocrats in order to preserve order and security and to act in the name of the people.[45]

During the Depression years conservatives would have to combat the rise of the masses to power. The question of economic recovery from depression was tied into the social and cultural questions concerning how to organize society and who should rule in such a society. During the 1930s the masses were on the side of the further extension of state power—many conservatives feared this would lead to an American fascism—and fought the New Deal for bringing it about. How conservatives could preserve their view of elite power during an age when the state empowered the "people" like never before proved to be a difficult dilemma for conservatives in the Depression decade.

DEALING WITH THE NEW DEAL

Conservatives had many reasons to be happy with the state of the economy during the 1920s. While not exactly laissez-faire, the Republican administrations of Warren Harding, Calvin Coolidge, and Herbert Hoover did promote business expansion, lower taxes, and smaller government. The economy in the eight years between 1921 and 1929 grew tremendously, with new technologies, consumer goods, and the housing market leading the way. There were problems in the economy to be sure—farm prices remained low and the stock market proved a drain on constructive investment—but during the 1928 presidential campaign no one thought twice about Herbert Hoover's comment that "we are nearer now to the final conquering of poverty than at any other time in American history." Who would not have believed it?

A year after Hoover's landslide election the story was much different. The nation was on its way into the Great Depression. No one could have foreseen the difficult times on the horizon. It seemed impossible that a nation so rich and abundant could be turned into a nation of want, hunger, and misery. Hoover attempted to assuage business by jawboning with business leaders to keep production going and labor employed, but by the end of 1930 the nation was mired in a severe slump which only seemed to worsen in spite of the programs Hoover enacted to deal with the downturn.

Hoover was not a believer in laissez-faire. In fact he has been described as a forgotten progressive by one biographer for holding beliefs that the state had a role to play in balancing the interests between capital and labor. However, he had also written on how the individual should remain free from governmental interference and while government might have some role to play in promoting economic recovery, the federal government had no role to play in providing relief to individuals. "If the individual surrenders his own initiative and responsibilities, he is surrendering his own freedom and his own liberty," Hoover stated. Running for reelection in 1932 Hoover articulated a belief in "ordered liberty." "The function of government in these times," he argued, "is to use its reserve powers and its strength for the protection of citizens and local governments. . . . It is not the function of the government to relieve individuals of the responsibilities to their neighbors, or to relieve private institutions of their responsibilities to the public."[46] Roosevelt would utter similar sentiments about welfare and the dole, but not during an election year.

The election of Franklin Delano Roosevelt in 1932 and the inauguration of the New Deal marked a turning point not only in American politics—the Democrats secured a stable presidential and congressional majority for the first time since the Civil War and maintained it until the late 1960s—but also in the way government, business, and citizens interacted. Far more than during the progressive era or during World War I, liberal Democrats helped create a powerful administrative state combined with programs binding the people to government like never before.

Roosevelt assured a nervous public that his administration would take action against the Depression. During the first hundred days he secured legislation to deal with the farm crisis, creating the Agricultural Adjustment Administration (AAA), which paid farmers to grow less food and thereby raise commodity prices; he supported industrial recovery through the creation of the National Recovery Administration (NRA) to get business and government officials to collude in the drafting of "codes of competition" governing prices and wages in a variety of industries. He provided relief for the unemployed through the Federal Emergency Relief Administration (FERA), jobs for unemployed young people through the Civilian Conservation Corps (CCC), and public works projects like the Tennessee Valley Authority (TVA). Yet for all the programs and for all Roosevelt's amazing political skills in putting together a framework for recovery, "the Depression still hung darkly over the land." By the end of 1934, historian David Kennedy wrote, "as the third year of the New Deal was about to open, recovery was nowhere in sight."[47]

Conservatives were dubious about Roosevelt and his schemes to promote recovery. Roosevelt's New Deal drew hostile criticism from some conservative figures such as *Chicago Tribune* publisher Robert McCormick. A former classmate of Roosevelt's at Groton prep school, McCormick objected to the NRA and other attempts to create a planned economy. As the *Tribune* opined about NRA, the collectivist influence of the New Dealers left "the shadow of Hitler on the government's walls." In 1934 McCormick delivered a radio address on NBC, "The Rising Red Tide in America," in which he called Congress dupes of the president, "willing to pass without reading it further legislation written in the little red house in Georgetown in the spirit of the big red house in Moscow." He asked one of his reporters to inquire of the State Department about "rumors that [Leon] Trotsky is in this country directing a revolution."[48]

H. L. Mencken agreed with the analysis of the New Deal, writing that Roosevelt's Brains Trust represented "a forbidding gang of quacks and shysters." There was certainly reason for concern. As early as 1927 a group of intellectuals and trade union representatives, many of them future Roosevelt advisors—including Columbia University professor Rexford Tugwell, economist Stuart Chase, union leader John Brophy, and Al Smith advisor Belle Moskowitz—boarded ship in New York for a junket to study the economy and conditions in the Soviet Union. They were met in Europe by other Americans doing the same thing, including University of Chicago economist (and future U.S. Senator) Paul Douglas.

They toured Soviet farms and factories, had discussions with workers—all of whom bragged about living conditions in the USSR—and toured the massive new power plant on the Dnieper River constructed to provide electrical power to the Ukraine. They met with Josef Stalin for hours at the end of their tour and were mesmerized by the Soviet leader. Many came back enamored with the Soviet Union as a model. Tugwell would become a member of FDR's Brains Trust and an advocate of planning in agriculture. Chase wrote a book glorifying Soviet collectivism at the very time when Stalin was forcing peasants into collective farms and killing millions of people to do so. "Russia, I am convinced," Chase wrote, "will solve for all practical purposes the economic problem." He wished the same spirit could exist here—"why should Russians have all the fun remaking a world?"[49]

The equation of the planning model recommended by some of the Brains Trust with that of the Soviet model was enough to convince conservatives of the revolutionary character of the New Deal. So was Roosevelt's rhetoric. Roosevelt waged an unrelenting war on business, which has led some scholars to contend that this negatively impacted business investment decisions and helped delay recovery. As early as his first inaugural address Roosevelt attacked businessmen, calling them "money changers [who] have fled from the high seats in the temple of civilization." He attacked those who resisted the trend toward governmental action against business: "whenever the unethical competitor, the reckless promoter, the Ishmael or Insull, whose hand is against everyman's, declines to join in achieving an end recognized as being for the public welfare . . . the government may properly be asked to apply restraint." No one, least of all unemployed workers who depended on business recovery most of all to provide for their own recovery from the Depression, benefited from such rhetoric. Few saw that then except for conservatives, who saw much to despise about Roosevelt.

Yet conservatives could do very little to challenge Roosevelt politically. FDR had secured passage of two key reforms in 1935, the Wagner Act, which recognized the right of labor unions to collectively bargain with their employers, and Social Security, an elderly pension fund that also created unemployment insurance. Congressional elections had broadened Roosevelt's secure lock on the country politically, and even while he faced political challenges from his Left wing in the persons of Huey Long and Charles Coughlin, Roosevelt was able to cement his political coalition and had an easy road to reelection. The GOP seemed dead and any remaining conservatism within it seemed a distant memory of the good times of the 1920s.

ROADS NOT TAKEN

Conservative intellectuals attempted to create different alternatives to address the economic problems facing the nation. Many of the cultural conservatives turned to solutions far outside the norm of a modern industrial society. Some even advocated fascism as a solution to the problems of the Depression. None of these alternatives became prominent within the mainstream of American conservatism; they represented instead roads not taken, ineffective and unpalatable alternatives to the path of limited government and laissez-faire that had shaped conservatism in the first three decades of the twentieth century.

One criticism of modern America was its reliance on industrialism to promote economic growth. The industrial revolution had sundered man from the soil and had allowed a plutocratic capitalism to develop, replacing the localist economy of the nineteenth century with one controlled by the malefactors of great wealth. One region particularly tied to the soil and to the agrarian economy once so vital to American life, was the South. Since the American Civil War the South had languished behind the rest of the nation economically. While some regions of the South embraced industrialization, the landscape and social patterns in the region remained unchanged. Particularly troubling was segregation, which reaffirmed a rigid inequality between the white and black races. Blacks were denied basic civil rights by law and they were also denied voting privileges and equality of opportunity in every other sphere of Southern life. Many Southern writers and intellectuals worried about a dilemma inherent in the region: "how could the South modernize and remain its essential self?"[50]

That question became the basis for a revival in Southern letters. A group of poets, writers, and essayists, all of them professors at Nashville's Vanderbilt University, contended with modernism and tradition in their work. Known as the Fugitives, they were dissatisfied with the call for simply a literary revival in the South; some of them sought a return to the traditional culture of agrarian life in the old South, sans slavery. In 1930 a group of them, writing under the nom de plume Twelve Southerners, published a manifesto *I'll Take My Stand*, articulating a new conception of Southern society called the new agrarianism. "There is a melancholy fact that the South . . . has . . . shown signs of wanting to join up behind the common or American industrial ideal," wrote John Crowe Ransom in the book's introduction. "It is against that tendency that this book is written."[51]

The agrarians diagnosed "the economic evils" they believed followed "in the wake of machines." In contrast they called for a return to the "culture of the soil" where all the amenities of civilized life—named as "manners, conversation, hospitality, sympathy, family life, romantic life"—could long endure. Working the soil was "the best and most sensitive of vocations and that therefore it should have the economic preference and enlist the maximum number of workers." "The responsibility of men," Ransom wrote, "is for their own welfare and that of their neighbors; not for the hypothetical welfare of some fabulous creature called society."[52]

Many of the essays extolled the South as a region where the traditional basis of society was best represented by the agrarian lifestyle. The authors spoke not at all about the legacy of slavery or of the reality of segregation. They offered no program or political solution to the problem of industrialism. Donald Davidson expressed what the book stood for best when he wrote, "it is true that we don't (at present) have an actual candidate for some office, and a platform for him to stand on. . . . It would be fairer to say that we represent principles that are looking for a party. . . . It will take a long time for ideas to work. But nothing in the end is quite so powerful as ideas."[53]

To what audience were such ideas addressed? Davidson later admitted that the "reviews [for the book] were terrible." When conservative author Richard Weaver later wrote that "the philosophical doctrines were as far above the average Southern farmer as the empyrean," in an essay published about *I'll Take My Stand*, Davidson retorted: "until he had been corrupted by the New Deal subsidies, war, and socialist intimidation, the average Southern farmer, wherever he could be physically approached, was naturally, in the early 1930s, a more sympathetic and understanding person than another crowd, who were our real enemies—the 'liberals,' the educated jackasses."[54]

The audience and a program for the agrarian vision never materialized and the agrarians remained frustrated by the lack of interest in their ideas outside the South. One northerner who paid attention was a "wealthy and eccentric" publisher, Seward Collins. Collins was editor of the once distinguished monthly literary magazine *The Bookman*. By the late 1920s when Collins took over the publication it had fallen on hard times. One of his first actions as publisher was to dedicate the journal primarily to the new humanism and especially to the writings of Irving Babbitt and Paul Elmer More. This was not popular with some longtime readers, including Collins's friend socialist author Upton Sinclair, who told Collins, "I am going to enter my plea against your turning the 'Bookman' into a propaganda organ for those two literary mummies, More and Babbitt." Yet, Collins persisted, letting Babbitt know that it was his work "that swung me around to sympathy with tradition."[55]

Collins was eclectic and attracted to a large variety of writers associated with what he called "revolutionary conservatism." Not only did he publish the new humanists but he also sought far and wide for other authors who approached the problem of industrial plutocracy in a headlong manner. With the collapse of the economy during the early 1930s Collins sought an economic answer to the Depression by focusing on the widespread distribution of property as a solution. He studied the English distributists G. K. Chesterton and Hilaire Belloc, and admired Belloc's conception of property in land as "foundational" to freedom. Belloc had published *The Servile State* (1913), in which he argued that "the arrangement of society in which a considerable number of the families and individuals are constrained by positive law to labor for the advantage of other families and individuals as to stamp the whole community with the mark of such labor is the servile state."[56] Belloc argued instead that in order to be free men must possess property in land.

In 1933 Collins suspended publication of the *Bookman* and turned the struggling publication into a monthly journal focusing on the political, social, and economic problems of the modern world. Known as the *American Review*, Collins published the first issue in March 1933. Soon after its publication Collins published agrarian contributors such as Allen Tate and Donald Davidson. Yet Collins turned more toward monarchism as a solution to the ills of modern America. He sought a strong man and ultimately advocated fascism for America.

Collins viewed fascism as a transitional form of government from a plutocracy, which existed in the late nineteenth century, to an authoritarian rule, which he believed necessary to check the power of the masses, who, if unchecked would bring about a communist system. "The question of politics resolves itself broadly," Collins wrote, "into a discussion of the succession of Fascism to parliamentarianism; or at least some form of authoritarian government supplanting Pluto-democracy, and Fascism seems to be the most convenient word."[57] His praise of Italian fascist leader Benito Mussolini in one editorial drew a harsh response from his friend Sinclair:

> Your idea that your monarch-hero, Mussolini, is putting an end to plutocracy sounds like a joke—when he is the hired ruffian of that same plutocracy. . . . Mussolini can't solve the social problem, nor can Hitler; and hence fascism is only a step towards communism. All your monarch-heroes plan war, one against the other; and when they lose the war—Stalin! You, and all of your ruling class, are offered peaceful and humane socialism; and rejecting it, you will get Bolshevism.[58]

Collins could not be dissuaded and continued to argue for increased executive power. He, alone among many of the conservatives discussed thus far, called for more power for the state. "My aim right now," he told journalist Walter Lippmann, "is to get more and more power for the President, whoever holds the office—I hope it may be Roosevelt for some time to come. Perhaps I am wrong in thinking that this purpose will be aided by an extreme and impossible monarchical position . . . but [it] might help to win a decent amount of increased power as a sort of 'lesser evil.'"[59] Such a view differed markedly from the views expressed by laissez-faire conservatives like Albert Jay Nock, who wrote that "Hegel's doctrine of the state [epitomized by the rule of fascism in Italy] . . . is distinctly offensive to us, and we congratulate ourselves on our freedom from the 'yoke of dictator's tyranny.'"[60] Collins felt differently, a result of how intellectuals from a variety of conservative viewpoints were dealing with the crisis of capitalism during the Depression years.

Collins went further than simply embracing the economic conceptions of fascism. He also accepted the anti-Semitism inherent in Nazi ideology. He told socialist Norman Thomas that attacks on Jews by the Nazis in Germany were "exaggerated" by Hitler's opponents. "I began to realize that there was after all a Jewish problem . . . that Jews are a race apart, unassimilable." In an interview with communist journalist Grace Lumpkin for the popular front magazine *FIGHT Against War and Fascism*, Collins argued that the Jews in Germany were not persecuted. "The Jews make trouble. It is necessary to segregate them. . . . They make dissension and trouble wherever they are."[61]

Such remarks led the remaining agrarians who had continued to publish in *American Review* to break with Collins. Herbert Agar, a journalist in Louisville who had published "The Task for Conservatism" in the March 1934 issue of the journal, wrote Collins announcing a break with him and the establishment of a new journal dedicated to the agrarian viewpoint called *Free America*. He was also coediting, with agrarian Allen Tate, a new volume of agrarian thinking on the problem of industrialism entitled *Who Owns America?* and was particularly concerned with being linked in the public mind with Collins. Agar told Collins, "I'd like to state that I do not want a king, that I do not want a return to the Middle Ages, that I do not want to abolish all factories, that I do not want to give 'each person' a piece of land, and that I would die in order to diminish the changes of fascism in America. If you really have decided—which I hope is not the case—to appear before the public as a friend of fascism, you and I must be opponents to the end."[62] Tate made a similar argument in an open letter on the subject in *The New Republic*: "I would choose communism if it were the alternative to [fascism]."[63]

The turn toward fascism marginalized the *American Review* and Collins lost the journal's most important contributors. Only a few more issues appeared and more space was dedicated to a pro-Franco position regarding the Spanish general's revolt against the Republic and fascism's dedication to a struggle against communism. In a draft of a letter to Idaho Senator William Borah, a consistent isolationist voice, Collins accused him of accepting the communist line when it came to "alleged atrocity stories at Guernica" (a Spanish town bombed by the German *Luftwaffe*). He chided Borah, telling him "I thought it was your duty to make inquiries before lending your great prestige to atrocity stories alleged against a people locked in a death struggle with communism."[64] In order to facilitate support for Franco, Collins opened a book shop on West Fifty-eighth Street in Manhattan—"New York's only Right-wing bookshop"—advertisements hailed it, to sell anticommunist literature as well as books and publications dedicated to the fascist cause. Increasingly isolated and with fewer allies on the Right, Collins, whether due to lack of finances or health problems, shut down *American Review* in 1937 and retired in virtual seclusion on his New Hampshire farm until his death in 1952.

Collins was by no means the only intellectual figure propagating a fascist viewpoint in the 1930s. Lawrence Dennis was another. Born in 1894 in Atlanta of mixed-race parentage, Dennis was educated at Phillips Exeter Academy and at Harvard. He worked for the State Department as a Latin American expert before leaving government service for Wall Street and a job in the prestigious Seligman banking house. Alarmed by the collapse of capitalism during the Great Depression, Dennis left Wall Street, convinced that the plutocratic capitalism he served was to blame for the downturn. He became an editorial writer for *The Awakener* and in that capacity published his first book. *Is Capitalism Doomed?* (1932) focused on how capitalism was a dead economic system; unfortunately, he worried, the system emerging to replace it was communism.

He updated his argument a few years later. In *The Coming American Fascism* (1936) Dennis argued that fascism and communism were vying for international economic power; of the two systems, Dennis argued, fascism was preferable since it left intact a vestige of capitalism while communism obliterated capitalism entirely. The new capitalism would bear little resemblance to laissez-faire; rather it would be corporatist. "The ultimate objective," Dennis wrote, "is welfare through a strong national state."[65] Even the New Deal did not go far enough for Dennis.

By the late 1930s Dennis was contributing essays on foreign affairs to a pamphlet published under the auspices of a Russian émigré, V. D. Gravenhoff, entitled *The Weekly Foreign Letter*. Privately circulated, the publication had over one thousand subscribers and by 1940 was being run by Dennis himself, who wrote most of the content. The focus was primarily noninterventionist when it came to war in Europe. After Germany invaded Poland in 1939, Dennis argued that Germany would win the conflict and that America should get used to living with a world where the Nazis controlled the European continent. Dennis labeled Roosevelt a "semiparalyzed country squire" and thought Winston Churchill "a senile alcoholic who [had] never been good at anything except writing alibis for his failures." Hitler, on the other hand, was viewed as a "genius" for his diplomatic skills in the late 1930s.[66]

Not surprisingly the choice of vituperative language, as well as allegations that Dennis had accepted money from the German embassy to support his publication, led to his isolation even from the isolationists. As a self-identified apologist for an American fascism—based on the corporatist model of Mussolini's Italy rather than the anti-Semitic nationalism of Hitler's Germany— Dennis drew fire from the communist Left, who challenged him to debates and wrote often about his critique of capitalism.[67] Forced by dwindling support for his views, he stopped publication of his newsletter in July 1942 after stating that he unequivocally supported the war after Japan's attack on Pearl Harbor. However since many of his articles were published in newsletters of the pro-Nazi German-American Bund, Dennis, along with twenty-nine others, was indicted and tried for sedition in a massive 1944 conspiracy trial. Dennis later wrote about the trial in a book published with his attorney Maximilian St. George and defended himself as a victim of the government looking to indict those who dissented from "the war hysteria" propagated by the Roosevelt administration. The trial dragged on for months before a mistrial was declared after the death of the presiding judge.[68] It would fuel Dennis in the postwar period to resist the rising tide of fascism in America he saw resulting from grand crusades abroad.

Agrarianism and fascism never became prominent alternatives for conservatives to follow during the 1930s. When one considers the number of Americans who either joined the communist party or sympathized with its political and international policies, especially when measured up against the paucity of those who joined radical Right-wing or fascist groups in America during the decade, it is clear that the 1930s remained a "red decade" and not a brown-or-black one. Later revelations concerning the significant influence of communist espionage within the New Deal agencies and within World War II government agencies supported anticommunist charges that liberals had been less than vigilant in their conduct of matters crucial to national security.[69]

THE RETURN OF LAISSEZ-FAIRE

Conservatives had never given up on the idea of laissez-faire but it was difficult to articulate such a cure for the Depression in the face of the rhetorical war Roosevelt had declared against business. Several organizations kept the flame of free enterprise alive during the decade however. Especially important were the efforts made by a group of businessmen in the National Association of Manufacturers (NAM) who called themselves the "Brass Hats." These individuals, counting among their coterie J. Howard Pew, the chairman of the Sun Oil Company, Ernest T. Weir, president of National Steel Corporation, Robert Lund of Lambert Pharmaceuticals, and Thomas Girdler of Republic Steel Corporation, dedicated themselves to saving NAM and the idea of free enterprise after the Depression began to take its toll on NAM membership. Paternalistic and defenders of free enterprise, the Brass Hats sought nothing less than to preserve their social and economic power in the teeth of the New Deal's rhetorical and legislative war against capitalism.

NAM found itself at war against the New Deal concept of industrial planning and its concept of collective bargaining. NAM lobbied against passage of the Wagner Act and fought the government's decision to allow labor unions to have collective bargaining rights in privately owned companies. The Brass Hats saw programs like the National Recovery Administration as socialistic. Thomas Girdler, who initially welcomed the NRA believing it would help "little steel" compete against behemoths like U.S. Steel, quickly turned against the program, especially due to provisions in the law that empowered labor unions. Girdler told the American Iron and Steel Institute, "we are not going to recognize any professional union" and he argued that he would rather shut down Republic Steel and "raise apples and potatoes" before he did recognize labor. After sit-down strikes paralyzed the auto industry in January and February 1937, Girdler decried the tactics of the newly formed Congress of Industrial Organizations (CIO), whose member union, the United Auto Workers, had won an agreement with General Motors as a result of the strike, stating that "I wouldn't have a contract, verbal or written, with an irresponsible, racketeering, violent Communist body like the CIO."[70]

Girdler's hostility to unions eventually led to a violent clash outside the gates of the South Chicago Republic Steel plant in 1937 when striking workers celebrating Memorial Day engaged in a melee with Chicago police; ten strikers were killed—many shot in the back—and sixteen police were wounded. The press, particularly McCormick's *Chicago Tribune*, described the strikers as "lusting for blood" and a "trained revolutionary body." Girdler had been involved in the creation of the Mohawk Valley formula, an anti-union public relations campaign devised by "little steel" company presidents that painted any strikers as communists and attacked labor leaders as revolutionaries. Given the coverage in McCormick's paper it was easy to see that the strategy was successful. Only during World War II, with production expanding and with defense contracts awarded to companies who recognized collective bargaining rights, did "little steel" recognize labor unions.

NAM's effort against the New Deal was primarily educational. The organization spent close to $800,000 in 1937 on a public relations campaign extolling the benefits of free enterprise and the importance of private property. Pew took the most active role in this effort by encouraging and subsidizing the publication of pamphlets and books dedicated to exposing the flaws in government planning and state socialism. One correspondent told Pew "the only way the New Deal can be uprooted is through a strong affirmative attack on the *intellectual* front. . . . Only as the nation's thought leaders show a change to the conservative position will the public begin to question what it now takes as semi-divine revelation."[71] Pew purchased thousands of copies of books, such as Brown University President Henry Wriston's *The Challenge to Liberty* (1942) and F. A. Hayek's *The Road to Serfdom* (1944), donating them to college libraries and securing attention for such ideas in the media.

Pew also gave thousands of dollars to the American Liberty League, a nonpartisan organization founded in 1934 and directed by Jouette Shouse, a former executive director of the Democratic Party. Shouse recruited the former governor of New York and Democratic presidential nominee Al Smith and Wall Street millionaire John Jacob Raskob to the effort. The League's purpose was "to defend and uphold the Constitution . . . to teach the necessity of respect for the rights of persons and property . . . to foster the right to work, earn, save and acquire property, and to preserve the ownership of property when acquired." "It was definitely not anti-Roosevelt," historian George Wolfskill wrote; indeed, Shouse had met with FDR and told him about the purpose of the Liberty League and the president pledged his full support for the organization.[72]

Bitter political antagonism between Roosevelt and Smith derailed the organization's original purpose and moved the Liberty League toward open opposition against the New Deal. The Liberty League published 135 pamphlets and twenty-four bulletins, many of them written by Raskob, defending the Constitution and attacking the collectivism of the New Deal. Shouse argued that the New Deal was designed "to set up a totalitarian government," while New York congressman James Beck, a friend of the Liberty League, argued that it was moving the country "towards a totalitarian socialistic state."[73]

Roosevelt gave the Liberty League every reason to believe they were correct in their depiction of the president and the New Deal. In the 1936 State of the Union address, Roosevelt attacked big business: "we have earned the hatred of entrenched greed. They realize that in thirty-four months we have built up new instruments of public power. In the hands of a people's government this power is wholesome and proper. But in the hands of political puppets of an economic autocracy such power would provide shackles for the liberties of the people. Give them their way and they will take the course of every autocracy of the past—power for themselves, enslavement for the public."[74]

Al Smith gave the rebuttal at a February Democratic dinner. Arguing that the president had not carried out the platform in 1932—which had called for budget cuts—he contended that the country was threatened by too much government spending. Alluding to what was at stake, he concluded "the young brain-trusters caught the socialists swimming and ran away with their clothes. . . . There can only be one capital, Washington or Moscow. There can be only the pure, fresh air of free America, or the foul breath of communistic Russia. There can be only one flag, the Stars and Stripes, or the flag of the godless Union of the Soviets. There can be only one national anthem,

The Star-Spangled Banner or the *Internationale*."[75] Smith's equation of the New Deal with communism was to no avail. Roosevelt easily won reelection in 1936, winning a huge landslide against Kansas Governor Alf Landon and securing a seemingly impenetrable Democratic majority in Congress. The GOP seemed in its death throes; within a few months after the election, the Liberty League ended operations.

Roosevelt entered his second term intent on securing the unfinished business of the people—"the need to find through government the instrument of our united purpose to solve for the individual the ever-rising problems of a complex civilization." He had promised during the campaign to never again go back "to the philosophy of the boom era, to individualism run wild." He focused his attention instead on "one-third of a nation, ill housed, ill clad, ill nourished" and promised action to alleviate the distress of the old poverty in America. Roosevelt was poised for action and with huge congressional majorities; conservatives expected the worst.[76]

Three issues derailed the New Deal and helped to revitalize conservative opposition to Roosevelt. The sit-down strikes that erupted in Michigan in January 1937, leading to fears of worker revolution, were blamed on New Deal labor legislation. The second reason had to do with Roosevelt's frustration with a conservative Supreme Court, which had declared unconstitutional his agricultural and industrial recovery programs. Roosevelt feared the worst for New Deal reforms like the Wagner Act and Social Security and came up with a solution: pack the Court with assistant justices for every justice over seventy years of age. His packing plan, couched in terms of assisting elderly judges with a crowded docket—the docket was no more crowded than usual—would have given FDR five appointments to the Supreme Court immediately and hundreds of additional appointments at the appeals and circuit court levels.

Roosevelt proved too clever. It was clear to most Americans, even those who supported the New Deal, that FDR seemed intent on establishing more power within the executive branch. Walter Lippmann wrote, "the mere proposal of this scheme is an immeasurable injury to the cause of democracy in the world" and came at a time when the United States faced growing threats to democracy abroad in Europe and Asia. Roosevelt sprung this on an unwary Senate, dominated by Southern Democrats grown increasingly frustrated with the New Deal, and the bill stalled before a compromise was struck which preserved nothing in the original legislation. However FDR's stunt may have convinced one justice that his interpretation of the Constitution was problematic. Justice Owen Roberts, appointed by Herbert Hoover, moved to the liberal side of the Court, voting in the affirmative on a federal minimum wage provision (two years after he had voted against such a provision). Roberts's decision, dubbed "the switch in time which saved nine," moved the Court away from its conservative views; by the end of the year two justices had retired and by the time Roosevelt died in 1945, he had thoroughly remade the Court, appointing all nine justices.

The damage worsened when Roosevelt, believing the economy had recovered enough that he could cut spending, slashed the budget for the New Deal; the economy sank back into Depression. Unemployment skyrocketed to 19 percent by 1938. "Being poor now seemed like a permanent fact of life," Amity Shlaes wrote. The so-called Roosevelt recession lasted until 1942, ending only in the massive government-funded spending on the war. The GOP capitalized in 1938, making significant gains in Congress. In alliance with Southern Democrats, conservatives in Congress blocked the further extension of New Deal programs.[77]

Conservatives took the offensive in the late 1930s, not only content with voting against New Deal programs but investigating those already in operation. Using the newly established House Committee on Un-American Activities (HUAC), conservative Democrats and Republicans investigated communist influence in labor unions and New Deal agencies like the Works Progress Administration (WPA). Formed initially as the Dickstein Committee after its chairman, New York congressman Samuel Dickstein—who turned out to be working for Soviet intelligence—HUAC was charged with investigating Nazi influence in America; under the leadership of Texas Democrat Martin Dies after 1937, it began to investigate the New Deal, becoming more interested in communist infiltration of the government. In 1938 HUAC held hearings on the WPA art projects, with Dies especially interested in the theater project. He called their productions "sheer propaganda for Communism or the New Deal."[78] A year later Congress killed the project. Conservatives began to regain confidence as the decade ended and as the looming threat of war took attention away from reform.

ISOLATIONISM AND WAR

Franklin Roosevelt was an internationalist and believed instinctively that during the 1930s the Great Depression had not only allowed for the rise of dictatorship in nations like Germany and of militarism in Japan, but that it also imperiled democracy. Yet he acted at times against the internationalism he professed, torpedoing the London Economic Conference in 1933 designed to promote worldwide solutions to economic recovery; he also removed the dollar from the gold standard and set the price of currency himself over breakfast, an irresponsible position which led many officials to resign in dismay.

He also signed the Neutrality Acts into law, a series of bills which forbade American trade, travel, and loans to belligerent powers in the desire to keep America out of a second European war. Roosevelt had to tread carefully within his own party between the internationalists, most of whom supported strengthening the relationship with Great Britain and France, and the noninterventionists, who wanted to isolate America as much as possible from European power politics. Roosevelt's juggling of these competing interests led him often to take action in ways which departed from his own "conceptualization of foreign policy" which, historian Alonzo Hamby wrote, "contained the synthesis of moralism and power politics that one can find in [Teddy Roosevelt]; to this he added the vision of collective security and world organization that Wilson expressed."[79]

Conservatives for the most part supported the noninterventionist position throughout the decade. Laissez-faire conservatives believed that the buildup for war and an interventionist foreign policy signified a movement toward dictatorship and the involvement of the Republic in foreign wars not in America's best interest. They were joined in such views by progressives such as Republican Gerald Nye and Democrat Burton Wheeler. Most progressives were influenced by their Midwestern or Western isolationism and by the experience of Americans during World War I.

During the Depression years the historical legacy of World War I was hotly debated. Many Americans had come to the view that the war itself was not worth entering and that America had entered only to enhance financial interests, not because of the idealism expressed by Wilson in 1917. A popular book by H. C. Englebrecht and Frank Hanighen, *The Merchants of Death* (1934), as well as books written by well-respected academic historians Charles Tansill and Charles Beard, promoted the view that the armament industry and banks had profited from the First World War and stood to profit from a second. The United States had entered the war through the back door, primarily due to the influence of economic elites. These revisionist arguments had an impact leading Nye to hold congressional hearings to investigate business collusion in getting the country into war. The hearings produced no evidence revealing such collusion, yet mobilized by public sentiment that agreed with the need to stay out of future wars in Europe, Nye secured passage of the Neutrality Acts, which restrained American rights to travel, trade, or aid belligerent nations. By 1937 the isolationist mood was dominant, with 70 percent of Americans claiming entering World War I was the wrong thing to do.[80]

Roosevelt was stuck and could only take the country so far from the isolationist sentiment dominating American politics. He invoked the Neutrality Acts when Italy invaded Abyssinia in 1935; he did the same when civil war broke out in Spain in 1936. The next year after Japan invaded China, FDR did

not invoke the acts, allowing America to aid the Chinese with money and munitions (which also meant that it bound America to sell war material to Japan as well). In Europe, meanwhile, Adolf Hitler occupied the Rhineland in 1936, annexed Austria in 1938, and demanded the German-speaking Sudetenland from Czechoslovakia. British and French prime ministers Neville Chamberlain and Pierre Daladier agreed providing Hitler demanded no further territory and promised no aggression. Hitler concurred; Chamberlain arrived back in London waving the agreement and promising "peace in our time." The scene was witnessed by a young William F. Buckley Jr. on his way from the airport to boarding school.[81] Six months later Hitler took the remainder of Czechoslovakia. The British and French now guaranteed Polish security. To secure Soviet acquiescence to a long-planned move into Poland, Hitler signed a nonaggression pact with Stalin that contained secret codicils allowing for the Soviet occupation of the eastern third of Poland. With this secured, on September 1, 1939, Germany invaded Poland and Britain and France declared war on Germany. FDR invoked neutrality.

The fall of France in June 1940 changed everything for Roosevelt. The British now stood alone against the Nazis. Winston Churchill became prime minister in May, after some in the British government had urged a separate peace with Germany. Churchill was defiant and mobilized the British public to fight on after evacuating the British Expeditionary Force from the beaches of Dunkirk. While the American public remained leery of aiding the British directly, Roosevelt was determined to do so. In September 1940 Roosevelt signed the "destroyer deal," which transferred vintage World War I destroyers to the British in exchange for base rights in the Caribbean. The administration also announced a cash-carry provision to allow Britain to purchase goods in the United States with cash as long as they carried the material on their own ships.

These actions were the final straw for the noninterventionists. That same month a group of prominent Chicago businessmen formed a pressure group, the America First Committee, designed to keep the U.S. out of war in Europe. Headquartered in Chicago and run by recent Yale University graduate H. Douglas Stuart, the membership of America First was made up of a diverse group of conservatives, progressives, socialists, radicals, and reactionaries. America First "contained many mansions and the bitterest of enemies might agree on only one premise: the necessity of avoiding full scale American involvement in World War II."[82] The only members it refused to countenance were Nazis and communists.

The key figures in the organization were all conservatives. Chicago businessman William H. Regnery provided the organization much of its financing. General Robert Wood, the CEO of Sears, Roebuck & Co., served as president and he used his influence in the business community to recruit associates from the Chamber of Commerce or NAM. Many prominent businessmen joined as a result, including Sterling Morton Jr., CEO of Morton Salt, and politicians such as Kansas Senator Arthur Capper, New York Congressman Bruce Barton, and Wisconsin progressive Robert LaFollette Jr. Former head of the National Recovery Administration, Hugh Johnson, served on the board of directors.

America First saw the war in Europe as "another chapter in the series of conflicts between European states that have been going on in war and peace for hundreds of years." Nazi Germany was not intent on world revolution, America First pamphlets claimed, and was no threat to America. Formed too late to influence the selection of candidates for the 1940 presidential campaign, America First vainly sought to persuade GOP nominee Wendell Willkie of their position on intervention. His failure to do so proved detrimental to a campaign where there was little discussion of the looming specter of war; it assured the reelection of Roosevelt to an unprecedented third term. FDR proved so confident during the campaign that he mocked noninterventionist congressmen Joseph Martin, Bruce Barton, and Hamilton Fish by getting crowds to chant "Martin, Barton, and Fish" after questions concerning American preparedness for war.

America First continued to fight against intervention, yet events were moving beyond their control. The British government informed Roosevelt they could not much longer continue resistance against Germany unless they received more assistance. Roosevelt proposed Lend-Lease, submitted to Congress as H.R. 1776, which passed Congress in March 1941 after intense debate. Robert Taft later wrote, "I feel very strongly that Hitler's defeat is not vital to us, and that even the collapse of England is to be preferred to participation for the rest of our lives in European wars."[83] Burton Wheeler called Lend-Lease "New Deal foreign policy. It will plow under every fourth American boy," referring to the AAA program which paid farmers not to grow food. Yet Lend-Lease passed and eventually Britain received $31 billion; after Germany's invasion of the Soviet Union in June 1941 Congress authorized Lend-Lease aid to the Soviets as well (some $11 billion was sent there during the war). Aviator Charles Lindbergh, a key supporter of America First, encapsulated many conservatives' views when he told a rally, "I would a hundred times see my country ally herself with England, or even with Germany, with all her faults, then the cruelty, the godlessness and the barbarism that exists in Soviet Russia."[84]

Throughout 1941 Roosevelt moved the United States closer to war with Germany. He fought an undeclared naval war against German submarines, allowing the Navy to escort British convoys, declared that the Monroe Doctrine now

applied to territory as far from America as Greenland, and had the Marines occupy Iceland. He met with Churchill in August off the coast of Newfoundland
and signed the Atlantic Charter, a statement of war aims. He encouraged discussion concerning Nazi designs on South America, and claimed he had plans
that showed a Nazi intention to occupy Brazil, exposed as a falsehood by
Colonel McCormick's *Chicago Tribune*. By the end of the year the only issue
that remained was not whether the United States would join the war against
Germany, but when.

Yet war did not come from Europe. It came instead from the Far East. On
December 7, 1941, Japanese naval warplanes struck the American fleet at
Pearl Harbor; the next day Roosevelt declared war on Japan and on December 10, Germany declared war on the United States. America First voted to
disband and supported the war effort. Robert Wood later expressed what
many America Firsters felt after the attack on Pearl Harbor: "I fought our involvement in World War II as long as I could, but, when the issue was decided
by the attack on Pearl Harbor, I did my best to aid my country."[85]

While America First failed in its efforts to keep America out of war, its activities helped crystallize a growing conservative political opposition to Roosevelt and to liberalism. Critics like Garet Garrett pointed out how Roosevelt
was concentrating power in the executive branch in a manner which practically
annulled the Constitution. FDR's desire to seek a third term violated the very
principles of limited executive power charted by George Washington. During
the war, so emboldened by their newfound influence, conservative politicians
made headway ending many New Deal programs, such as the CCC and WPA,
made redundant by a rejuvenated economy. Roosevelt himself caught the drift
when he told the press in early 1942, much to the consternation of liberals like
his wife Eleanor, that "Dr. Win the War had replaced Dr. New Deal."

Business had regained its lost social authority during the war years, a product of helping bring about victory against Germany and Japan. The outcome
of the war, as historian Thomas Fleming noticed, created a "remarkable revival of confidence" among conservatives. "The roots of the modern conservative movement," Fleming wrote, "can be found in the New Dealers' war."[86]
The war that many conservatives had opposed would help bring the conservative doctrine into fruition. The war helped engender a transition from the
older conservatism, dismissive as it was to the idea of mass democracy, to one
where the people seemed to possess the virtues lacking among the liberal
elites. This transition, which began in the years after World War II, helped
conservatives compete for, and eventually claim, political power. In the
process much of what had passed as conservatism before the war was marginalized; it never disappeared entirely but it was no longer at the center of
conservative thought and politics.

NOTES

1. For a biography of Garrett see Carl Ryant, *Profit's Prophet: Garet Garrett (1878–1954)* (Selingsgrove, N.Y.: Susquehanna University Press, 1989); for the quote, see Garet Garrett, *Salvos Against the New Deal: Selections from the Saturday Evening Post, 1933–1940*, ed. Bruce Ramsey (Caldwell, Idaho: Caxton, 2002), 13.

2. Garet Garrett, *The Revolution Was*, reprinted in *The People's Pottage* (Caldwell, Idaho: Caxton Press, 1953), 18.

3. Garrett, *The Revolution Was*, 44–45, 73.

4. Albert Jay Nock, *Our Enemy, the State* (San Francisco: Fox and Wilkes Books, 1994; first published 1935), 10.

5. The critique of mass democracy and managerialism remains a staple for the paleoconservatives in contemporary times. See Paul Gottfried, *After Liberalism: Mass Democracy and the Managerial State* (Princeton: Princeton University Press, 2001).

6. George H. Nash, *The Conservative Intellectual Movement in America: Since 1945*, 2nd ed. (Wilmington, Del.: Intercollegiate Studies Institute, 1996), xv.

7. The best books about the Old Right have been written by paleoconservatives interested in recapturing the movement's legacy to help in their claim as "true conservatives" in contemporary debates over the movement. See Justin Raimando, *Reclaiming the American Right: The Lost Legacy of the Conservative Movement* (Burlingame, CA: Center for Libertarian Studies, 1993); and Joseph Scotchie, *The Paleoconservatives: New Voices of the Old Right* (New Brunswick, N.J.: Transaction, 1999).

8. For a history of conservatism within the GOP, see Donald T. Critchlow, *The Conservative Ascendancy: How the GOP Right Made Political History* (Cambridge, Mass.: Harvard University Press, 2007).

9. The term *laissez-faire* conservatism was used by Clinton Rossiter, *Conservatism in America*, 2nd ed. (Cambridge, Mass., 1962), to define what is typically called classical liberalism. I have chosen to borrow the term not necessarily because it precisely defines what classical liberals advocated; rather I want to avoid confusion when I speak throughout the book of liberalism as a philosophy of expanded state power.

10. Robert Green McCloskey, *American Conservatism in the Age of Enterprise, 1865–1910* (Cambridge, Mass.: Harvard University Press, 1951), 169.

11. Sidney Fine, *Laissez-Faire and the General Welfare State: A Study of Conflict in American Thought, 1865–1910* (Ann Arbor: University of Michigan Press 1956), 32.

12. William Graham Sumner, "Socialism," in Bannister, ed., *On Liberty, Society, and Politics: The Essential Essays of William Graham Sumner* (Indianapolis: Liberty Fund, 1992), 165.

13. Sumner, "The Forgotten Man," in Bannister, ed., *On Liberty, Society and Politics*, 202.

14. McCloskey, *American Conservatism*, 123–26.

15. See Christopher Lasch, *The True and Only Heaven: Progress and Its Critics* (New York: Norton, 1991), 206. The quote from Rockefeller is from Michael McGerr, *A Fierce Discontent: The Rise and Fall of the Progressive Movement in America, 1870–1920* (New York: Free Press, 2003), 8.

16. See Richard Hofstadter, *The Age of Reform* (New York: Vintage, 1960). For a strong analysis of the tradition of populist insurgency within American political culture, see David A. Horowitz, *Beyond Left and Right: Insurgency and the Establishment* (Urbana: University of Illinois Press, 1997), 1–18.

17. See the first issue for the quote, *Conservative* 1 (July 14, 1898): 1; for a good summary of the journal, see Ronald Lora and William Henry Longton, eds., *The Conservative Press in Twentieth-Century America* (Westport, Conn.: Greenwood, 1999), 23–36. For the attitudes of gold Democrats see David T. Beito and Linda Royster Beito, "Gold Democrats and the Decline of Classical Liberalism, 1896–1900," *The Independent Review* 4, no. 4 (Spring 2000): 555–75. Contemporary libertarians point to the Cleveland administration as a prototype for classical liberal government.

18. Fine, *Laissez-Faire and the General Welfare State*, 388–89.

19. William Graham Sumner, "The Fallacy of Territorial Expansion," and "The Conquest of the United States by Spain," in Bannister, ed., *On Liberty, Society and Politics*, 268–69, for the quote.

20. David Nasaw, *Andrew Carnegie* (New York: Penguin, 2006), 547–53.

21. These events are well described in David M. Kennedy, *Over Here: The First World War and American Society* (New York: Oxford University Press, 1980).

22. Thomas Fleming, *The Illusion of Victory: America in World War I* (New York: Basic, 2003), 94.

23. Alan Dawley, *Changing the World: American Progressives in War and Revolution* (Princeton: Princeton University Press, 2003), 109–16, discusses the conservative nationalists.

24. *The Constitutional Review*, edited by Henry Black and published from 1917–1928, was one of the strongly nationalist, anti-immigrant journals of the decade.

25. Letter from Nock to Ruth Robinson, Sept. 23, 1913, Box 1, Series I, Folder 18 (Ruth Robinson Corr., Sept.–Oct. 1913), Albert Jay Nock Papers, Sterling Library, Yale University.

26. See Albert Jay Nock, *Memoirs of a Superfluous Man* (Tampa, Fla.: Hallberg Publishing, 1994 ed.); and Lora and Longton, eds., *Conservative Press*, 308–16. See Brian Doherty, *Radicals for Capitalism: A Freewheeling History of the Modern Libertarian Movement* (New York: PublicAffairs, 2007), 55, 56, 67–111.

27. John Lukacs, *Remembered Past: John Lukacs on History, Historians, and Historical Knowledge*, ed. Malvasi and Nelson (Wilmington, Del.: Intercollegiate Studies Institute, 2005), 80.

28. See Peter Gay, *Modernism: The Lure of Heresy from Baudelaire to Beckett and Beyond* (New York: Norton, 2008), 3–4; Stephen J. Kern, *The Culture of Time and Space, 1880–1918* (DeKalb, Ill.: Northern Illinois University Press, 1986).

29. Russell Kirk, *The Conservative Mind: From Burke to Santayana* (Chicago: Regnery Publishing, 1953), 7–8.

30. Rossiter, *Conservatism in America*, 157–58.

31. George Panichas, *The Critical Legacy of Irving Babbitt* (Wilmington, Del.: Intercollegiate Studies Institute, 1998), 8–9; and J. David Hoeveler Jr., *The New Humanism: A Critique of Modern America, 1900–1940* (Charlottesville: University Press of Virginia, 1977), 3.

32. Irving Babbitt, *Rousseau and Romanticism* (New Brunswick, N.J.: Transaction, 2004).

33. Babbitt, *Rousseau and Romanticism*; Panichas, *Critical Legacy*; Claes G. Ryn, "Introduction to the Transaction Edition," in Babbitt, *Rousseau and Romanticism*, x–liii.

34. Irving Babbitt, *Democracy and Leadership* (Indianapolis: Liberty Fund, 1979), 314.

35. Ralph Adams Cram, *My Life in Architecture* (New York: Little, Brown, 1937).

36. Ralph Adams Cram, *The Nemesis of Mediocrity* (Boston: Marshall Jones Co., 1917).

37. Cram, *The Nemesis of Mediocrity*, 21–22, 25–26.

38. Cram's essay is reprinted in Robert Crunden, ed., *The Superfluous Men: Conservative Critics of American Culture*, 2nd ed. (Wilmington, Del.: Intercollegiate Studies Institute, 1999), 122–34.

39. Terry Teachout, *The Skeptic: A Life of H. L. Mencken* (New York: HarperCollins, 2002), 14. For a recent complete biography of Mencken, see Marion Elizabeth Rodgers, *Mencken: An American Iconoclast* (New York: Oxford University Press, 2005).

40. Teachout, *The Skeptic*, 191.

41. Edward J. Larson, *Summer for the Gods: The Scopes Trial and America's Continuing Debate over Science and Religion* (New York: Basic, 2006).

42. H. L. Mencken, "The Hills of Zion," in *A Mencken Chrestomathy* (New York: Vintage, 1982 ed.), 396–98.

43. H. L. Mencken, "In Memoriam: WJB," in *A Mencken Chrestomathy* (New York: Vintage, 1982 ed.), 243–48.

44. H. L. Mencken, *Notes on Democracy* (New York: Knopf, 1926), 212.

45. Jose Ortega y Gasset, *The Revolt of the Masses* (New York: Norton, 1932), 18.

46. Gordon Lloyd, *The Two Faces of Liberalism: How the Hoover-Roosevelt Debate Shapes the 21st Century* (Salem, Mass.: M & M Scrivener Press, 2007), 35, 36.

47. David M. Kennedy, *Freedom From Fear: The American People in Depression and War, 1929–1945* (New York: Oxford University Press, 2001), 189.

48. Richard Norton Smith, *The Colonel: The Life and Legend of Robert R. McCormick, 1880–1955* (New York: Houghton Mifflin, 1997), 331.

49. H. L. Mencken "The New Deal," in *A Mencken Chrestomathy*, 426–28; Amity Shlaes, *The Forgotten Man: A New History of the Great Depression* (New York: HarperCollins, 2007), 47–84 (on the junket); quotes from pp. 83–84.

50. Paul V. Murphy, *The Rebuke of History: The Southern Agrarians and American Conservative Thought* (Chapel Hill: University of North Carolina Press, 2001), 14.

51. Twelve Southerners, *I'll Take My Stand: The South and the Agrarian Tradition* (Baton Rouge: Louisiana State University Press, 1977; first published 1930), xliii.

52. Twelve Southerners, *I'll Take My Stand*, xlvi.

53. Letter from Donald Davidson to [Finney], November 6, 1930, Box 1, Folder 16 (Outgoing Corr., 9/27/30–11/26/30), Donald Davidson Papers, Special Collections and University Archives, Heard Library, Vanderbilt University, Nashville, Tennessee.

54. Letter from Davidson to Richard Weaver, March 13, 1949, Box 1, Folder 3 (Essays) Agrarianism in Exile (draft), Richard M. Weaver Papers, Heard Library, Vanderbilt University.

55. Upton Sinclair to Seward Collins, January 16, 1930, Box 11, Series I, Folder 306 (Upton Sinclair Corr., 1929–1934) ; and Collins to Irving Babbitt, September 30, 1929, Box 2, Series I, Folder 29 (Irving Babbitt Corr., 1929–1930), Seward Collins Papers, Beinecke Rare Book and Manuscript Library, Yale University.

56. Hilaire Belloc, *The Servile State* (Indianapolis: Liberty Fund, 1977; first published 1913), 50.

57. Seward Collins, "The *American Review*'s First Year," 3, no. 1 *American Review* (April 1934): 124.

58. Letter from Sinclair to Collins, May 31, 1933, Box 11, Series I, Folder 306 (Upton Sinclair Corr., 1929–1934), Collins Papers.

59. Albert R. Stone Jr., "Seward Collins and the *American Review*: Experiment in Pro-fascism, 1933–1937," *American Quarterly* 12, no. 1 (Spring 1960): 7. See also Edward S. Shapiro, "American Conservative Intellectuals, the 1930s and the Crisis of Ideology," *Modern Age*, 6, no. 4 (Fall 1979): 370–80.

60. Nock, *Our Enemy the State*, 11.

61. Stone, "Seward Collins," 15–16.

62. Herbert Agar to Seward Collins, May 26, 1936, Box 1, Series I, Folder 10 (Herbert Agar), Collins Papers. Only Donald Davidson expressed his support for Collins, telling him "we might differ with you, as you have indicated, on some matters of procedure, or even, here and there, of theory. But it seems to me that on matters of fundamental importance we agree about as well as Americans interested in the same general ends can hope to agree." Davidson to Collins, May 27, 1936, Box 4, Series I, Folder 115 (Donald Davidson Corr., 1936), Collins Papers.

63. Stone, "Seward Collins," 17.

64. Letter from Collins to Borah, n.d. Box 1, Series I, Folder 55 (William Borah Corr.), Collins Papers.

65. Lawrence Dennis, *The Coming American Fascism* (New York: Harper, 1936).

66. Quotes on Dennis's views of FDR, Churchill, and Hitler are from Justus Doenecke, "Weekly Foreign Letter," in Lora and Longton, eds., *Conservative Press*, 286–87.

67. Ronald Radosh, *Prophets on the Right: Profiles of Conservative Critics of American Globalism* (New York: Simon & Schuster, 1975), 290–91.

68. Lawrence Dennis and Maximilian St. George, *The Trial On Trial* (New York: National Civil Rights Committee, 1946), 409–11.

69. The revelations concerning the penetration by Soviet intelligence into the executive branch of government before and especially during World War II became public in 1995 when the top secret Venona Project was declassified by the federal government. There is now a large literature on Venona that confirms that individuals once accused of being communists by Elizabeth Bentley and Whittaker Chambers were indeed working for Soviet intelligence. See Herbert Romerstein and Eric Breindel, *The Venona Secrets* (Washington, D.C.: Regnery, 1999); John Earl Haynes and Harvey Klehr, *Venona* (New Haven, Conn.: Yale University Press, 2000).

70. Robert Shogan, *Backlash: The Killing of the New Deal* (Chicago: Ivan R. Dee, 2006), 190, 191; see Thomas Girdler, *Bootstraps* (New York: C. Scribner's Sons, 1943), for his account.

71. Letter from Bronson Batchelor to J. Howard Pew, August 31, 1943, Box 3, Folder B (1943), Pew Papers.

72. George Wolfskill, *Revolt of the Conservatives: The American Liberty League, 1934–1937* (New York: Houghton Mifflin, 1963), 21–22.

73. Wolfskill, *Revolt*, 35–36; Morton Keller, *In Defense of Yesterday: James M. Beck and the Politics of Conservatism, 1861–1936* (New York: Coward-McCann, 1958).

74. Lloyd, *Two Faces of Liberalism*, 260.

75. Wolfskill, *Revolt*, 151–53.

76. Quotes from Lloyd, *Two Faces of Liberalism*, 304, 306.

77. Shlaes, *Forgotten Man*, 334; James T. Patterson, *Congressional Conservatism and the New Deal: The Growth of the Conservative Coalition in Congress, 1933–1939* (Lexington: University of Kentucky Press, 1967).

78. Walter Goodman, *The Committee: The Extraordinary Career of the House Committee on Un-American Activities* (New York: Farrar, Straus & Giroux, 1968); Richard Gid Powers, *Not Without Honor: The History of American Anti-Communism* (New York: Free Press, 1996).

79. For Roosevelt's foreign policy see Robert Dallek, *Franklin D. Roosevelt and American Foreign Policy* (New York: Oxford University Press, 1972); Warren Kimball, *The Juggler: Franklin Roosevelt as Wartime Statesman* (Princeton: Princeton University Press, 1994); for the London conference, see Raymond Moley, *After Seven Years* (New York: Harper, 1939); for FDR setting the price of gold over breakfast, see Shlaes, *Forgotten Man*, 147–49; for the quote, see Alonzo L. Hamby, *For the Survival of Democracy: Franklin Roosevelt and The World Crisis of the 1930s* (New York: Free Press, 2004), 393.

80. John E. Wiltz, *From Isolation to War, 1931–1941* (New York: Thomas Y. Cromwell, 1968).

81. Buckley as witness to Chamberlain in London, see John O'Sullivan, "Man of Thought, Man of Action," *National Review* (March 28, 2008): 18. See William F. Buckley Jr., *Miles Gone By: A Literary Autobiography* (Washington, D.C.: Regnery, 2004), 22–24.

82. Justus Doenecke, *Storm on the Horizon: The Challenge to American Intervention, 1939–1941* (Lanham, Md.: Rowman & Littlefield, 2000), 8.

83. Remarks of Robert A. Taft on CBS Radio, June 25, 1941, *Congressional Record*, Vol. 87, Part 12, 77th Congress, First session, page A3077, Box 435, Political File (1952 Campaign—Communism), Robert A. Taft Papers, Library of Congress.

84. A. Scott Berg, *Lindbergh* (New York: Berkley Books, 1998), 422.

85. Letter from Robert Wood to William Henry Chamberlin, January 16, 1959, Box 2 (Corr.—William Henry Chamberlin, 1950–1959), Robert Wood Papers, Herbert Hoover Presidential Library, West Branch, Iowa.

86. Thomas Fleming, *The New Dealers' War: F. D. R. and the War within World War II* (New York: Basic, 2001), 549.

Chapter Two

Prophets, Proselytizers, and Pundits

The early conservative movement was a community. . . . One could come into a strange town and find immediate hospitality and companionship. . . . There was a bond of friendship. . . . A room full of five hundred people eating rubber chicken is no substitute for a night at Mecosta, Woodstock or Three Oaks.

—Stephen J. Tonsor

In August 1945, a few days after atomic bombs were dropped on Japan, Albert Jay Nock, one of the key intellectual figures in pre–World War II conservatism, passed away. The year before his death he had published his engaging and literate *Memoirs of a Superfluous Man*, written in the third person and, in keeping with the title, utterly devoid of any specific personal revelations about his own life. Nock had despaired about the chance of restoring the heritage of Western civilization to its former greatness and took comfort in the idea that, at least, a remnant of believers could still be found willing to preserve what remained.[1] The idea of the remnant anchored a view held by many pre-war conservatives dismayed by the degenerate nature of mass democracy.

Ten years later, one of the young people influenced by Nock, William F. Buckley Jr.—Nock had been a personal friend of Buckley's father and had often visited the Buckley home in Sharon, Connecticut—launched a new weekly magazine, *National Review*, which advocated an intellectual defense of Western civilization but also recommended action against the dominant liberalism. The young Buckley, while effete and urbane, could also be a populist—as in his defense of anticommunist Senator Joseph McCarthy. His famous quip that he would rather be governed by the first two hundred names in the Boston phone book than by all the professors at Harvard was not a statement one could imagine being made by Nock. With the founding of *National Review*, the direction conservatism had taken in its development up to the 1940s was irremediably altered. How did this occur and what impact did such a shift have on conservatism?

The main issues that altered conservatism were communism, both as an internal and an external threat, and the continued prominence of liberalism in American politics. The development of an effective opposition to both necessitated a "plunge into politics," the need to create electoral majorities to make conservatism the dominant political idea in America. But what conservatism could effectively appeal to electoral majorities? The answer was not the conservatism of Cram, Irving Babbitt, or the Southern Agrarians, or even the noninterventionism of America First. Before the task of challenging liberalism politically was mounted, conservatism would have to define its principles and proselytize its ideas. That is what conservatives set out to do, constructing in the end a movement with a definable, though not always agreed upon, intellectual position.

REAWAKENINGS

As World War II entered its climactic phase, many conservatives were worried. Russian troops had crossed the Polish frontier in 1944, having liberated most of the Soviet territory taken by the Nazis three long years before. In some of the most savage fighting ever witnessed in human history, Soviet troops destroyed and killed Polish and German civilians as they moved westward, repayment for the millions of Russians who had been killed in the German occupation of *Russland.*

On the home front, America was regimented like never before. Government spending had increased drastically, the number of people paying federal taxes had increased as well, and the means for government to secure tax dollars, the withholding tax, was developed. During the war, prices and wages were controlled by the Office of Price Administration (OPA) but inflation still proved a problem and fears of its continuance after the war worried businessmen and workers.[2]

Government spending on the war had a positive impact as well. It provided a cure for Depression, with unemployment sinking to an artificially low level of 1.2 percent in 1944. It led to economic development in the South and West, particularly California, areas that would soon become bastions not of liberalism but of conservatism. Cities like Detroit, Chicago, and Oakland burgeoned with migrants from the South and Midwest, drastically changing the makeup of those cities in terms of race, values, and religious belief.[3] The nation was on the move as more than 11 million men joined the services and as many as 20 million more people left home in search of new jobs.

Business executives as a result had regained much of the economic and social authority they had lost during the Depression, and they intended to keep it. The National Association of Manufacturers was revitalized and developed campaigns to sell free enterprise to the American public. Much of this involved the exposure of labor unions and an attack on government regulations, such as the OPA, and postwar Democratic efforts to secure a Keynesian full employment law, providing a trigger for government-induced spending to maintain "full employment."[4]

Certain conservative businessmen, like Sun Oil Company CEO J. Howard Pew, encouraged an "intellectual assault on the New Deal" and on liberalism. Pew endorsed the views in books written by Brown University President Henry Wriston and especially that of the Austrian economist Friedrich Augustus von Hayek, *The Road to Serfdom* (1944), which he called "a great book." He considered plans to get "Hayek's book in all college libraries in sufficient quantity." One correspondent told him that "I believe Hayek's book will be revolutionary in academic circles and it may be that the push it gives will cause the pendulum to swing back again toward more rational and more practical thinking."[5]

Hayek was an Austrian economist, born in Vienna in 1899, who had studied under the guidance of prominent free market economists such as Eugen Von Bohn-Bawerk and Ludwig Von Mises. He moved to London before the start of World War II and spent the war years teaching at the University of London. While there, surrounded by socialist academics not only in the economics department but in every other discipline, Hayek wrote a polemical essay, "dedicated to socialists of all parties," which was published by the University of Chicago Press. The book was a staggering success, was excerpted in *Reader's Digest*, and received attention from prominent journals and newspapers throughout the world.[6]

Hayek's argument was that England and America were replicating the road traveled by Germany between the World Wars. "It is necessary now to state the unpalatable truth that it is Germany whose fate we are in danger of repeating," Hayek warned. "For at least twenty-five years before the specter of totalitarianism became a real threat, we had progressively been moving away from the basic ideas on which western civilization has been built. . . . We have progressively abandoned that freedom in economic affairs without which personal and political freedom has never existed in the past. Although we had been warned by some of the greatest political thinkers of the nineteenth century, by De Tocqueville and Lord Acton, that socialism means slavery, we have steadily moved in the direction of socialism."[7]

The only solution to the drift toward socialism in the Western democracies was to enhance individual liberty and to maximize economic freedom based on the rule of law. Statist policies represented the "road to serfdom." Hayek's insight came at a time when classical liberal economics was on the defensive, not taught in most universities and colleges.[8] Planning was the norm and Hayek competed for prominence with John Maynard Keynes, the prominent British economist whose ideas about taxing and spending to promote economic growth (countercyclical spending, as theorists called it) were in vogue within government and in economics departments. Free market economics, it was generally thought, had been responsible for the worldwide depression and for the awful consequences that followed. The trend in the Western democracies when Hayek wrote was toward greater and greater economic control by government; indeed, in England, the Labor Party, elected in 1945, would embrace socialist planning and government control over the economy, with disastrous effects for British industry over the long term.

Hayek's book had a huge impact in the United States and he was given a position in the Committee on Social Thought at the University of Chicago. In 1947 Hayek formed an organization of economists, journalists, and philosophers in Switzerland. Named the Mont Pelerin Society, after the name of the resort where it first met, the organization dedicated itself to reestablishing the sundered intellectual, legal, and economic basis for liberty. Thirty-six academics attended the first meeting, including future Nobel Prize–winning economists Milton Friedman and George Stigler. Hayek and von Mises represented the Austrian economists and a few American journalists dedicated to free market principles attended as well. A talking salon more than a think tank, the society flourished as a place for the articulation of free market ideas.[9]

That an audience existed for Hayek's ideas in America testified to the long duration and strength of free market principles and laissez-faire conservatism. Such ideas and their purveyors had been marginalized by the political success of New Deal liberalism. Yet they had never quit the fight. Many journalists and intellectuals propagated on behalf of such ideas, including Garet Garrett, John T. Flynn (whose 1950 book *The Road Ahead* prophesized a world similar to that described by Hayek), and an individualist philosopher and journalist named Frank Chodorov.

Chodorov was born in 1887 in New York City, the eleventh child of Russian-Jewish immigrants. He attended Columbia University and worked in various careers before heading up the Henry George School of Social Science in New York in 1937.

Henry George's *Progress and Poverty* (1889) inspired what became known as the single tax movement. George's basic proposition was that the ownership of land, especially as speculation, was a social evil. The charging of rent by landowners should be abolished and the means to do this was what George called the "single tax," an exorbitant tax on land that would end speculation. Single-tax clubs spread throughout the country in the late nineteenth and early twentieth centuries and Georgist mayors were elected in several cities, promising single-tax reforms as a part of their political platform.

Chodorov was never interested in single tax as a political strategy, but rather in George's individualist philosophy. Chodorov wrote, "George is the apostle of individualism; he teaches the ethical basis of private property; he stresses the function of capital in an advancing civilization; he emphasizes the greater productivity of voluntary cooperation in a free market economy, the moral degradation of a people subjected to state direction and socialistic conformity. His is the philosophy of free enterprise, free trade, free men."[10] In a nutshell, that became the philosophy of Frank Chodorov as well.

Chodorov lost his job in 1942, in conflict with the school administrators owing to his refusal to accept the single tax idea. Isolated, and with only Nock as an intellectual comrade, Chodorov began his own publication, the journal *analysis*, in November 1944. Four pages in length and published by Chodorov himself, *analysis* delved into questions of free market economics, taxation, and natural rights. William F. Buckley Jr. would call it "the testimony of a single man," and Chodorov himself would refer to it as "an individualist publication—the only one of its kind in America."[11]

The journal's focus was on the issue of state power and how it was maintained by "coercion." The evidence for this, according to Chodorov, lay in the power the state received from the income tax. Chodorov argued that "when you unmask it, by means of reason and historical investigation, you see that taxation is highwaymanry made respectable by custom, thievery made moral by law; there isn't a decent thing to be said for it."[12] It was robbery, pure and simple.

Aside from domestic concerns, the bulk of *analysis* was dedicated to foreign policy, particularly the emerging policy of containment devised by President Truman to prevent Soviet expansion in Europe. In a widely read editorial in the July 1947 issue, Chodorov, who remained a dedicated isolationist (a term he readily accepted), argued that the Cold War doctrines of Truman had made America an empire. "Currently, fear of communism, fear that it will engulf Europe, fear that it will eventually penetrate this country and destroy the cherished American 'way of life,' is seeping into our consciousness," Chodorov wrote. "If we don't help Greece and Turkey, we are told, European culture must give way to this horrible communism." This fear propaganda, he called it, obscured the evidence that "communism is already the religion of Europe." The only way to defeat it is a "policy of unlimited production," one which frees people and leaves them alone to produce. Truman's policy, which relied on American economic, and eventually, military aid, strengthened America's empire but would not defeat the poverty and despair that communism fed on.[13]

Chodorov believed communism was evil, part of the statist fallacy that threatened the freedom and liberty of individuals throughout the world. Yet he believed that efforts to combat communism both abroad and at home, through the House Committee on Un-American Activities, were wrongheaded, and would eventually create a totalitarian society in the United States. In "How to Curb the Commies," Chodorov wrote, "the menace of communism will not be removed by investigations, by legal prosecutions, or by legislation outlawing its advocates; all such measures are dangerous in that they open the way to attacks on freedom of thought. To curb communists, the government has all the power it needs or ought to have. If the communists succeed, it will be only because the politicians, by neglecting their duty to society, become their accomplices."[14] Chodorov remained committed to his prewar conservative noninterventionism and especially its commitment to individual liberty and hostility to empire.

Felix Morley was a conservative who agreed with both Hayek and Chodorov. Morley was born in 1892 on the campus of Haverford College. He served in World War I in the ambulance corps, had been appointed a member of the American delegation at Versailles, and had covered the tumultuous revolution in China during the 1920s. In the early 1930s he became editor of the *Washington Post* and became disenchanted with Roosevelt and the New Deal. At the end of the decade he was selected to be president of Haverford College, serving in that capacity until 1945.[15]

Morley was alarmed at events in Europe. He had opposed American entry into World War II but had never joined the America First movement. He watched events keenly, keeping a diary until the end of his tenure as Haverford president, where he commented on foreign and domestic affairs. In early 1944 he wrote, "the semi-Oriental . . . civilization of Russia, personified by [Josef] Stalin, that reincarnation of Genghis Khan, is steadily working to take over the ruins of Europe." "In Bulgaria, Greece and Yugoslavia," he wrote, "the communist movement is steadily gaining."[16] Reflecting conservative disenchantment with Roosevelt's war diplomacy, Morley believed that "so far as one can judge Stalin had everything his way at Teheran [a 1943 conference between the Allied leaders] and the Anglo-American role henceforth is really to 'soften up' western Europe for the eventual triumph of the Bolsheviks."[17]

Conservative commentators had been predicting such a result since before the war. Journalist William Henry Chamberlin, in *The Confessions of an Individualist* (1940), wrote: "Hitlerism and Stalinism stand exposed as com-

pletely opportunistic dictatorships, animated only by lust for power and plun-
der and disassociated from any social or economic ideas. . . . The Communist
and Nazi regimes now appear as devoid of any coherent consistent body of
principles as the predatory Goths and Vandals, with whom, indeed, they possess disconcertingly many traits in common." Much like after World War I,
Chamberlin feared revolution and further war as an outcome of World War II.
Yet he hoped for something different: "There is a chance—a very faint
chance, I am afraid—that the revolutions, violent or peaceful, which must follow the new war will be of a different character, individualist rather than collectivist."[18]

One way to make such a faint hope a reality was to proselytize on behalf
of freedom. On February 3, 1944, a new eight-page newsletter, *Human
Events*, appeared. Founded by Morley, Chamberlin, and journalist Frank
Hanighen, coauthor of *The Merchants of Death* (1934), the journal was to be
one dedicated to noninterventionism and a pro-Constitutionalist viewpoint.
Morley suggested a title of "Old Republic" to suggest its leanings, but the
words from the first line of the Declaration of Independence were chosen instead.

The newsletter was a weekly. To fund the venture, Hanighen secured the
America First movement donor list from Robert Wood, and within the first
year of publication about 4,500 subscriptions were secured (at its peak
Chodorov's *analysis* had about four thousand subscriptions). Joseph Pew,
Charles Lindbergh, and William Regnery were important financial contributors to *Human Events* and continued to share its outlook, the reestablishment
of an America First–styled noninterventionism after the war.[19]

The publication was dominated in its early years by foreign policy concerns. Morley argued in a widely distributed announcement of the newsletter
that "it seems . . . high time for careful, objective, and continuous examination of America's place in the postwar world, undertaken primarily from the
viewpoint of the essential American tradition." In one essay, "For Yalta, Read
Munich," Morley attacked Roosevelt's appeasement of Stalin at the February
1945 Yalta conference, equating the results with British Prime Minister
Neville Chamberlain's appeasement of Hitler at the 1938 Munich conference.[20] Chamberlin also contributed on foreign policy issues, focusing on
how Roosevelt's policy created the means for Soviet expansion in Europe.
Such views were echoed in his 1950 book, *America's Second Crusade*, which
argued that "failure to foresee the aggressive and disintegrating role which a
victorious Soviet Union might be expected to play in a smashed and ruined
Europe and Asia was the principal blunder of America's crusading interven-
tionists. . . . The majority erred out of sheer ignorance and wishful thinking
about Soviet motives and intentions."[21]

After a year in publication, Henry Regnery, the son of textile manufacturer William Regnery, became involved with *Human Events*, helping to establish a publishing firm around the newsletter dedicated to pamphlets and eventually, to books. He would establish the Henry Regnery Company, a book publishing firm headquartered in Chicago and dedicated to publishing works of enduring value and quality.

Regnery was born in 1912 in the Chicago suburb of Hinsdale, Illinois, an affluent area eighteen miles west of the city along the Chicago, Burlington, and Quincy Railroad. He wrote fondly of growing up in the burg, of playing in the woods near the Salt Creek, and of being educated in a one-room schoolhouse by dedicated female teachers. After graduation from public high school, Regnery attended Armour Institute of Technology on Chicago's South Side before transferring to MIT, where he received a degree in mechanical engineering. He studied in Germany for two years during the mid-1930s, establishing long-lasting friendships with anti-Nazi intellectuals and political figures, some of whom would play crucial roles in the creation of a democratic West Germany after World War II.

In 1936, then a supporter of Roosevelt's New Deal, Regnery entered graduate school in economics at Harvard University. In his memoirs, he claimed to have had an intellectual conversion at this point after he took courses with Austrian economist Joseph Schumpeter, who convinced him of the efficacy of the free market. The conversion was not immediate, however, as Regnery took a position with the Resettlement Administration (RA) in western Pennsylvania, working at a planned community funded by the RA known as Penn Craft.[22]

Regnery worked for his father's textile business in Chicago during the war but looked to establish a publishing venture. He joined with Morley and Hanighen at *Human Events*, initially to turn the publication into a slick weekly conservative journal. With Regnery's entrance, *Human Events* went through a small makeover, adding a political sheet "Not Merely Gossip," edited by Hanighen and dedicating larger, more philosophical issues to the pamphlet series published by Regnery.

By 1949, however, differences between Hanighen and Morley became more intractable and Morley left the newsletter, claiming that his health was beginning to be affected by his work. More important may have been the changing editorial position of the newsletter, and of conservatism. With the Cold War raging and with conservatives supportive of the efforts of Truman and the GOP Congress to extend military and economic aid to nations fighting communism, the older pre-war conservatism was being replaced by an internationalism that supported the fight against communism. Morley held fast to his prewar noninterventionism the remainder of his life; by the 1960s he would tell correspondents that *Human Events* had descended into "fanatical

obscurantism," blaming Hanighen and new editor Jim Wick for making the
publication one which seemed to "emphasize bitterness, xenophobia, and nar-
row nationalism."[23]

Along with *Human Events* and *analysis* there were a few other conservative publications in the early years of the Cold War. Isaac Don Levine published an anticommunist monthly, *Plain Talk*, from 1946 to 1950. But it
merged with *analysis* and was succeeded in 1950 by a new venture, *The Freeman*. The idea for *The Freeman* was to create a journal dedicated to classical
liberalism. Backed by industrialists J. Howard Pew, Jaspar Crane (DuPont
Chemical), and textile manufacturer Alfred Kohlberg, and with six thousand
subscribers its first year, the journal got off to a promising start, dedicated to
both principles of free market economics and, in theory, a criticism of the
Cold War. Edited by journalists John Chamberlain, Henry Hazlitt, and
Suzanne LaFollette (an old editor of Nock's journal of the same name), the
biweekly was to be dedicated to the freedom of the individual and to uncovering the principles behind the "institution of a liberal society."[24]

The journal struggled, however, between support for the Cold War—with
Chamberlain, LaFollette, and William Henry Chamberlin being convinced of
the efficacy of intervention (which they hoped would be of short duration)—
and those Old Right authors, like Chodorov, Garrett, and John Flynn, who
worried about the garrison state that would have to be established in America
in order to wage a global crusade against communism.

These debates moved the journal from its original purposes and investors
in the magazine began to worry about the publication's Cold War positions,
as well as its focus on political issues. Pew, who had given as much as
$150,000 in three years to the magazine, told Hazlitt that "my conception of
the *Freeman* was that it would be a magazine designed for the purpose of developing a strong economic and social philosophy. . . . My position is that we
should not be interested in putting out a Republican paper."[25]

Pew told Crane, who had also invested heavily in the journal, "I am not going to support a paper which is not dedicated to the one objective—that of
telling the truth and thereby contributing to the saving of America. If the paper is going to be used for the purpose of taking sides on issues which are not
in themselves fundamental, I have no further interest in the *Freeman*."[26]
Within a few years, *The Freeman* moved away from being a political and foreign affairs journal and rededicated itself to the philosophical defense of classical liberal economics. After 1955 it was published by the Foundation for
Economic Education in Irvington-on-Hudson, New York.

The Foundation for Economic Education (FEE) was founded in 1946 by
Leonard Read. Read was born in Michigan in 1898. A World War I veteran,
he entered the wholesale produce business before moving to California to
pursue a career in real estate (a gangland killing of one of his competitors in

the produce business served as the motivation for the move). He became active in the Chamber of Commerce and in 1939 was appointed general manager of the Los Angeles branch of the Chamber. Initially a supporter of the New Deal, Read's intellectual life was changed due to his friendship with William Mullendore, a former assistant to Herbert Hoover and vice president of Southern California Edison. It was Mullendore who convinced Read that the New Deal represented the road to socialism and urged him instead to embrace free market philosophies at the Chamber.[27]

Read was frustrated by businessmen who adjusted to the new realities of government control, which only worsened during the war. Wanting to propagate on behalf of the "freedom philosophy," Read established FEE, getting a personal check for $10,000 from retired motor oil executive H. B. Earhart (who would later establish a conservative foundation, the Relm-Earhart Foundation) to fund a new think tank dedicated to a classical liberal philosophy. By 1947 FEE had secured close to $250,000 in donations, allowing it to buy an old mansion on the Hudson and to make Read a well-paid think tank president at $25,000 per year. He traveled extensively each year trying to raise money, find like-minded individualists, and propagate on behalf of limited government and individual rights.

During those early years the FEE board chose a "great books" approach modeled on the success of Hayek's *Road to Serfdom*. One of their biggest successes came with the publication of Henry Hazlitt's *Economics in One Lesson* (1946) and French economist Frederic Bastiat's *The Law*. It was able to get these books, discussing in simple terms the primacy of free market economics and the dangers of government intervention, circulated widely to teachers, schools, libraries, and other outlets. Some 4 million copies of FEE literature were distributed in the first decade of the organization's existence, much of it due to the doggedness of the group's founder, Leonard Read.[28]

When FEE took over *The Freeman*, it published many important conservatives as contributors in the early 1950s, including William F. Buckley Jr., James Burnham, and Frank Meyer. The latter two were ex-communists. Increasingly, those who articulated a new conservatism came from the ranks of communism, and advocated a strong American foreign policy and vibrant intellectual challenge to communism. The conservative movement was altered profoundly by the entry into its ranks of former Reds.

THE ROAD FROM SERFDOM

One of the most prominent among these conservative converts was a former Trotskyite, and perhaps the most well-known Leftist intellectual in America,

James Burnham. Burnham was born in 1905 in Chicago, the son of a railroad executive. He attended Princeton University and Oxford's Balliol College before taking a position as a philosophy instructor at New York University. With the onset of the Depression and under the influence of his philosophy colleague Sidney Hook, Burnham became interested in Marxism and joined a Marxist party in New York, the American Workers Party (AWP). By 1934 he had become attracted to the principles of Leon Trotsky, the exiled Russian revolutionary who called for true internationalism as opposed to Josef Stalin's building of "socialism in one country." Under a death sentence from Stalin, Trotsky lived in the United States and Mexico, where he was eventually murdered by Stalin's agents in 1940. Burnham coedited the Trotskyite journal, *The New International*, and also wrote for journals such as *Partisan Review,* becoming one of the best known Left intellectuals during the depression years.[29]

With Trotsky's assassination and with war raging in Europe, Burnham began to have doubts about Marxism. In 1941 these doubts were displayed in his best-selling book *The Managerial Revolution: What Is Happening in the World*. Burnham argued that the world was experiencing a social revolution, a transition as consequential as Marx's analysis of the transition from feudalism to capitalism. "This transition is from the type of society which we have called capitalist or bourgeois to a type of society which we shall call managerial," Burnham wrote. "What is occurring in this transition is a drive for social dominance, for power and privilege, for the position of ruling class by the social group or class of the managers." The process, he argued, was already well under way, as evidenced by the social revolution in Germany and Soviet Russia. Burnham believed it was going to spread and by the end of this transition "there will be no direct property rights in the major instruments of production vested in individuals as individuals."[30] In other words, capitalism would be vanquished by managerialism.

Burnham increasingly analyzed the world situation in terms of power rather than class interests. He followed up *The Managerial Revolution* with *The Machiavellians* (1943), a book that explored the theories of power of political theorists and sociologists Vilfredo Pareta, Gaetano Mosca, and Robert Michels. The book discussed the virtues of Machiavelli's reasoned understanding of political power and his study of men who wielded it. Burnham found this understanding useful as it gave hope to those who confronted the new managerialism, perhaps offering a means whereby the slide toward dictatorship could be avoided.

In these two books and in many other essays published during the war and immediately after, Burnham's movement away from Marxism was clear. By the start of the Cold War, Burnham and many other Trotskyites became disaffected with the Stalinist conception of the Soviet Union as a "worker's state" and dedicated themselves to exposing the lies of Stalinism and the evil of communism. This would culminate in Burnham's appointment with the Central Intelligence Agency and with his role in constructing the Council on Cultural Freedom, an agency funded by the CIA that provided an intellectual defense of the traditions of Western civilization.[31]

For other ex-communists, the path to freedom and the defense of liberty was a bit more tortured. Whittaker Chambers was best representative of this journey. Born in 1901, Chambers had been one of the greatest literary talents on the American Left. He was educated at Columbia University, where he became a member of the communist party, and wrote for communist publications like *The Daily Worker* and *The New Masses*. A forlorn figure, living a secret homosexual life that he knew the party disproved of, Chambers decided to enter underground work on behalf of Soviet military intelligence, recruiting spies and agents within New Deal agencies in Washington, D.C. It was in his work as an underground agent that he recruited Alger Hiss, a well-connected lawyer for the Agricultural Adjustment Agency whose brother and wife were also communist sympathizers. After Hiss moved on to the State Department, Chambers received top secret documents from Hiss—giving Hiss a Bokhara rug as payment—and kept the documents hidden in a relative's apartment before moving them to his Maryland farm.

He grew disenchanted with underground operations, fearing for his life after a friend was called to Moscow and never returned, presumably killed in the Stalinist purges of the late 1930s. Chambers left the party, secured employment as an editor with *Time* magazine, and converted to Christianity. In 1940 he approached the FBI about his activities but Roosevelt refused to believe the stories. In 1947, Chambers testified before HUAC, following the testimony of "the Red spy queen," Elizabeth Bentley. He confirmed that the individuals Bentley named were on the Soviet payroll, including Undersecretary of the Treasury Harry Dexter White and former State Department official, Alger Hiss.[32]

Hiss was called before HUAC; he denied spying on behalf of the Soviets and denied knowing Chambers (who had used the name Crosley in his dealings with Hiss). At one meeting, Hiss even asked if he could inspect Chambers's teeth. After Chambers made the accusation against Hiss public (over radio), Hiss sued for libel. Chambers was ultimately persuaded by young Congressman Richard Nixon to provide evidence of Hiss's guilt to the committee; pressured to do so, Chambers produced the documents from a hollowed-out pumpkin on his farm. These top secret documents were enough to secure a perjury charge against Hiss (the statute of limitations on espionage had expired) and, after two trials, Hiss was convicted and imprisoned.[33]

Chambers was vilified by the press and by government officials, including President Truman, Secretary of State Dean Acheson, and others, for accosting Hiss. The Venona cables, released in 1995, have proven Chambers correct; Hiss was a Soviet agent in the 1930s. However, that did Chambers little good at the time. A melancholy figure, he considered suicide at several points during this drama; fortunately, he chose to write about his experiences instead, publishing a powerful and moving memoir, *Witness* (1953).

Chambers described communism as "the vision of man's mind displacing God as the creative intelligence of the world. . . . Communism restores man to his sovereignty by the simple method of denying God." With the denial of traditional religious faith in the early twentieth century, Chambers contended, man was attracted to the logical last step of rationalism: "if man's mind is the decisive force in the world, what need is there for God? Henceforth, man's mind is man's fate. This vision is the Communist revolution." The break with communism comes when "one night [one] heard screams." Though communism denies it, "in every man . . . there persists . . . a scrap of soul," and the screams testify to the agony experienced by those victimized by communism, by coming to terms with the fact that "economics is not the central problem of this century. . . . Faith is the central problem of this age." *Witness* proved an extraordinarily powerful testament to one man's journey from communism with its worship of man, to Christianity and its worship of God.[34]

Chambers was a soul in turmoil, and this is vividly depicted in the book. *Witness* reached a huge audience, serving as an inspiration for millions who read its lovely prose and took in the message of redemption therein, the message of moral witness against an ideology that denied faith. Still, Chambers had difficulty finding peace. Vilified by the press and by old friends, Chambers withdrew, virtually secluding himself on his farm, where he died in 1961, convinced the West had lost the Cold War.[35]

TRADITIONALISM REVIVED

Many conservatives approached the new dawn of the atomic age with trepidation. The American use of the atomic bomb against Japan and the utter destruction of the war alarmed many postwar intellectuals. Richard Weaver, a professor of English at the University of Chicago, compared modern war to a "lynching party." "The object now," Weaver wrote, "is to pulverize the enemy completely, men, women and children being lumped into one common target; it is to reduce the country to 'atomic ashes,' to recall a frightening phrase which I saw recently in a newspaper. And then, if anything remains, the next step is the unethical one of demanding unconditional surrender."[36]

Weaver was a traditionalist conservative, in the vein of Irving Babbitt. Born in Weaverville, North Carolina, in 1910, Weaver was the intellectual heir to the Southern Agrarian tradition. But there was a lot of mythology surrounding his earlier origins: "Dick remained a countryman. . . . He plowed his lands in Weaverville with a mule," wrote his friend Eugene Davidson.[37] That is doubtful, for Weaver was raised in Asheville, North Carolina, and Lexington, Kentucky, and it was not until 1953, according to his biographer, that he would return to Weaverville on a regular basis, and then only during the summer months. He was, instead, a prototypical New South denizen, seeking an education and residing most of his life in urban areas in and outside of the South.

Weaver attended the University of Kentucky, dabbled in socialist politics during the Great Depression, and then began graduate study in English at Kentucky, before leaving in 1933 to attend Vanderbilt. It was at Vanderbilt that Weaver began to construct his defense of the Southern tradition. While not yet a convinced antiradical (he toyed with the idea of going to Spain in 1936 in defense of the Republic), it was at Vanderbilt where he decided to "junk Marxism as not founded in experience" and came to embrace, instead, "the church of Agrarianism."[38]

After teaching stints at Texas A&M University and Louisiana State University, where Weaver completed his dissertation on Southern thought (published posthumously), he received an instructorship in the college at the University of Chicago. Weaver taught undergraduates and was not given time to complete much research; nevertheless, with a dedicated work ethic and without a family to take his time (he remained a lifelong bachelor), Weaver produced a significant body of scholarship. The most important work he produced, one which he outlined as the war ended and the cataclysm of the nuclear age was dawning, was *Ideas Have Consequences*, published in 1948 by the University of Chicago Press.

Weaver argued pointedly that "we have for many years moved with a brash confidence that man had achieved a position of independence which rendered the ancient restraints needless. Now, in the first half of the twentieth century, at the height of modern progress, we behold unprecedented outbreaks of hatred and violence; we have seen whole nations desolated by war and turned into penal camps by their conquerors. These signs of disintegration rouse fear, and fear leads to desperate unilateral efforts towards survival, which only forward the progress."[39]

What was responsible for the downward march of progress? It was not the New Deal or even World War II. Instead, Weaver claimed it was the nominalist heresy advocated by fourteenth-century monk William of Occam. Nominalism denied universals and "the denial of universals carries with it the denial of everything transcending experience. The denial of everything transcending experience means inevitably—though ways are found to hedge on this—the denial of truth. With the denial of objective truth there is no escape from the relativism of 'man the measure of all things.'"[40] It was this notion that set man on the path to the moral relativism that plagued the modern world.

Weaver's analysis of the philosophical condition of modern man was gloomy to say the least. If, as he contended, the roots of declension in the West lay at the feet of a monk six hundred years before, what could be done to change society? How could conservatives ever think about altering six centuries of history? Weaver's book was not programmatic and it was not meant to inspire conservative policy makers in Congress. But it did spark a revival of traditionalism, dormant since the 1920s, and through the cogency of Weaver's arguments, *Ideas Have Consequences* helped spark a conservative intellectual revival.

This revival was carried forward by a young professor at Michigan State University, Russell Kirk, who published *The Conservative Mind: From Burke to Santayana* (1953). Kirk's book was a historical and literary analysis of the conservative tradition in Anglo-American thought. Kirk himself had despaired of reawakening such a tradition, and like Weaver, seemed resigned to the fact of living in a world where truth and beauty had been routed. Kirk insisted that his book be entitled "The Conservative Rout." It was advice sagely rejected by his publisher, Henry Regnery.[41]

Kirk was born in Plymouth, Michigan, in 1918, the son of a railroad engineer. For a time, Kirk worked at the Dearborn factories of the Ford Motor Company. He came to despise the industrial revolution and embraced a traditionalist ethos that found him leaving Michigan State University and residing the remainder of his life in the small central Michigan town of Mecosta, living the life of a conservative sage from some premodern past. He received a doctor of letters from St. Andrew's in Scotland, the first American accorded that honor, and it was in pursuit of his degree that he became enamored not only with the Scottish lowland countryside but also of the writings of Edmund Burke.[42]

Burke infused Kirk's work. "Every conservative thinker discussed in the following chapters—even the Federalists who were Burke's contemporaries—felt the influence of the great Whig, although sometimes the ideas of Burke penetrated to them only through a species of intellectual filter."[43] Burke's *Reflections on the Revolution in France* (1790) was the beginning for Kirk of a "conscious conservatism."

Kirk developed six canons of conservative thought. First, "belief that a divine intent rules society as well as conscience. . . . Political problems, at bottom, are religious and moral problems"; second, an "affection for the proliferating variety and mystery of traditional life"; third, a "conviction that civilized society requires orders and classes. The only true society is moral equality"; fourth, "property and freedom are inseparably connected and that economic leveling is not economic progress"; fifth, "faith in prescription and distrust of 'sophisters and calculators.' . . . Tradition and sound prejudice provide checks upon man's anarchic impulses"; and sixth, the "recognition that change and reform are not identical. . . . Society must alter, for slow change is the means of its conservation" but revolution and economic and political leveling were not to be tolerated by the proper conservative.[44]

Kirk's work was reviewed widely and he has been credited with giving a name—conservatism—to the movement of traditionalists (and even classical liberals) who were criticizing the dominant liberalism. Whittaker Chambers, an editor at *Time*, dedicated the entire book page to a lengthy and positive review of Kirk's work. Regnery would later claim in his memoirs that "after the long domination of liberalism, with its adulation of the common man, its faith in mechanistic political solutions to all human problems, and its rejection of the tragic and heroic aspects of life, such phrases as 'the unbought grace of life' and the 'eternal chain of right and duty which links great and obscure, living and dead,' and a view of politics as the 'art of apprehending and applying the Justice which is above nature' came like rain after a long drought."[45]

Historian George Nash has written that Kirk's book "dramatically catalyzed the emergence of the conservative intellectual movement" in a manner that Weaver's more philosophical traditionalism did not. Kirk wrote about a heritage of conservatism that conservatives could point to.[46] Liberal critics countered Kirk's work with the appellation "new conservatism" that they contended differed little from the conservatism of the 1920s. Lionel Trilling, a professor of English at Columbia University, would write in *The Liberal Imagination* (1950) that no conservative tradition existed in America; Louis Hartz would argue that only liberalism, whether classical or modern, counted as traditions in American society.[47] Kirk proved otherwise, finding and analyzing a canon of conservative thought that existed in America, from John Adams to the author George Santayana (in later editions, Kirk would add a discussion of the poet T. S. Eliot).

Conservatism by the early 1950s had reached adolescence in terms of its definition of principles. But there was no unity among the various factions of conservatism. Hayek, for instance, would heap scorn on the designation of his views as conservative, writing a scathing denunciation of the term and idea in "Why I Am Not a Conservative." Hayek believed the new conservatism "by its very nature cannot offer an alternative to the direction in which we are moving.

It may succeed by its resistance to current tendencies in slowing down undesirable elements, but since it does not indicate another direction, it cannot prevent their continuance."[48] Hayek also discussed the collective nature of conservatism, finding in its doctrine little difference from socialism. Both would need to rely on a powerful institution—whether for conservatives that was the church, or for socialists the state—to bring about the change they sought.

One of the harshest criticisms of Kirk came from a former communist-turned-conservative, Frank Meyer. Meyer attacked Kirk for embodying a "collectivist trend." Meyer wrote that "the fundamental political issue today is that between, on the one hand, collectivism and statism which merge gradually into totalitarianism and, on the other, what used to be called liberalism, what we may perhaps call individualism: the principles of the primacy of the individual, the division of power, the limitation of government, the freedom of the economy." Kirk's conservatism "is not a body of principles, but a tone, an attitude." Kirk rejected the individual as the basis for a society and thereby, programmatically, the only way his conservatism could be established was through force, and while Kirk would reject the idea, "any society of status today, with the increased potentialities of power of our times, could only move inevitably towards totalitarianism."[49]

Kirk was livid and told Regnery that "the present number of *The Freeman*, you will perceive, is the anti-Kirk number. Kirk is a deviationist, and is so denounced by Chodorov, Meyer and [William F.] Buckley. It is amusing to behold two radical Jewish atheists—one an anarchist and the other a 'reformed' Marxist—setting themselves up as the infallible authorities on One Hundred Percent Americanism."[50] The bitterness was long-lasting; Kirk continued to refer to Meyer as an ex-Marxist in his literate memoir *The Sword of Imagination* (1995), published a year after his death.

Richard Weaver defended Kirk as well in a letter to Regnery, saying that "the new conservatism is not a new form of the collectivist spirit . . . and I don't see how he could have arrived at a conclusion so outrageous." However, Weaver also agreed that Kirk's lack of specific formulations pointed to Kirk's "difficulty showing just what his conservatism rests on and what it would demand of those who followed it. . . . I think this is where the real spadework for a conservative movement now needs to be done."[51] Meyer had set the stage for a discussion on where conservatism should go.

FUSION

How had a former communist, one who served as a recruiter for the party until his break from communism in 1945, become a defender of individualism?

The answer lay in his experience with communism, with "the dark night of the soul" as Chambers called it, which affected every convert from that doctrine. Meyer's struggle was not religious (only at the end of his life in 1972 did he convert to Catholicism). His struggle was one embodying the doctrine of individual rights versus collectivism.

Frank Meyer was born in 1909 in Newark, New Jersey. He attended Princeton University but dropped out due to bad health. When the Depression started he found himself at Oxford, where he entered the British communist party. He moved on to the London School of Economics but was expelled for distributing communist literature. When he returned to America, under party discipline, he was assigned to Chicago and by 1938 was named educational director for the Illinois-Indiana region. Despite the Nazi-Soviet pact, Meyer remained in the party through World War II but increasingly grew disenchanted with party work, and especially with Stalin's totalitarianism. He broke with the party in 1945 and went into isolation at a home in Woodstock, New York, where he and his wife reeducated themselves in the principles of Western philosophy and political theory. After cooperating with the FBI in hearings on communism, Meyer began publishing articles and reviews for *The Freeman*, eventually being named a contributor and the chief book reviewer for the journal.[52]

It was at *The Freeman* where Meyer met and developed a close friendship with a young contributor who had come to national attention with the publication of his first book, *God and Man at Yale* (1951). That person was William F. Buckley Jr. Born in New York in 1925, the son of an oil company president who instructed his ten Catholic children in the verities of Western civilization and free market economics, Buckley was raised in privilege in Sharon, Connecticut, and Camden, South Carolina. He was a precocious youth who would write a letter to the king of England protesting England's foreign policy. A noninterventionist, his father supported America First financially, with Buckley taking an active role in debates with his siblings over the course of foreign policy in the late 1930s.

Buckley joined the service during World War II and after the war attended Yale University, where he excelled at debate (alongside his future brother-in-law and conservative comrade, L. Brent Bozell). He also became editor of the *Yale Daily News*. Buckley was captivated by an eccentric political science professor, Willmoore Kendall, an Oklahoman who taught at Yale. Kendall had published a book on John Locke and majority rule that he sought to inject into conservative doctrine. It was Kendall who helped shape Buckley's sense of the importance of democracy in American society.[53]

After he graduated from Yale, Buckley wrote a book exposing his alma mater, published by Regnery in 1951. The book, *God and Man at Yale*, was a smash and Buckley became a controversial figure as a result. He attacked Yale for condoning the instruction of socialism in economics and agnosticism in religion. The Yale Corporation attacked the brashness of the author, having McGeorge Bundy write the official Yale reply in a review published in *The Atlantic Monthly*. Bundy attacked Buckley's religion, discussing how the Catholic faith differed markedly on educational matters from Protestantism. In other words, as a Catholic, Buckley could not grasp the educational mission of Yale and was not an authoritative spokesman for the education he received in New Haven.[54]

That same year Buckley joined the CIA, serving as an operative in Mexico City. Buckley was fluent in Spanish; indeed, it was the first language he learned as a child. But life in clandestine service in the CIA in Mexico lacked the romance and intrigue of life in clandestine service in Europe, and Buckley soon tired of intelligence work, returning to America to pursue other avenues in conservative journalism.

Buckley wrote pieces for both *The Freeman*, as well as H. L. Mencken's old journal *The American Mercury*, soon to become a rabidly anti-Semitic publication under the control of Russell Maguire. He was chosen by Frank Chodorov as the first president of a new student organization called the Intercollegiate Society of Individualists (ISI). ISI was formed by Chodorov in 1953 as a society to recruit young college students for conservative and individualist causes. Buckley served as the organization's first president but he still looked for something else to contribute to conservatism.[55]

It was at this time that he seized on the idea of beginning a weekly journal of opinion dedicated to conservatism. Buckley was convinced of the need for such a journal by Austrian immigrant and ex-communist Willi Schlamm, who worked for *Time* magazine. Buckley set out to raise funds for the new venture, initially called "National Weekly." He wrote businessmen about the need for a new journal, telling industrialist Herbert Kohler that "the few spasmodic victories conservatives are winning these days are aimless, uncoordinated, and inconclusive. This is so, we believe, because many years have gone by since the philosophy of freedom has been expounded systematically, brilliantly, and resourcefully. This is a job for a weekly journal of opinion whose impact will be felt by the nation's opinion molders."[56]

It took about a year for the dream to become reality. Buckley solicited money from businessmen but he became the sole shareholder in the venture, typically relying on fund-raising appeal letters to readers and friends of the magazine. On November 19, 1955, the first issue of *National Review* appeared. In the issue Buckley famously wrote: "[*National Review*] stands athwart history, yelling Stop, at a time when no one is inclined to do so, or to have much patience with those who so urge it." Among the convictions of the magazine, Buckley wrote, were a variety of different beliefs: from the classical liberals, "it is the job of centralized government (in peace-time) to protect its citizens' lives, liberty and property. All other activities of government tend to diminish freedom and hamper progress"; from the traditionalists, "the profound crisis of our era is, in essence, the conflict between the Social Engineers, who seek to adjust mankind to conform with scientific utopias, and the disciples of Truth, who defend the organic moral order"; from the anticommunists, "the century's most blatant force of satanic utopianism is communism. We consider 'coexistence' with communism neither desirable nor possible." Buckley then labeled liberalism, world government, and socialism as additional enemies of the magazine.[57]

Among the editors who joined Buckley was James Burnham, who had become an apostle for the global war against communism, and who would play an indispensable role for Buckley of being a sounding board for ideas. Burnham was perhaps the most important editor at the magazine until a stroke incapacitated him in 1979. Frank Meyer would be listed as a contributor but within a few years became a columnist and books and arts editor for the magazine. Russell Kirk and Richard Weaver were contributors, as was Frank Chodorov and journalist John Chamberlain. Ex-communists like Max Eastman and writer John Dos Passos also contributed regularly in early issues.

Buckley had done something truly extraordinary. He had created a journal of opinion on the Right that brought together the various factions of conservatism. Traditionalists mingled with ex-communists. Classical liberals communed with traditionalists. Every other journal, from *Human Events* (by 1955 a political weekly only) to *analysis* to *The Freeman*, had emphasized a single aspect of conservative or anticommunist thought. Buckley's *National Review* created a conservative journal that waged unrelenting war against liberalism. Not all conservatives liked what *National Review* did. Some, like Whittaker Chambers, considered it, at times, to be "sophomoric," while others, like Kirk, believed it did not do enough to advance the traditionalist cause (in 1957 Kirk would form his own monthly journal, with Regnery's assistance, called *Modern Age*). As historian George Nash wrote, "to a very substantial degree, the history of reflective conservatism in America after 1955 is the history of the individuals who collaborated in—or were discovered by—the magazine William F. Buckley, Jr., discovered."[58]

While the magazine was representative of a consolidated conservatism, it still took several years for the movement to recognize that at the most basic level, different factions of conservatism could be reconciled. The person most responsible for working out this problem was Frank Meyer. How could positions such as the maximization of freedom for the individual and an insistence on establishing an organic social order be reconciled? Meyer would work on an answer over the course of five years in a column he wrote for *National Review* called "Principles and Heresies."

The culmination of Meyer's search for a defensible conservative position was revealed with the publication of *In Defense of Freedom: A Conservative Credo* (1962). In the book, Meyer argued about how classical liberalism and the new conservatism could be reconciled. He argued, "What I am defining is essentially the consensus of contemporary American conservatism. . . . At the source to which American conservatism inevitably returns—the Declaration of Independence, the Constitution and the debates at the time of its adoption—this simultaneous belief in objectively existing moral value and in the freedom of the individual person was promulgated in uncompromising terms. From that source it radiates the active present scene of American conservatism."[59]

Conservatives defended the freedom inherent in America's founding principles, which were the basis of American social order—republican democracy—and individual liberties. Within this "fusion" of principles, as *National Review* editor L. Brent Bozell labeled Meyer's new theory, both factions could accommodate and reconcile around American principles and ideas. Outside these principles lay the challenge of modern liberalism, what Meyer called throughout the book "collectivist liberalism," as well as totalitarian movements like Nazism and communism. These forms of political organization were detrimental to a "good society" whose premises were embodied by the ordered liberty the Founders created in America.

Meyer's fusion—a term he never much liked—became the basis around which an organized conservative movement would function until the end of the Cold War. Crucial to its success was the fact that ordered liberty could be accepted by individuals as diverse as Kirk and Hayek. Hayek might refute the label *conservative*, but that is what he was in the manner in which Meyer defined it. Kirk might not care much for Meyer or for individualism as a doctrine worth defending, but in the conservative movement Meyer helped construct, Kirk was a fusionist as well. Anticommunists who were conservative could also accept the fusionist mantle as both classical liberals and traditionalists opposed communism. In many ways it was anticommunism that provided the glue around which fusion worked. When the Cold War ended, political conservatism fractured.[60]

Fusionism never became an ideology of conservatism. It was more a tactic, a means for reconciling seemingly disparate intellectual positions. It also allowed conservatives to promulgate a movement of political activism, to propagate and proselytize a distinct conservative viewpoint, as opposed to the dominant liberal viewpoint in society. The fusionist ethos was centered at *National Review*, and while that flagship of conservatism was dominant, fusion remained the dominant creed.

But other varieties of conservatism never entirely went away. Individualism continued to be represented by individuals like Felix Morley, but also in radical forms by writers like Ayn Rand. Noninterventionism remained alive as well, with Lawrence Dennis promulgating such views in his privately distributed but well regarded *Appeal to Reason*. John Flynn never felt comfortable with Buckley or *National Review*. Other conservatives felt equally marginalized by the new journal's emergence and fought a rearguard action against *National Review*. But such actions only marginalized many of these individuals even more. William F. Buckley became a celebrity, which drove his publication to greater fame. He was charming, urbane, witty, conversational, everything that conservatism needed after a long time in the wilderness. He wrote books, sailed, played the harpsichord, and added a new literate quality to the English language. He ran for mayor of New York in 1965, telling voters he would demand a recount if he won. He hosted a program on Public Broadcasting for thirty-five years where intellectuals of all opinions jousted with Buckley. He became a public face for conservatism, only replaced by the equally charming and handsome visage of Ronald Reagan. He began to challenge the liberal consensus. He did not succeed at stopping history, but he helped chart its course in a more Rightward direction.

NOTES

1. Nock borrowed the idea of the remnant from his friend Ralph Adams Cram. He initially described this view in an essay entitled "Isaiah's Job," originally published in *The Atlantic Monthly* in 1936. It can be found in Albert Jay Nock, *The State of the Union: Essays in Social Criticism*, ed. Charles H. Hamilton (Indianapolis: Liberty Fund, 1991), 125–35.

2. A good overview of the conflicts within liberalism during the war can be found in Thomas Fleming, *The New Dealer's War: FDR and the War within World War II* (New York: Basic, 2002); Alan Brinkley, *The End of Reform: New Deal Liberalism in Recession and War* (New York: Knopf, 1995); see also, Brian Waddell, *The War Against the New Deal: World War II and American Democracy* (DeKalb: Northern Illinois University Press, 2001).

3. There is an extensive literature on the impact of demographic changes in postwar America in the urban north. See Robert O. Self, *American Babylon: Race and the Struggle for Postwar Oakland* (Princeton: Princeton University Press, 2005); and Thomas Sugrue, *The Origins of the Urban Crisis: Race and Inequality in Postwar Detroit* (Princeton: Princeton University Press, 1994).

4. A good description of these efforts can be found in Elizabeth Fones-Wolf, *Selling Free Enterprise: The Business Assault on Labor and Liberalism, 1945–1960* (Urbana: University of Illinois Press, 1995); and Robert M. Collins, *The Business Response to Keynes, 1929–1964* (New York: Columbia University Press, 1982).

5. Letter from Bronson Batchelor to J. Howard Pew, August 31, 1943, Box 3, Folder B (1943), J. Howard Pew Papers, Hagley Library and Museum, Wilmington, Del.

6. See Alan Ebenstein, *Friedrich Hayek: A Biography* (New York: Palgrave Macmillan, 2001).

7. Friedrich A. Hayek, *The Road to Serfdom* (Chicago: University of Chicago Press, 1994; first published 1944), 4, 5, 16.

8. One exception to this was the University of Chicago where a number of free market economists had established a veritable center for such thinking within the university. See Gregory Eow, "Fighting a New Deal: Classical Liberal Thought in the Depression Years" (PhD Dissertation, Rice University, 2007).

9. For a short history of the Mont Pelerin Society see Edwin Feulner, *Intellectual Pilgrims: The Fiftieth Anniversary of the Mont Pelerin Society* (Washington, D.C.: self-published, 1999); Max Hartwell, *A History of the Mont Pelerin Society* (Indianapolis: Liberty Fund, 1995); see also Alfred S. Regnery, *Upstream: The Ascendance of American Conservatism* (New York: Threshold, 2008), 30–34.

10. Frank Chodorov, *Out of Step: The Autobiography of an Individualist* (New York: Devin-Adair, 1962).

11. William F. Buckley Jr., *The Jeweler's Eye: A Book of Irresistible Political Reflections* (New York: Putnam, 1968), 343–49.

12. Frank Chodorov, *Fugitive Essays: Selected Writings of Frank Chodorov*, ed. Charles Hamilton (Indianapolis: Liberty Fund, 1980), 267–69; originally published as *Human Events* pamphlet "Taxation Is Robbery" (1947).

13. Frank Chodorov, "A Byzantine Empire of the West?" *analysis* (May 1947): 1–4.

14. Chodorov, "How to Curb the Commies," *analysis* (May 1949): 1–4.

15. Felix Morley, *For the Record* (Washington, D.C.: Regnery, 1979).

16. Felix Morley, Diary, [n.d.], Felix Morley Papers, Herbert Hoover Presidential Library, West Branch, Iowa.

17. Morley, Diary, December 11, 1943, Box 53, Volume 8 (Nov. 1942–June 1944), Morley Papers, Hoover Presidential Library.

18. William Henry Chamberlin, *Confessions of an Individualist* (New York: Macmillan, 1940).

19. See Frank Hanighen to Felix Morley, October 19, 1943, on recruiting financing for Human Events. Box 16, Corr. and Subj. File (Human Events Corr., 1943), Morley Papers, Hoover Presidential Library. For general details on the founding of Human Events, see Henry Regnery, *Memoirs of a Dissident Publisher* (Chicago: Regnery Publishing, 1985), 26–30.

20. Felix Morley, "For Yalta, Read Munich," *Human Events* (October 1945): 1–4.

21. William Henry Chamberlin, *America's Second Crusade* (Chicago: Regnery Publishing, 1950), 343.

22. Biographical information from Regnery, *Memoirs of a Dissident Publisher*; also, see Henry Regnery, *Perfect Sowing: Reflections of a Bookman* (Wilmington, Del.: Intercollegiate Studies Institute, 1999), 38–64.

23. Letter from Morley to Jim Wick, March 22, 1964, Box 22 (Corr. and Subj. Regnery), Morley Papers, Hoover Presidential Library. He would tell Regnery similar things about *Human Events*, calling it "angry, shrill and superficial," January 27, 1964, Box 53, Folder 1 (Morley Corr.), Regnery Papers, Hoover Institution.

24. Letter from J. Howard Pew to Henry Hazlitt, November 9, 1950, Box 111 (Freeman Magazine, 1950), Pew Papers.

25. Pew to Hazlitt, November 9, 1950, Box 111 (Freeman 1952), Pew Papers.

26. Pew to Jaspar Crane, July 10, 1952, Box 111 (Freeman 1952), Pew Papers.

27. Brian Doherty, *Radicals for Capitalism: A Freewheeling History of the Modern American Libertarian Movement* (New York: PublicAffairs, 2007), 149–50, 155–65.

28. Doherty, *Radicals for Capitalism*, 164.

29. Daniel Kelley, *James Burnham and the Struggle for the World: A Life* (Wilmington, Del.: Intercollegiate Studies Institute, 1997), 1–90.

30. James Burnham, *The Managerial Revolution: What Is Happening in the World* (New York: The John Day Company, 1941), 71.

31. Kelley, *James Burnham*, 115–81.

32. Sam Tanenhaus, *Whittaker Chambers: A Biography* (New York: Random House, 1995), 49–119.

33. Allen Weinstein, *Perjury: The Hiss-Chambers Case* (New York: Vintage Books, 1977).

34. Whittaker Chambers, *Witness* (New York: Regnery, 1980; first published 1954).

35. See William F. Buckley Jr., ed., *Odyssey of a Friend: The Correspondence of Whittaker Chambers and William F. Buckley Jr., 1954–1961* (New York: Putnam Publishing, 1969), for a sampling of letters revealing Chambers's turmoil.

36. Richard M. Weaver, "Up From Liberalism," *Modern Age* 3, no. 1 (Winter 1958–1959): 21–32.

37. Eugene Davidson, "Richard Malcolm Weaver—Conservative," *Modern Age* 7, no. 3 (Summer 1963): 227.

38. Ted Smith III, "Introduction," in Smith, ed., *Defense of Tradition: Collected Shorter Writings by Richard M. Weaver, 1929–1963* (Indianapolis: Liberty Fund, 2000), xi–xlviii, provides a complete biography of Weaver, taking issue with some of the myths in his background. See, also, Joseph Scotchie, *Barbarians in the Saddle: An Intellectual Biography of Richard Weaver* (New Brunswick, N.J.: Transaction, 1997), and Fred D. Young, *Richard M. Weaver, 1910–1963: A Life of the Mind* (Columbia: University of Missouri Press, 1995).

39. Richard Weaver, *Ideas Have Consequences* (Chicago: University of Chicago Press, 1948), 2.

40. Weaver, *Ideas Have Consequences*, 4.

41. Kirk contacted Regnery concerning the book in 1952 after it had been rejected by Knopf. See Letter from Russell Kirk to Henry Regnery, July 31, 1952, Box 39, Folder 9 (Russell Kirk Corr., 1952–1954), Henry Regnery Papers, Hoover Institution on War, Revolution, and Peace, Stanford University.

42. Russell Kirk, *The Sword of Imagination: Memoirs of a Half-Century of Literary Conflict* (Grand Rapids, Mich.: Eerdmans, 1994).

43. Russell Kirk, *The Conservative Mind: From Burke to Santayana* (Chicago: Regnery, 1953), 8–9.

44. Kirk, *Conservative Mind*, 9.

45. Regnery, *Memoirs of a Dissident Publisher*, 155–56. Regnery would write Kirk: "I am amused by Bill Buckley; he has adopted the name or rather, description, 'conservative.' Until fairly recently he called himself a libertarian, and it was only last

July [1954] that man [Frank] Meyer was equating conservatism with collectivism. Now all three of you—Russell Kirk, Bill Buckley and Frank S. Meyer seemed to have joined forces as conservatives." Regnery to Kirk, November 28, 1955, Box 39, Folder 10 (Russell Kirk Corr., 1955–1956), Regnery Papers.

46. George H. Nash, *The Conservative Intellectual Movement in America: Since 1945*, 2nd ed. (Wilmington, Del.: Intercollegiate Studies Institute, 1996), 104.

47. See Lionel Trilling, *The Liberal Imagination: Essays on Literature and Society* (New York: Viking, 1950), ix–x; Louis Hartz, *The Liberal Tradition in America* (New York: Harcourt, 1955).

48. Friedrich A. Hayek, "Why I Am Not a Conservative," in *The Constitution of Liberty* (Chicago: University of Chicago Press, 1960), 397–411.

49. Frank Meyer, "Collectivism Rebaptized," *The Freeman* (July 1955): 259–62.

50. Letter from Russell Kirk to Henry Regnery, July 5, 1955, Box 39, Folder 10 (Kirk Corr., 1955–1956), Regnery Papers.

51. Letter from Richard Weaver to Regnery, Regnery Papers.

52. Kevin Smant, *Principles and Heresies: Frank S. Meyer and the Shaping of the American Conservative Movement* (Wilmington, Del.: Intercollegiate Studies Institute, 2002).

53. On Kendall's influence on Buckley, see Nash, *Conservative Intellectual Movement*, 350–66; William F. Buckley Jr., *Miles Gone By: A Literary Autobiography* (Washington, D.C.: Regnery Publishing, 2004), 58–59.

54. Controversy over this is described in Nash, *Conservative Intellectual Movement*, 2nd ed., 204–5.

55. Lee Edwards, *Educating for Liberty: The First Half-Century of the Intercollegiate Studies Institute* (Washington, D.C.: Regnery Publishing, 2003), 11–12.

56. Letter from William F. Buckley, Jr. to Herbert Kohler, January 6, 1955, Box 3 (WFB Corr.)—Folder (Herbert V. Kohler, 1955–1957), William F. Buckley Papers, Sterling Library, Yale University.

57. Statement of Principles and Credenda, *National Review* (November 19, 1955): 1–3 reprinted in Schneider, ed., *Conservatism in America since 1930: A Reader* (New York: New York University Press, 2003), 201–5.

58. Nash, *Conservative Intellectual Movement*, 2nd ed., 233; Jeffrey Hart, *The Making of the American Conservative Mind: National Review and Its Times* (Wilmington, Del.: Intercollegiate Studies Institute, 2006).

59. Frank Meyer, *In Defense of Freedom: A Conservative Credo* (Washington, D.C.: Regnery, 1962). See also, Meyer, ed., *What Is Conservatism?* (Chicago: Regnery Publishing, 1964).

60. For disputes over fusionism, see Niels Bjerre-Poulsen, *Right Face: Organizing the American Conservative Movement, 1945–1965* (Copenhagen: Museum Tusculanum, 2003), 39–54.

Chapter Three

Getting to Know
(and to Like) the People

Communism is not a disease of poverty—it is a disease of the mind. The children of the very rich are far more susceptible to it than the children of the poor.

—Fred Koch

On May 1, 1950, the town of Mosinee, Wisconsin, was taken over by communists. The mayor and police chief were arrested, churches were closed (one enterprising minister hid the Bible), and restaurants served nothing but stale bread and potato soup at highly inflated prices. A prison camp was built on the outskirts of town to hold class enemies, library books were seized, and mass meetings were held in the town's center, renamed Red Square. Was Mosinee an unreported communist takeover, or is this a lost episode of the Rod Serling television series *Twilight Zone*?

It was neither, but it more closely resembled the latter in that the American Legion put on a real-life play involving most of the town's 1,400 inhabitants in order to showcase what would happen to freedom should an actual town in America succumb to Soviet takeover. Mosinee's passion play gained media attention as a result and served to buttress the idea that freedoms had to be guarded, both from internal enemies and from external ones, however unlikely the scenario of communist invasion in the nuclear age.[1]

Fear of communism and of communist subversion was deeply felt by millions of Americans. The Cold War climate intensified this fear. The presence of Soviet armies in the ravaged landscape of central Europe, poised to strike on a helpless and devastated West—the Genghis Khan imagery described by Felix Morley and others—was troubling to Americans in the uncertain climate of American foreign policy at the dawn of the atomic age. Despite

America's "preponderance of power," the specter of communist expansion haunted policy makers and officeholders, but mostly the American people, during the 1940s and 1950s. Eschewing their hostility to mass democracy, conservatives reached out to the majority of Americans based on their fear of, and hostility to, communism.

FROM ISOLATIONISM TO INTERNATIONALISM

The origins of the Cold War are still hotly debated by historians. Some historians have focused blame on Harry Truman, unknowledgeable about foreign affairs; others have blamed Josef Stalin and his seemingly insatiable demands for security. Stalin wanted a buffer zone controlled by pro-Soviet governments in eastern Europe to prevent a third German invasion of Russia in thirty years—an unlikely and implausible scenario to us today. Such demands drove western European governments and the United States to seek accommodations on a variety of security issues, including reconstruction aid for war-ravaged Europe, and, eventually, a military alliance, NATO, formed in 1950 to defend against a potential Soviet invasion.[2]

President Harry S. Truman, inexperienced when it came to foreign policy, made some momentous decisions in the face of this emerging threat. He authorized and supported a policy of containment, devised by State Department official George Kennan, to "contain Soviet expansive tendencies" in Europe, Japan, the Middle East, and in America. Turkey was threatened by Soviet diplomatic and military pressure; Greece, embroiled in a civil war between communists and the monarchy, faced collapse and communist control if the monarchy could not prevail. When Great Britain informed the U.S. government it could no longer support militarily its traditional interests in the eastern Mediterrenean, Truman secured $350 million from Congress in economic and military aid to prevent "external aggression" from bringing about the collapse of both governments. The aid worked. Turkey withstood the pressure, eventually becoming a strong ally to the United States and a member of NATO, and the communist insurgency in Greece was defeated.

That same spring, Truman offered Europe reconstruction assistance. Known as the Marshall Plan, after Secretary of State George Marshall, the economic assistance was offered to both western and eastern European governments. The Soviets flatly turned it down and forced client governments in eastern Europe to do so as well. The Republican Congress was hesitant concerning the costs of such assistance, but supported it after the Czechoslovakian government—which wanted to receive the aid—was overthrown in a Soviet-supported coup. Congress appropriated the funds; initially more than $11 billion in aid was sent to Europe. The aid did not entirely rebuild Europe—the western European governments, especially market-driven policies devised by Ludwig Erhard in West Germany, did much of that—but the Marshall Plan provided a psychological boost to the war-ravaged European nations.[3]

The early years of the Cold War were successful for Truman's containment policies. He devised a strategy, implemented it, and kept western Europe from succumbing to communism. He had overseen the creation of what would become known as the Cold War consensus. Both Democrats and Republicans could agree on the strategy of containing communism, a remarkable political achievement, especially since the GOP controlled Congress and still remained, for the most part, a noninterventionist party.

The shift among conservatives from the Old Right tradition of noninterventionism in foreign affairs to one of internationalism was helped immensely by the fact that the Republican Party controlled Congress between 1947 and 1949. It is possible to think of another scenario in which embittered noninterventionist conservatives refused to extend Truman any carrot regarding foreign policy. But the majority of the American public feared communism and supported politicians who recommended a continued defense of "the West" against it. Even though noninterventionists may have opposed, in principle, an extension of American military and economic aid in peacetime to Europe, they understood the practicality of such policies when it came to communism. As the Cold War intensified in the late 1940s and early 1950s, noninterventionism was increasingly implausible in a world of nuclear weapons, especially after the Soviets acquired the bomb in 1949.

Many of the pre-war noninterventionists became Cold War internationalists as a result. Communism was the main reason for the shift. Journalist William Henry Chamberlin, in *America's Second Crusade* (1950), a book critical of American policy in World War II, could argue about the Cold War: "the broad goal of American foreign policy is clear. It is to promote a worldwide cooperation of anti-Communist nations. . . . In the present state of the world this is no sentimental undertaking, no Third Crusade. This is an enterprise vital to American security, and America is the natural leader."[4] Chamberlin became an ardent defender of the Cold War and even urged military action against communist China during the 1950s.

Other conservatives who made the transition easily were publisher Henry Regnery and journalist William F. Buckley Jr. Journalist John Flynn became one of the more zealous defenders of anticommunist Joseph McCarthy in the 1950s. He also blamed Truman for losing China, accepting the arguments of the so-called Asia-lationists, former isolationists who became ardent defenders of Chiang Kai-shek and supported the China Lobby to prevent any normalization of relations with communist China.[5]

Many of the pre-war noninterventionists, like Felix Morley, journalist Garet Garrett, and Lawrence Dennis, never made the transition to Cold War internationalism. Morley remained hostile to the idea of the Cold War crusade, and accordingly, became marginalized in the new direction conservatism took following World War II. He would write Dennis in 1954, "I am half-amused and half-horrified by the way so many Americans dash from one end of the extreme to another. The former isolationists who now crave to start a hopeless war with Red China are a case in point."[6] Morley would consistently excoriate rising political stars on the Right, referring to supporters of Barry Goldwater (in the 1960s) as "a fascist element" and to Ronald Reagan (in the 1970s) as "a phony of the first order. . . . Robert Taft was the last intelligent leader [of the GOP] and the GOP now seems to me a tattered remnant actively preparing for *hari kari*."[7]

Garrett would continue to focus his writing on the subject of the welfare state and American empire. In *The Rise of Empire* (1953), Garrett wrote, "we have crossed the boundary that lies between Republic and Empire." The rise of the executive in the government, the increase of military expenditures, a system of satellite nations, the subordination of domestic policy to foreign policy, and the emotionalism of fear all signified the turn toward empire. Garrett glumly concluded, "The people know that they can have their Republic back if they want it enough to fight for it and to pay the price. The only point is that no leader has yet appeared with the courage to make them choose."[8]

Lawrence Dennis also opposed the Cold War in his self-published weekly broadsheet *The Appeal to Reason*. Dennis focused on the internal dangers of the Cold War, not simply the threat of communist subversion in government but also the impact of inflation, considering the high cost of Cold War defenses. He told Sterling Morton that the Korean War "proves that FDR and Truman did not know how to handle Russia and were too much influenced by pinks on the inside. As I see it, these results could not have been avoided once we were committed to unconditional surrender and the general ideology of religious war."[9] Harry Elmer Barnes, an America First supporter and sociologist, told Dennis in 1957, "all the America Firsters are now Formosa Firsters, Israel Firsters, Indo-China Firsters, Hungary Firsters and so on. The best one I have run on to recently is a very rich and very rightist foundation which is supporting a combination of 'Operation Israel,' 'Operation Vatican,' and 'Operation Cecil Rhodes.' It is the most extreme vindication of your Dumbrightist theme that I have turned up so far."[10]

Yet it was indeed the postwar trend away from noninterventionism that gave the conservative disposition in America the chance to implement the changes many of them sought, not only to oppose liberalism (as Buckley's *National Review* would set out to do in 1955), but also to support the prosecution of the war against communism. The noninterventionists who continued to oppose the Cold War, however principled their arguments, were not interested in the political ramifications of such principles. The Cold War had changed the political equation drastically, causing many conservatives to embrace a popular cause—anticommunism—and leading them to embrace mass democracy in the process.

HAD ENOUGH? ANTICOMMUNISM AND CONSERVATISM

What may have led to this development most was the electoral victory Republicans won in 1946, the stunning takeover of Congress after thirteen years out of power. Unlike in the New Deal era, where conservatives lacked the political power to influence events, the growing reaction against political controls over the economy and the deep fear of communist intrusion into government allowed the GOP and conservatives to take the initiative against liberalism. Running on the campaign slogan "Had Enough?" the GOP victory came at a crucial juncture. While their political control was short-lived—only two years—a precedent was established. Political power could be harnessed for conservative ends.

The GOP Congress focused their attention on two major concerns: opposition to further economic controls and hostility to the growing political influence of organized labor. The Republicans were elected due to their opposition to price controls embodied by the World War II Office of Price Administration (OPA), which Truman wanted to make permanent. Congress refused to extend the OPA beyond 1946, ending price controls and seeking to speed up the transition to a peacetime economy, including the demobilization of millions of men in the armed forces. Truman sought a full employment bill to maintain a full employment level—if unemployment sunk below a certain level, the government would intervene to ensure employment. The GOP watered down the bill and gave Truman instead a Council of Economic Advisors.

Truman faced a particularly difficult domestic situation after the war, similar to that experienced by Woodrow Wilson in the tumultuous year after World War I. Strikes were an immediate problem for the president as more than 4 million workers struck various industries, interested in higher wages after years of price controls. When railroad workers threatened to strike in late 1946, Truman said he would draft them into the military. Labor was not too enthusiastic for Democratic candidates in 1946 as a result.

One of the 80th Congress's most effective pieces of legislation was the Taft-Hartley Act, enacted into law in 1947 over a Truman veto. In the short run, the legislation led to the GOP losing Congress in 1948, as labor was still strong enough to influence elections; in the long run, however, Taft-Hartley was spectacularly successful at minimizing the power of organized labor, whose tentacles had reached so deep into the industrial economy. Big labor was never again as powerful as in the twenty or so years after World War II, its influence on the wane due to Taft-Hartley, as well as the declining industrial economy.[11]

The issue of communism in government was not only a major concern for postwar conservatives, but also for most Americans. Historian Richard Fried has argued that "public attitudes were molded by the political elites, but they were already strongly anti-communist . . . few citizens doubted that communism was an alien presence and a threat to the 'American way of life.'" Poll data show this. Some 36 percent of those polled in 1946 urged that communists be dealt with harshly, such as "get[ting] rid of them, deport[ing] them, shoot[ing] them, or jail[ing] them." Another 16 percent said they should be banned from public office. By 1947 61 percent urged outlawing membership in the Communist Party; by 1948 that number rose to 77 percent. As Fried concluded, "these levels of loathing had little to do with administration rhetoric."[12]

Catholics were at the forefront of such opposition. American Catholics had been key members of the New Deal coalition and would consistently support Democrats until the 1980s. But they wanted a hard line against communism. The Soviet takeover of Poland was one reason for this view (and the fact that such a takeover may have come about as a result of communist infiltration in the State Department—an assertion that remained unproven then—may have hastened their embrace of anticommunism). In 1946, 40,000 Catholics in Philadelphia protested the Soviet imprisonment of Yugoslav Archbishop Aloysius Stepinac, who was accused of collaboration with Nazis. Bishop Fulton Sheen spoke out against what he called "Red fascism" and "fellow travelers" on a nationally syndicated radio program.

In the 1946 elections, Catholic opposition to communism was crucial for the defeat of Democrats at the polls (the Democrats lost close to 40 percent of their seats in heavily Catholic cities like Chicago, Detroit, New York, and Los Angeles). Republicans capitalized on such disaffection by claiming that they would clean out "the Communists, their fellow travelers and parlor pinks from high positions in our government." Joseph McCarthy, a Catholic war veteran, ran against Robert LaFollette Jr., the incumbent senator from Wisconsin, in the primaries and used the Red issue to attack him; in the general election he referred to his opponent as "communistically inclined." Richard Nixon used similar tactics against his opponent Jerry Voorhis.[13]

The mood of the country had indeed shifted. Investigations into communism in government were being conducted by J. Edgar Hoover's FBI. Hoover had concluded that Truman was indifferent to the issue of communism in government. While Truman had established a federal loyalty program designed to investigate charges of disloyalty on the part of federal workers, the administration was lax in conducting the investigations. On March 26, 1947, in a famous appearance before HUAC, Hoover told the committee that it was up to them to make the fight against communism, that the administration was unwilling to do so. "I feel that once public opinion is thoroughly aroused as it is today, the fight against communism is well on its way. Victory will be assured once communists are identified and exposed, because the public will take the first step of quarantining them so they can do no harm. Communism, in reality, is not a political party. It is a way of life—an evil and malignant way of life."[14]

Hoover also testified that the FBI had done all in its power to allow the Truman administration the ability to expose communists in government. According to Hoover biographer Richard Gid Powers, "out of 6,193 cases the Bureau had investigated under the Hatch Act, there had been only 101 firings, 21 resignations, and 75 cases of administrative action."[15] This showed HUAC the way to credibility: seizing the reins of investigation away from the executive branch.

Congress had two committees, the House Committee on Un-American Activities, and the Senate Internal Subcommittee on Investigations, which kept the pressure on exposing communism in government. The former committee would score a touchdown with the October 1947 testimony of Elizabeth Bentley and Whittaker Chambers, who named Alger Hiss (then president of the Carnegie Endowment for International Peace) and Undersecretary of the Treasury Harry Dexter White as communist agents during the 1930s. White denied he was a communist but died from a heart attack before appearing as a witness; Hiss denied his spying as well but Richard Nixon eventually coaxed a reluctant Chambers to provide evidence. Chambers produced State Department cables from a hollowed-out pumpkin. Hiss was charged with perjury and after two trials was convicted and sentenced to five years in prison.

Probably the most famous HUAC investigation concerned Hollywood. In October and November 1947 HUAC moved its hearing to Los Angeles to investigate communism in the movie industry. A lineup of famous stars cooperated with the investigation, including Gary Cooper, who testified that "communism isn't on the level" and Screen Actors Guild (SAG) president Ronald Reagan. Reagan had fought against communist infiltration into the union after he was elected SAG president in 1946. He came to believe that the movie industry was threatened by communism and sought to keep it out of SAG. Yet Reagan refused to name names in public (he had done so with the FBI in private). Instead, despite the fears he had due to communist infiltration in SAG (he later revealed that he slept with a loaded pistol under his pillow due to threats from communists that they would throw acid on his face), he was moderate in tone, telling the committee that "I would hesitate to see any political party outlawed on the basis of its political ideology. We have spent one hundred-seventy years in this country on the basis that democracy is strong enough to stand up and fight against the inroads of any ideology."[16]

HUAC was interested in specific figures, named the previous spring in closed-door meetings with studio executives, of the so-called Hollywood Ten, screenwriters and directors who were (or had been), in fact, members of the Communist Party. They were defended by a group of actors including Humphrey Bogart, Frank Sinatra, Danny Kaye, Gene Kelly, and Lauren Bacall, known as the Committee for the First Amendment, which the "Ten" took instead of the Fifth. They all declined to speak about any involvement in communist activities and were summarily charged with contempt citations. Within a month, eight of the ten were fired from their jobs with the studios and the studio executives agreed not to hire communists in the future. The so-called blacklist was a response not only to the pressure of HUAC's investigation but also to the fact that the Cold War climate had made the activities of the Ten highly suspect with the majority of the American public, the ones who would buy tickets to Hollywood movies. It was a pragmatic decision for Hollywood executives to make regarding the Ten, who were indeed longtime Stalinists and supporters of the Soviet Union (although clearly not spies).[17]

In 1949 both Truman's domestic war against communism and his foreign policy imploded. In early 1949 communist forces led by Mao Zedong, who had fought a long revolution against the American-supported government of Chiang Kai-shek, took Beijing. A month later, Shanghai and the Nationalist capital of Nanjing fell to the communists. Chiang fled to Taiwan promising to return and liberate China. The loss of China to communism was blamed on State Department employees who had produced a "White Paper" saying that Chiang's government was corrupt and collapsed despite millions of dollars in American aid. They also claimed that Mao was better organized and more representative of the wishes of the Chinese people. Republicans turned on the so-called "China hands" who wrote the report and formed the backbone of Joseph McCarthy's attacks on communism in the State Department.

The China Lobby came about as a result. Made up of a bipartisan mix of politicians and proselytizers, what they had in common was a resolute defense of Chiang Kai-shek. *Time* publisher Henry Luce, Congressmen Walter Judd (R-Minn.) and Richard Nixon (R-Calif.), Senators Styles Bridges (R-Conn.)

and William Knowland (R-Calif.), journalists like George Sokolsky, and Chinese textile importer Alfred Kohlberg supported the venture, which provided an effective lobby in favor of Chiang and against "Red China." Within a few years the Committee of One Million (Against the Admission of Red China into the United Nations), despite its awkward name, proved an effective lobby against China's admission into the UN and served as a vehicle for conservative anticommunist organizing in the 1950s.[18]

A second problem for Truman in 1949 was the Soviet explosion of the atomic bomb. Only four years after the Americans dropped the bomb on Japan, the Soviets now had the awesome weapon. Within a few months, Truman authorized the construction of a hydrogen bomb, a "super" bomb advocated since the Manhattan Project by physicist Edward Teller.

How did the Soviets get the bomb so fast? American intelligence predicted a 1953 date at earliest before the Soviets would get the weapon. What intelligence did not take into account was the network of spies working on behalf of the Soviets at Los Alamos. Klaus Fuchs, a Danish physicist working for the British, was arrested. So were Americans Julius and Ethel Rosenberg, who were fingered for espionage by Ethel's brother David Greenglass (who was at Los Alamos). In 1953, the Rosenbergs were executed for treason, their case becoming a cause célèbre for the postwar Left. Suspicion fell on Manhattan Project director J. Robert Oppenheimer, who lost his security clearance as a result. Oppenheimer, while never a spy, certainly kept intact risky political acquaintances during his tenure as science director at Los Alamos. The price was steep and colleagues like Teller, who wanted to develop the "super" bomb, testified against Oppenheimer during his government hearing.

The communist issue exploded in full fury in late 1949. But Truman may have been able to weather the storm if not for the antics of the junior senator from Wisconsin, Joseph McCarthy. In a February 9, 1950, speech in Wheeling, West Virginia, McCarthy told the audience that he had a list of 205 communists in the State Department. A few days later the number became 57 communists. McCarthy, not widely known before February 1950, soon became a media dynamo and a national figure. He used the media, tantalizing them with tidbits of information. When he returned to Washington, his colleagues demanded that he reveal some names. He refused to do so and Millard Tydings (D-Md.) demanded an investigation into McCarthy's allegations (McCarthy eventually named several people, including former China hand Owen Lattimore; most he named no longer worked, or never did work, at the State Department).[19]

While the Tydings committee engaged in its work, which ultimately revealed that there was nothing sustainable in McCarthy's charges, Truman was dealt his worst setback yet. On June 25, 1950, communist North Korean armies invaded the South. Stalin had given his consent to the invasion. Truman went to the United Nations to condemn the aggression (the Soviets were boycotting the Security Council because of China's nonadmittance). General Douglas MacArthur, who was presiding over the occupation of Japan, was put in charge of UN troops, and in September 1950, MacArthur launched a risky invasion at Inchon, slicing the North Korean lines in half and taking thousands of prisoners.

Truman decided to go north, prompted by politics at home showing support for ending communist occupation of the peninsula, as well as his conviction that China would not enter the war. By Thanksgiving, with American troops nearing the Yalu River border with China, communist Chinese troops entered the war. More than two million People's Liberation Army troops drove south, pushing the UN forces back across the 38th parallel, retaking the southern capital of Seoul before finally the line stabilized. It was the worst retreat in American military history.

MacArthur called for a wider war against communist China, arguing "there is no substitute for victory." Victory for MacArthur meant the atomic bombing of Chinese cities and the "unleashing" of Chiang Kai-shek from Taiwan (whose army was in no position to invade China). Truman was livid and met his general on Wake Island to give him a medal. Truman gained assurances from MacArthur that he would end such statements. But within a few days of their meeting, MacArthur was again issuing calls for a war against the mainland. Truman fired him. His replacement, Matthew Ridgway, solidified the lines in Korea. The war dragged on for another two years. Eventually more than 35,000 Americans would die in what historians have labeled "the forgotten war."

Korea gave McCarthyism its momentum, feeding anxieties about communism in government. Someone was to blame for the failures in American policy since Truman's reelection. McCarthy seemed to pinpoint where the blame lie, with Dean Acheson's "striped pants boys" in the State Department. McCarthy broadened the appeal of anticommunism, deliberately choosing class imagery to showcase his opposition to liberal elites. Historian Michael Kazin has shown that the capture of such populist symbols by anticommunists explained much about conservative success in the postwar era. It was now representative figures like McCarthy who seemed to speak for the people; Truman, whom biographer Alonzo Hamby labeled "a man of the people," was now seen as representative of establishment concerns. Liberals had become defensive of the status quo, and if conservatives had not quite yet become revolutionaries, that moment was getting closer.[20]

The 1952 Republican presidential nomination depicted the shift to populism quite well and further intensified the grievances between the liberal eastern GOP establishment (Wall Street internationalists) and Midwestern conservative Republicans (America First nationalists). With Truman floundering in the polls and deciding not to seek reelection, the GOP was assured of at least a competitive chance to win the presidency. Conservatives pressed for the nomination of Robert A. Taft, the Ohio senator who had been denied the nomination by liberals within the party since 1940. Taft had strong delegate support and positioned himself as champion of conservative concerns on domestic and foreign policy.

Taft had supported the original containment policy but by 1950 he became increasingly critical of where American policy was headed. In 1951 he published *A Foreign Policy for Americans*, a campaign statement on American policy that recommended greater militancy than Taft had ever expressed before, including "a propaganda campaign on behalf of liberty," which would involve the infiltration of foreign governments. He also wanted to maintain the status quo in Europe.[21]

Taft was not an inspiring or charismatic candidate. While he led the delegate count coming into the convention in Chicago that summer, the entrance of General Dwight David Eisenhower into the fray excited GOP delegates, who placed more emphasis on winning the presidency than in nominating a principled conservative. In polls, Eisenhower beat any candidate the Democrats would pick; Taft would lose to specific candidates. With a better organized and better funded operation, Eisenhower prevailed, won the nomination, and as a sop to conservatives, nominated Richard Nixon as his vice presidential candidate. Sterling Morton expressed conservative frustration when he wrote, "the rejection of Taft is a repudiation of a devoted band of men who have fought creeping socialism, financial instability and endless costly foreign adventures."[22] One Taft delegate, not an intellectual, put it much more simply after Ike won: "this means eight more years of socialism."

Eisenhower easily defeated Democratic nominee Adlai Stevenson in the fall. He kept a campaign promise by going to Korea to investigate conditions there; the war ended by truce within a year. Josef Stalin's death in March 1953, and not Eisenhower's policy, had more to do with the truce than anything else. Korea had fundamentally altered containment doctrine, globalizing the Cold War (Truman signed onto the policy of NSC-68, which greatly increased America's military budget and authorized the construction of the hydrogen bomb). Military spending during the Korean War, at 12 percent of GNP, was the highest it would ever be during the entire Cold War. Such spending promoted inflation and spurred economic growth in western states as a result. Eisenhower came into office determined to change that, cutting back on the Army's budget and relying more on strategic nuclear deterrence to keep the peace.

He also employed rhetoric concerning liberating communist regimes and rolling back Soviet control over eastern Europe. He used such rhetoric to please conservatives, whose calculation of the Cold War had changed. Containment policy, as James Burnham had argued, was too defensive and surrendered the initiative to communist governments. It also contained a fundamental spiritual flaw. As Burnham described, who would "willingly suffer, sacrifice and die" for containment policy? In *Containment or Liberation?* (1953), Burnham argued instead for a policy of political warfare against communist governments, one involving a strategy of liberation for eastern European regimes. There was tremendous hyperbole in what he envisioned: the ability of "winged soldiers, air cavalry able to raid two thousand miles behind the lines tonight and be gone before the defense arrives tomorrow ready to liberate a Siberian slave labor district this week, spearhead a revolt in the Caucasus the next, and blow up an enemy powerhouse over the weekend."[23]

Burnham's imaginative construct for waging Cold War struck a chord with many Americans who believed the Cold War had gone horribly wrong. Ethnic Americans consistently supported a stronger policy toward Soviet regimes in eastern Europe. Such nations were renamed "captive nations" to reflect their temporary status as Soviet satellites. Captive Nations Week was celebrated each year. It was routine for young Catholics to pray for the liberation of Russia. In November 1956, after Soviet troops invaded Hungary to quell an uprising there, killing 20,000 Hungarians in the process, hundreds of Americans, including movie actors Bela Lugosi and Zsa Zsa Gabor, picketed outside the Soviet consulate in New York. *National Review* urged readers to sign the Hungary Pledge, which stipulated that "until all Soviet troops and police are withdrawn from Hungary, I will enter into no economic, social, political or cultural relations with that regime."[24]

McCarthy tapped into this sensibility and attacked those elites who were responsible for the wrong turn in American policy. This in itself was not the best strategy, sure to produce resistance from elites who were victims of McCarthy's charges, but it was worth the question asked by John Flynn about the senator. McCarthy "has insisted that Communists and their sympathizers have no place in our government councils. . . . Why should he not have, in this, the whole-hearted support of every loyal American?"[25]

Yet McCarthy was his own worst enemy, giving the Democrats and the Republican president (who detested the senator) the opportunity to challenge his charges on many occasions. When McCarthy accused the Army of harboring communists, the climax of McCarthyism was reached. In televised hearings McCarthy looked harried, mean, and vindictive. That the Army defense attorney, Joseph Welch, was equally mean and vindictive mattered very little to a public who, for the first time, saw McCarthy in action and was unimpressed.

After the hearings, the Senate condemned the senator in 1955; McCarthy was finished, dying of cirrhosis of the liver (from acute alcoholism) in 1957.[26]

GRASSROOTS RIGHT

The "loyal Americans" who supported McCarthy saw an opportunity for action at the grassroots. Throughout the 1950s the grassroots Right was accelerating its activities both in opposition to communism and to liberalism. Many grassroots activists believed that the country was imperiled, that the nation's constitutional governance was threatened, that the "do-gooders" and "one-worlders" were going to destroy America's constitutionalism and its liberty. McCarthy's populism had spurred a wide array of popular concerns on the grassroots Right.

One figure who was crucial to the development of a grassroots Right in the 1950s and afterward was Phyllis Schlafly. Born Phyllis Stewart in St. Louis in 1924, Schlafly's values were influenced by the Great Depression, when her father lost his job and the family became dependent on her mother as the main breadwinner. A smart and talented young woman, Schlafly attended Catholic high school and transferred to Washington University where she took her undergraduate degree, working to support herself in an ammunition factory during the war years testing ordnance. In 1944 she attended Radcliffe, where she pursued a master's degree in political science. After graduation she worked for a year at one of the first conservative organizations in Washington, the American Enterprise Association (AEA), founded by Lewis H. Brown, of the Johns Manville Corporation, who formed the organization as a vehicle by which business and conservative politicians could study complex policy issues. AEA became the first conservative think tank.

It was at the AEA that Schlafly became a convert to conservative principles regarding taxes and the welfare state. Many of these values were imbued in her by her father's hostility to Roosevelt and the New Deal and by her traditional Catholicism, but now she began to explore issues from a policy perspective, something that would serve her well during the remainder of her long career.

She returned to St. Louis, married Fred Schlafly, an attorney for the Olin Corporation, and became active in Republican politics, chosen by a committee of local Republicans in her Alton, Illinois, district to run for a congressional seat in 1952 against an entrenched Democrat incumbent. While she lost the race, she was an impressive candidate, proper, prim, and pretty, but with the ability to articulate clearly her conservative views in public. After the GOP convention that year, Schlafly returned to local politics, becoming a popular speaker with women's groups such as the Daughters of the American Revolution and the Illinois Federation of Republican Women.

A prominent theme of her speeches throughout the 1950s was the issue of communism, particularly its impact on domestic issues like education and the home. The intersection between communist intrusion in government, the defense of constitutionalism, and the morality of the home was central to women's grassroots activism during the postwar era. Such themes were long engrained in women's activism, dating back to the nineteenth century and to progressive reformers at the turn of the century. Schlafly articulated these themes well, telling audiences that communism "was an international criminal conspiracy founded on atheism, materialism, and economic determinism, organized with the Dictatorship of the party as its central feature and dedicated to use any illegal and immoral means toward the achievement of its goals." Communists "expect to destroy our Church, our country, our freedom, the institution of the family, and everything else we hold dear." Such a message resonated with thousands of Christian women throughout the country.[27]

The linkage between anticommunism and the defense of Christian values was explicit in much of the grassroots anticommunist movement of the 1950s and 1960s. In 1958 Phyllis and Fred Schlafly formed the Cardinal Mindszenty Foundation, named after a Hungarian Catholic archbishop who opposed the Soviet invasion and was living in exile within the U.S. embassy in Budapest. An educational organization designed to awaken Catholic priests and laypeople to the dangers of communism, the Foundation distributed literature, organized conferences, and urged the establishment of study groups designed to promote active interaction between Catholic anticommunists on the local level. One of its crucial supporters was Father John Rigney, once president of a Catholic university in China, who was imprisoned and tortured by the Chinese communists, writing about his experiences in *Four Years in a Red Hell* (1956), published by Regnery. The Foundation eventually established study groups in every state as well as in Canadian provinces. Schlafly reminded audiences that "Communism can only be stopped by the individual actions of little people."[28] She did her part to establish the means whereby the little people could work to challenge communism.

Others were contributing as well. As historian Don Critchlow notes, "one report written by a conservative in 1955 estimated that there were some 185 organizations and 135 publications 'on our side,' with 'about 100 that have as their objective the fight against communism, socialism, internationalism, and one-worldism.'"[29] There were some that deserved the label "extremist," such as the Willis Carto's Liberty Lobby, Bill Hargis's Christian Crusade, Gerald L. K. Smith's organization, and the Minutemen. Such groups were never large and never effectively brought into the web of conservative activism.

William F. Buckley, for one, engaged in a lengthy correspondence with Smith through the late 1950s in which Buckley rebuked him for his anti-Semitism and racism.[30]

More effective organizations existed, such as the Protestant-evangelical dominated Christian Anti-Communist Crusade (CACC), founded by Australian physician Fred Schwarz in 1953 in Australia after a suggestion by evangelist Billy Graham that such an organization was needed in America. The CACC thrived in the 1950s and early 1960s. Schwarz gave up his practice and came to the United States to oversee the organization, returning to Australia for six weeks out of the year. He was an expert at diagnosing communist tactics and was well-read in communist literature. Far from telling his audiences that communist books and literature should be banned, he recommended instead that they dedicate their time to learning about communism, including reading Karl Marx's and Fredrick Engels' *Communist Manifesto*.

His audiences were primarily church groups, civic clubs, and schools. His friendships with leading evangelical ministers such as Graham, Carl McIntire, and others, including a close friendship with the Schlaflys, helped him get his message out to a variety of Christian and evangelical audiences. Much like Phyllis Schlafly, Schwarz believed that communism was immoral. Schwarz wrote, "We believed that God existed; that Christian doctrines were true while communist doctrines were delusional; and that the Communist danger was real." The organization was funded with small speaking fees and donations from church groups—it never possessed an Internal Revenue Service tax deduction status. It was an educational organization designed to invoke knowledge about communism and to provoke action.[31]

CACC's most effective accomplishments were anticommunist schools held throughout America. One of the most important schools was held in Southern California in 1961. Over 15,000 people attended in Los Angeles, with four nights of the school's proceedings televised. Ronald Reagan, John Wayne, Pat Boone, and many other anticommunist Hollywood actors spoke. A similar school in Orange County that spring drew seven thousand people, many of them high school students excused from class by their school boards. Locally organized and funded by Walter Knott, owner of Orange County attraction Knott's Berry Farm, Schwarz spoke at the event and at others being organized throughout the country.[32]

Within a few years, the anticommunist schools ran out of steam, finding it difficult to recruit people to attend. Interest in publications and the organization of study groups from the Cardinal Mindszenty Foundation sagged as well. The cause seemed to be the new spirit of détente that galvanized the American public in the early 1960s, even though in retrospect, the tensions between the United States (then led by Democrat John F. Kennedy) and the

Soviets were never higher, culminating in the nuclear standoff between the two powers over Soviet missiles in Cuba.

More likely, it was the controversy that swirled around the John Birch Society (JBS), whose conspiratorial thinking and the controversial views of its founder, Robert Welch, worked against the grassroots anticommunist movement in the early 1960s. The John Birch Society seemed to prove for many liberal intellectuals and politicians that the Right wing was truly antidemocratic, that it represented what social scientists called "status anxiety," and that its leaders possessed an "authoritarian personality" that reminded them of the German lower-middle-class embrace of Hitler in the 1930s.

The JBS was founded in 1958 by Robert Welch, a candy manufacturer from Massachusetts. Born in 1899 in North Carolina, Welch was a child prodigy, graduating from the University of North Carolina at age sixteen. He entered Harvard Law School but never finished, instead starting a candy business in Cambridge, Massachusetts, before joining his brother's firm, the James O. Welch Company, in the Depression years, eventually becoming famous for his sales techniques, especially his development and marketing of popular brands such as Sugar Daddy and Slo-Poke suckers. Welch became active in the National Association of Manufacturers, rising to a position of prominence within that organization, and like most businessmen within NAM, he opposed the drift toward collectivism at home, embodied by the New Deal and Truman's Fair Deal.

In 1951 Welch wrote a pamphlet, published by Regnery, entitled *May God Forgive Us*. Funded by Welch himself, he established a company to distribute the pamphlet. More than 200,000 were given away by Welch. The focus of the pamphlet was on the creeping socialism embodied in American politics, foreshadowing his later view that American politics had already succumbed to communism. In 1954, also with Regnery, Welch published *The Life of John Birch*, a testament to the short life of a Baptist soldier killed by the Chinese communists in 1946, ostensibly the first American victim of communism in the Cold War. It was from his study of Birch's life, which Welch claimed was that of an exemplary Christian and principled anticommunist, that the seeds of Welch's organization were planted.[33]

In 1955 Welch wrote J. Howard Pew, one of his friends in NAM, about his intentions. Welch was to give a lengthy talk entitled "What Is Happening to America Abroad" at the NAM annual convention and he told Pew, "I am thinking of it in my own mind as more or less the opening gun in the campaign into which I shall be plunging not long thereafter, with all of the mental resources and energy I have left at the age of fifty-five. It will be a campaign . . . to supply some of the fighting leadership so desperately needed to keep America from going completely over the brink of collectivism."[34] A year later, Welch had begun distributing lengthy letters that were entitled "One Man's Opinion," a magazine of sorts dedicated "to the crusade to save our country from its Communist-socialist enemies."[35]

As Welch worked out what would become the Birch Society, he did so by relying on friends and acquaintances in NAM. At the founding meeting of the Birch Society, held in an Indianapolis, Indiana, home, many of those in attendance were either business executives, like Wichita, Kansas, oil pipeline magnate Fred Koch, or others who traced their grassroots involvement back to the Bricker amendment (a failed effort to make foreign treaties ratified by a majority vote), such as Clarence Manion and T. Coleman Andrews. During the weekend-long meeting, Welch spoke for over twenty hours, laying out, in excruciating detail, what the communist threat portended for America (this was later published by the Birch Society as *The Blue Book*). But the founding members were convinced of Welch's facts and supported the organization, lending both their names and finances to the cause.

Welch spoke throughout the country to increase membership, to similar audiences of businessmen and prominent civil leaders. Always it was a long weekend of Welch speaking and convincing the assembled men and women of the communist threat. One who he could not convince was Pew, who remained elusive and refused to attend the weekend meetings, or even to join the Society. Welch continually pestered Pew about coming to hear his message, telling him on one occasion "we have a program designed here, Howard . . . one in which the long range positive and constructive purposes are far more important than the merely negative purpose of stopping the communists."[36]

But Welch was his own worst enemy. By the late 1950s he had become convinced that even Eisenhower was "a conscious, articulate agent of the communist conspiracy." He asserted this in a lengthy letter, over three hundred pages in length, which he privately circulated and later published as *The Politician* (1963). In the book Welch described how Eisenhower was a dupe of the communists. It was conspiratorial in its presentation and even argued that Ike's brother, Milton, who was president of Johns Hopkins University at the time, actually ran the government.[37]

When the contents of the book were revealed in 1961, Welch backed away from his charge, saying that *The Politician* was meant for private circulation only and was never meant to be a published book. He said this on NBC's *Meet the Press*, disavowing his conclusion that Ike was a communist. His charge worked for many who were already convinced that they too had unraveled the communist plot against America. But for the great majority of Americans, including many conservatives, Welch had contributed to frightening people in a way that provoked a backlash against his more irresponsible comments.[38]

Still, during the early 1960s the John Birch Society dominated the nation's media outlets as an example of the Right-wing lunatic fringe. It grew tremendously during the early part of the decade, claiming over 100,000 members (though a report filed with the state of Massachusetts claimed less than 35,000). It was largest in places like Orange County, California, where "little old ladies in tennis shoes" held coffee klatches to distribute the Birch Society's publications, such as *American Opinion*, and discuss the issue of communism in their own communities.[39] The Birch Society was strong as well in west Texas and in cities like Wichita, Kansas. It also had a lot of support (but membership numbers are unclear) in the South, in cities like New Orleans, where Kent and Phoebe Courtney had established the Conservative Society of America in 1955, and in Dallas and Houston, Texas, as well.

It was in the South where the anticommunist politics of the Birch Society intermingled and intermeshed with the issue of race. Welch, a Southerner by upbringing, possessed conventional views about the South and race. His view was best expressed in a letter written in 1957, "Letter to the South on Segregation," in which he argued that communists were to blame for the 1954 Supreme Court decision *Brown v. Board of Education of Topeka, Kansas.* Communists were to blame for turmoil in the South. Whites needed to look beyond civil rights protests to get at the root of the problem, communism in government. He concluded, "Communists do not have either the slightest real interest in the welfare of either the colored people or the white people of the South. It is not desegregation as an end in which they are interested, but the bitterness, strife, and terrors of mob action which can be instigated while that end is supposedly being sought."[40]

Pew told Welch in response to his letter that "the Constitution not only prohibits the Federal Government from usurping the rights reserved to the states, but it virtually outlines the way in which these rights can be taken away and prohibits the use of such procedure."[41] Accordingly, Welch struck out against the radicalism of the Supreme Court and urged Birch Society members to impeach Earl Warren, the chief justice responsible for the Brown decision. *American Opinion* later focused on the linkages between communism and the civil rights movement. In 1964 the magazine opined that the Civil Rights Act was "part of the pattern for the communist takeover of America." It also referred consistently to links between civil rights leader Martin Luther King Jr. and communism, a view that was widely propagated among White Citizen's Councils in the late 1950s and early 1960s, referring to his attendance at the Highlander Folk School in Tennessee.

But JBS opposition to civil rights never deviated from Welch's central mission: to expose the connections between protests in favor of civil rights and communism. He consistently maintained that blacks were not responsible for communist advancement, but rather were victims of forces behind such protests—the intellectuals, politicians, and other leaders who encouraged protests for the sake of advancing communism. Like Americans generally, Welch argued, blacks "can easily be misled by clever agitators."[42]

While JBS membership in the South is unknown, it is clear that the organization would have found fertile ground among white segregationists who believed, in myriad ways, that civil rights protests were inspired by communists. The White Citizen's Councils, formed throughout the South after the *Brown* decision, explicitly maintained that the push for integration was "communism in action." Commissions in states like Mississippi and Alabama were authorized to investigate the links between groups like the National Association for the Advancement of Colored People (NAACP) and the communist party. Given information from a variety of extremist groups, the conclusions they reached were not surprising. Even the American Nazi Party, under the leadership of Lincoln Rockwell, "exposed" Martin Luther King's connections to the communist party. Of course, to the Nazis, all communists were Jewish, so this justified their belief, which the Ku Klux Klan's publication, *The Fiery Cross*, propagated as well, of a "Jewish-communist conspiracy."[43]

King did possess some rather loose communist connections. He had attended meetings at the Highlander Folk School, a notorious communist-dominated institution in the Tennessee hills. One of his key advisors was Stanley Levison, a former member of the party, whom King continued to rely on for advice and support even after he was warned by John F. Kennedy of FBI wiretaps that had revealed this connection. The Bureau under Hoover saw a close connection between communism and civil rights and developed "Racial Matters," an investigative unit within the agency to examine "communist influence" in the civil rights movement. The FBI was particularly interested in exposing King as a fraud and taped his secret sexual liaisons and mailed tapes of his dalliances home to his wife with threatening letters attached, one of them seemingly recommending suicide: "You are done. There is but one way out for you. You better take it before your filthy fraudulent self is exposed to the nation."[44] Eventually, the Bureau would establish COINTELPRO (Counter Intelligence Program) to investigate, harass, and intimidate radical groups like the Black Panther Party and anti–Vietnam War groups.

For the conservative movement in general there was a benign neglect of civil rights as an issue. The vast majority of conservatives were far more interested in the communist issue than in civil rights. Two Southern conservatives who did make civil rights a forefront of their activism in this era were Donald Davidson, a holdover from the Southern Agrarian movement of the Depression years, and *Richmond Times-Leader* editor and columnist James Jackson Kilpatrick.

While many of the Southern Agrarians had departed the South in search of better paying teaching positions elsewhere, Davidson remained at Vanderbilt throughout his career and became a leading apologist for segregation in Nashville. He supported Strom Thurmond's Dixiecrat Party in 1948 and helped organize, and chair, the Tennessee Federation for Constitutional Governance, which served for all purposes as a White Citizen's Council. Davidson accepted the view that communism and civil rights were linked, telling one correspondent that the NAACP was a front for communists. "Behind it all, in the last analysis, is Communist and Socialist pressure and their long-distance planning."[45] He later wrote, "anything that weakens state governments and swells the power of blind bureaucracy makes it that much easier for Russian Communism to take over the United States from the inside."[46] He grew pessimistic about the chances of defending a segregated South and the historical tradition in which he had wrapped himself. Allen Tate would write about Davidson, "I fear his Southernism, for all its cunning and learning, is now at the level of White Supremacy."[47]

A much less overt racial defense of states' rights came from the pen of James Jackson Kilpatrick. Entitled *The Sovereign States* (1957), Kilpatrick's book (and his many columns and speeches) defended the states' rights position from encroachment by the federal government. Kilpatrick's book was an examination of the historical tradition of the compact theory of government, arguing that states were governments unto themselves who had entered into a compact with other states to form the national government. Their rights were protected by the Tenth Amendment to the Constitution and were not invalid even after the Confederacy's defeat in the Civil War and the ratification of the Fourteenth Amendment. Kilpatrick saw *Brown* as unnecessary federal intervention on the states and urged a doctrine of interposition to prevent further "federal intrusions."[48]

Kilpatrick believed that the government that was closest to the governed was the best. Of his many travels to Washington, he wrote, "I gaze from the House galleries at the awesome scene below. A few good men excepted, it offers only a milling gaggle of chiropractors, foot doctors, country clowns, elevated plumbers, and second-rate lawyers—and these, God save the mark, are the statesmen who would discard the charter of our liberties!"[49] Despite his Mencken-esque bromide, Kilpatrick argued out of conservative conviction that the imposition of law by the federal government on the South was immoral and should be resisted. "The intelligent South," Kilpatrick said at one debate on the issue, "the South that to this day reflects the thoughtfulness and compassion of Jefferson and Madison and Lee, this South recognizes a great rightness on the Negro's side."[50] But under the constitutional prerogatives given the states, Kilpatrick argued, Southerners had to resist.

Kilpatrick was not saying Southerners should engage in massive and violent resistance. He told one correspondent that he was horrified by the manners and dress of whites who opposed black student protestors in the 1960s sit-in movement. Blacks were dressed properly, minded their manners, and protested civilly, while whites acted like brutes. The problem for Kilpatrick's intelligent resistance based on principle was that it could ignite the fiery and brutish kind, and more often did (Kilpatrick subsequently changed his views in the late 1960s).

Yet Kilpatrick's theory of sovereign states became the basis for *National Review's* opposition to civil rights. William F. Buckley set the tone for the magazine in a 1957 editorial, "Why the South Must Prevail." *"National Review* believes that the South's premises are correct. If the majority wills what is socially atavistic, then to thwart the majority may be, though undemocratic, enlightened. It is more important for any community, anywhere in the world, to affirm and live by civilized standards, than to bow to the demands of the numerical majority. . . . The problem in the South is not how to get the vote for the Negro, but how to equip the Negro—and a great many whites—to cast an enlightened and responsible vote."[51] It appeared that for Buckley the ghost of Ortega y Gassett was still very much alive.

National Review's line on the disruption in the South as a result of the *Brown* decision was expressed in an editorial calling the *Brown* case a result of the Court's "obsession with an egalitarian ideology." As a result, "Negro-White relations in the South, and in many northern cities also, have catastrophically worsened." "It is easy enough," the editorial concluded, "for Earl Warren and Felix Frankfurter, at the turn of an ideological spigot, to lecture their 175 million countrymen about instant and total obedience to 'the law of the land,' but plentitudes [*sic*] from the bench . . . will not, overnight, transmute the ingrained sentiments and convictions of self-reliant communities. Tragically, the resistance by self-reliant and decent men to what they deem the usurpations of the Court . . . tends to promote a general atmosphere of civil disobedience, and disrespect not only for the Warren Court but for the law; in which the dregs of society break through to the surface."[52]

National Review would go further, however. In 1960 it editorialized on "the crisis in the Senate and the South." "In the Deep South the Negroes are, by comparison with whites, retarded ('unadvanced,' the NAACP might put it). Any effort to ignore the fact is sentimentalism and demagoguery. Leadership in the South, then, quite properly, rests in White hands."[53] As Jeffrey Hart, a long time editor of *NR*, has written in a history of the magazine, "Everyone has a bad day. This [editorial] wanders off into the tall grass."[54] Consistently thereafter, however, the magazine and conservatism remained more committed to constitutionalism and judicial inertia on the subject of civil rights, a position for which the intelligent white South (not the segregationists and Klansmen) would eventually concede as well, as they made their way into the GOP.

It should not be surprising to scholars that grassroots conservatives, many of them Christian activists, were not chanting "we shall overcome" in Mississippi peace marches—nor should anything nefarious be inferred about them not doing so. Communism remained their vital concern; despite the views that many of more radical elements at the grassroots held concerning the linkage between communism and civil rights. Historian Don Critchlow wrote, "Southern anti-semitism and segregation were not integral to conservative thought in the South." For activists like Schlafly, and even to a large degree, Robert Welch, "the struggle against communism dictated all aspects of political life from the local to the national level."[55]

It was a struggle that many saw heating up in the late 1950s and early 1960s. But conservatives still lacked a champion, a political figure who could gather all the diverse forces of conservatism under his banner, and one who could articulate the cause of anticommunism and discuss the necessity for victory in the Cold War. The emergence of such a figure in the person of Barry Morris Goldwater, a senator from Arizona, would push conservatives into a new phase of activism. It would plunge them into politics. Conservatives had gotten to know and to like the people. Now it was incumbent on conservative politicians to see if the people liked them too.

NOTES

1. See Richard M. Fried, *The Russians Are Coming! The Russians Are Coming! Pageantry and Patriotism in Cold War America* (New York: Oxford University Press, 1998), 67–86.

2. The Cold War's origins are still hotly debated by historians. Some useful starting points are John Lewis Gaddis, *The United States and the Origins of the Cold War* (New York: Columbia University Press, 1972), and Gaddis, *The Cold War: A New History* (New York: Penguin, 2006); for a revisionist perspective see Melvyn Leffler, *A Preponderance of Power: National Security, the Truman Administration, and the Cold War* (Stanford, Calif.: Stanford University Press, 1993); for a new thorough study of Truman's policies in the early Cold War years, see Wilson Miscamble, *From Roosevelt to Truman: Potsdam, Hiroshima, and the Cold War* (Cambridge: Cambridge University Press, 2006).

3. For a discussion of these events, see John Lewis Gaddis, *Strategies of Containment: A Critical Appraisal of American National Security Policy During the Cold War*, rev. exp. ed. (New York: Oxford University Press, 2005).

4. William Henry Chamberlin, *America's Second Crusade* (Chicago: Regnery Publishing, 1950), 354.

5. Flynn's conversion story is well told in John E. Moser, *Right Turn: John T. Flynn and the Transformation of American Liberalism* (New York: New York University Press, 2005); for useful discussions of the shift from noninterventionism to Cold War internationalism, see Michael Miles, *The Odyssey of the American Right* (New York: Oxford University Press, 1980) and Justus Doenecke, *Not to the Swift: The Old Isolationists in the Cold War Era* (Cranbury, N.J.: Associated University Presses, 1979).

6. Letter from Felix Morley to Lawrence Dennis, July 2, 1954, Box 13, Correspondence and Subject Files (Lawrence Dennis, 1954), Felix Morley Papers, Herbert Hoover Presidential Library.

7. Morley expressed his frustration with where the Right was headed in a series of letters to Henry Regnery. See, for the fascist quote, Letter from Morley to Henry Regnery, June 25, 1969, Box 53, Folder 1 (Morley Corr.), Henry Regnery Papers, Hoover Institution, Stanford University. Also, see Morley to Alf Landon, June 20, 1964, Box 1, Name and Subject File (Alf Landon, 1958–68), Morley Papers. There is also much correspondence on this issue between Morley and Lawrence Dennis, and Morley and Harry Elmer Barnes, available in the Morley Papers, Hoover Presidential Library.

8. Garet Garrett, *The Rise of Empire*, published in *The People's Pottage* (Caldwell, Idaho: Caxton Press, 1953), 117.

9. Letter from Lawrence Dennis to Sterling Morton Jr., July 18, 1951, Box 13 (July 16–31, 1951), Sterling Morton Jr. Papers, Chicago Historical Society.

10. Letter from Harry Elmer Barnes to Lawrence Dennis, October 23, 1957, Box 2 (Barnes Corr., 1957–68), Lawrence Dennis Papers, Hoover Institution.

11. There is an extensive literature on Truman's presidency and the domestic issues in postwar America. See Alonzo Hamby, *Beyond the New Deal: Harry Truman and American Liberalism* (New York: Columbia University Press, 1973); see also, Michael Lacey, ed., *The Truman Presidency* (Cambridge: Cambridge University Press, 1991).

12. See Richard M. Fried, "Voting against the Hammer and Sickle: Communism as an Issue in American Politics," in Chafe, ed., *The Achievement of American Liberalism: The New Deal and Its Legacies* (New York: Columbia University Press, 2003), 99–127.

13. Richard M. Fried, *Nightmare in Red: The McCarthy Era in Perspective* (New York: Oxford University Press, 1990); and George J. Marlin, *The American Catholic Voter: 200 Years of Political Impact* (South Bend, Ind.: St. Augustine's, 2004), 220–27; Irwin Gellman, *The Contender: Richard Nixon: The Congress Years, 1946–1952* (New York: Free Press, 2007 ed.). Gellman's book is the most well-researched work on Richard Nixon's congressional career.

14. J. Edgar Hoover, "Testimony before HUAC," *Congressional Record*, Appendix, March 28, 1947, A1409–A1412.

15. Richard Gid Powers, *Not Without Honor: The History of American Anticommunism* (New York: Free Press, 1996), 216–17; M. Stanton Evans, *Blacklisted by History: The Untold Story of Senator Joe McCarthy and His Fight Against America's Enemies* (New York: Crown Forum, 2007), 87–175, details the lax security investigations in World War II, as well as in the Truman White House.

16. Peter Schweizer, *Reagan's War: The Epic Story of His Forty-Year Struggle and Triumph over Communism* (New York: Doubleday, 2002), 15–16.

17. On communism in Hollywood, see Ronald Radosh and Allis Radosh, *Red Star over Hollywood: The Film Colony's Long Romance with the Left* (San Francisco: Encounter, 2003), 137–206. See also Kenneth Lloyd Billingsley, *Hollywood Party: How Communism Seduced the American Film Industry in the 1930s and 1940s* (Rocklin, Calif.: Prima Lifestyles, 1998).

18. Miles, *Odyssey of the American Right*, 94–120, provides a valuable general discussion of China's role in the postwar Right; see also Stanley D. Bachrack, *The Committee of One Million: "China Lobby" Politics, 1953–1971* (New York: Columbia University Press, 1976).

19. Evans, *Blacklisted by History*, 206–312, provides a well-researched account of McCarthy and the best analysis of the political investigation into McCarthy's charges by the White House and Congress; for other views, see David Oshinsky, *A Conspiracy So Immense: The World of Joe McCarthy* (New York: Oxford University Press, 2005 ed.); Fried, *Nightmare in Red*; and Arthur Herman, *Joseph McCarthy: Reexamining the Life and Legacy of America's Most Hated Senator* (New York: Free Press, 1999).

20. Michael Kazin, *The Populist Persuasion: An American History* (Ithaca: Cornell University Press, 1998); Michael Federici, *The Challenge of Populism: The Rise of Right-Wing Democratism in Postwar America* (Westport, Conn.: Praeger, 1991), disputes the idea that getting to know the people has been a good thing for conservatives.

21. Robert A. Taft, *A Foreign Policy for Americans* (New York: Doubleday, 1951).

22. Letter from Sterling Morton to C. Warren Mapes, July 10, 1952, Box 16 (July 1952), Morton Papers.

23. James Burnham, *Containment or Liberation?* (New York: John Day, 1953), 147–52.

24. Embassy protests described in Gregory L. Schneider, *Cadres for Conservatism: Young Americans for Freedom and the Rise of the Contemporary Right* (New York: New York University Press, 1998), 20–21; Hungary Pledge in *National Review*, reprinted in Schneider, ed., *Conservatism in America since 1930: A Reader* (New York: New York University Press, 2003), 167–68.

25. Moser, *Right Turn*, 180–91, describes Flynn's defense of McCarthy.

26. Evans, *Blacklisted by History*, 542–70, and Herman, *Joseph McCarthy*, 273–76, provide a revisionist view of the Army hearings and of Counsel Joseph Welch.

27. Donald T. Critchlow, *Phyllis Schlafly and Grassroots Conservatism: A Woman's Crusade* (Princeton: Princeton University Press, 2005), 75; for context into the conservative activism of women in the twentieth century, see Catherine E. Rymph, *Republican Women: Feminism and Conservatism from Suffrage through the Rise of the New Right* (Chapel Hill: University of North Carolina Press, 2006); June Melby Benowitz, *Days of Discontent: American Women and Right-Wing Politics, 1933–1945* (DeKalb: Northern Illinois University Press, 2002); Mary C. Brennan, *Wives, Mothers, and the Red Menace: Conservative Women and the Crusade Against Communism* (Boulder: University Press of Colorado, 2008); and Lisa McGirr, *Suburban Warriors: The Origins of the American Right* (Princeton: Princeton University Press, 2001).

28. Critchlow, *Phyllis Schlafly*, 82.

29. Critchlow, *Phyllis Schlafly*, 70.

30. Gerald L. K. Smith to William F. Buckley Jr., and W. F. B. Jr. to Smith, William F. Buckley Jr. Papers, Sterling Library, Yale University, New Haven, Connecticut.

31. Fred Schwarz, *Beating the Unbeatable Foe: One Man's Victory over Communism, Leviathan, and the Last Enemy* (Washington, D.C.: Regnery, 1996).

32. McGirr, *Suburban Warriors*, 54–63.

33. Jonathan M. Schoenwald, *A Time for Choosing: The Rise of Modern American Conservatism* (New York: Oxford University Press, 2001), 62–99.

34. Letter from Robert Welch to J. Howard Pew, July 1, 1955, Box 112 (Robert Welch Corr.), J. Howard Pew Papers, Hagley Library and Museum, Wilmington, Delaware.

35. Letter from Welch to Pew, April 7, 1956, Box 112 (Robert Welch 1956), Pew Papers.

36. Letter from Welch to Pew, April 20, 1959, Box 112 (Robert Welch 1959), Pew Papers.

37. Robert Welch, *The Politician* (Belmont, Mass.: Western Islands, 1963).

38. Schoenwald, *Time for Choosing*, 93–97.

39. McGirr, *Suburban Warriors*, 82–87.

40. Welch, "Letter to the South on Segregation" in Box 112 (Welch 1957), Pew Papers.

41. Letter from Pew to Welch, January 7, 1957, Box 112 (Welch 1957), Pew Papers.

42. Schoenwald, *Time for Choosing*, 90.

43. See Jeff Woods, *Black Struggle, Red Scare: Segregation and Anti-Communism in the South, 1948–1968* (Baton Rouge: Louisiana State University Press, 2003), 105–7, 159–68; for the views of the American Nazi Party, see Frederick J. Simonelli, *American Fuehrer: George Lincoln Rockwell and the American Nazi Party* (Urbana: University of Illinois Press, 1999), which is especially useful on Rockwell's anti–civil rights activism.

44. David Garrow, *The FBI and Martin Luther King* (New York: Norton, 1981), documents these efforts quite well, as does Kenneth O'Reilly, *"Racial Matters": The FBI's Secret War on Black America, 1960–1972* (New York: Free Press, 1991).

45. Paul Murphy, *The Rebuke of History: The Southern Agrarians and American Conservative Thought* (Chapel Hill: University of North Carolina Press, 2001), 203.

46. Murphy, *Rebuke of History*, 203.

47. Murphy, *Rebuke of History*, 205.

48. James Jackson Kilpatrick, *The Sovereign States* (Chicago: Regnery Publishing, 1957). Kilpatrick gave many speeches outside of the South defending his doctrine of states' rights and interposition. He often described the situation in the South as a war over school integration. A good sample of the type of speeches he gave is "School Integration in the South: The Greater Meaning," March 14, 1959, City Club, Cleveland, Ohio, Box 2 (March 14, 1959), James Jackson Kilpatrick Papers, Special Collections, University of Virginia, Charlottesville.

49. James Jackson Kilpatrick, "The Case for States Rights," University of Chicago Public Affairs Conference Center, 1961, Box 12, Kilpatrick Papers.

50. Excerpts from remarks by James Jackson Kilpatrick, in a debate before the Morristown (N.J.) Forum, November 20, 1958, p. 14, Box 1 (1958), Kilpatrick Papers.

51. William F. Buckley Jr., "Why the South Must Prevail," *National Review* (August 24, 1957): 148–49.

52. Jeffrey Hart, *The Making of the American Conservative Mind: National Review and Its Times* (Wilmington, Del.: Intercollegiate Studies Institute, 2006), 100.

53. "Crisis in the Senate and the South," *National Review* (March 1960), cited in Hart, *The Making of the American Conservative Mind*, 103.

54. "Crisis in the Senate and the South," 104.

55. Critchlow, *Phyllis Schlafly*, 62–63.

Chapter Four

Plunging into Politics

The time will come when we entrust the conduct of our affairs to men who understand that their first duty as public officials is to divest themselves of the power they have been given.

—Barry Goldwater

On July 16, 1964, at San Francisco's Cow Palace, the culmination of years of hard work by conservatives paid off when Barry Goldwater, a senator from Arizona, received the Republican nomination for the presidency. While he faced a herculean task in the fall campaign—challenging the incumbent Lyndon Johnson, who had taken over the presidency a year earlier after the tragic assassination of John F. Kennedy—the evening was one for celebration. After decades in the political wilderness, after suffering defeat after defeat at convention after convention by better organized and funded eastern establishment figures within the party, conservatives had finally prevailed: a conservative was the presidential nominee.

The bubble of euphoria was burst however when Goldwater addressed the delegates. In his speech, Goldwater defended a principled conservatism, defining the concept of freedom and urging its renewal in the face of "bureaucratic government." "It is the cause of Republicanism to resist concentrations of power, private or public, which inflict . . . such despotism," Goldwater added. After outlining how the Republican Party had been the "historic home" of freedom, Goldwater stated the penultimate lines, the words his speech became best known for: "Anyone who joins us in all sincerity is welcome. Those who do not care for our cause, we don't expect to enter into our ranks in any case. . . . I would remind you that extremism in the defense of liberty is no vice. And let me remind you also that moderation in the pursuit of justice is no virtue!"[1]

That phrase did more damage to Goldwater than anything else he said or did the entire campaign. It stuck in the minds of Goldwater's enemies who argued that the candidate was defending extremists like the assassin of John F. Kennedy, or Robert Welch of the John Birch Society, or any other number of "crazies" who were purportedly working in association with conservatives to threaten democracy. While many young conservatives in the audience cheered when Goldwater uttered these words, other delegates understood that the candidacy was doomed. Journalist Theodore White quoted one delegate as saying, "My God! They're going to let him run as Barry!"[2]

PATHS TO POWER: THE SEARCH FOR A CANDIDATE

Conservatives had long sought political power and had been frustrated ever since the New Deal years in their pursuit of an avowed conservative presidential candidate. Robert Taft had been their standard-bearer for years, but he failed to win the party's nomination three times, the last time losing it to the popular war hero Dwight Eisenhower. A year after Ike's 1952 election, Taft was dead from cancer.

Throughout the 1950s conservatives never were entirely comfortable with Eisenhower, finding his domestic policy too redemptive of the New Deal and his foreign policy too accommodating toward the Soviet Union and communism. It was in the Eisenhower years where a brief thaw, known as peaceful coexistence, developed between America and Russia, encouraged by Josef Stalin's death in 1953. Conservatives hated the policy and believed it to be responsible for America's failure to intervene in the Soviet crackdown in Hungary in 1956.

National Review was particularly hostile to Eisenhower. Willi Schlamm, the ex-communist who helped form *National Review* with William F. Buckley Jr., wrote in October 1956, "Mr. Dwight Eisenhower, an inconsistent Liberal, is in firm control of the Republican Party. For conservatives, the strategic job in this year's election is to break that control. It can be broken only by defeating Mr. Eisenhower. . . . Both parties are trying to elect a Liberal."[3] Schlamm represented a minority position at the magazine, however; Buckley had decided that Eisenhower was "the most conservative electable candidate" in 1956 and thus, without an official endorsement, *NR* backed Ike as the lesser of two evils. It would not be the last time conservatives made such a choice.

It is quite odd, in retrospect, that conservatives would have been so upset with Eisenhower. On the surface the Ike age was one of peace and prosperity, of continued support for the Cold War, and of continued hostility toward Mao's China, which became, in the words of historian Gordon Chang, "the main enemy" during the decade. Certainly given the tumultuous decade that followed, the 1950s looked like a conservative time.[4]

Yet there was tremendous dissatisfaction at the grassroots with where the nation was heading. The 1950s was a time of great anxiety as well as of great affluence. Not only were social movements brewing on the Left, such as civil rights, the antinuclear movement, and the sexual revolution (it was in the 1950s when Alfred Kinsey, the famed sex researcher, and Hugh Hefner, with *Playboy* magazine, both gained fame), but there were also grassroots conservative and anticommunist movements disaffected with the reigning consensus during that decade.

But after Taft's death, to whom could conservatives turn for political leadership? Joseph McCarthy may have been one answer, but his Senate condemnation made him an impractical and unlikely choice. Some, like his Senate colleague William Jenner (R-Ind.), continued to push the McCarthy bandwagon, but few jumped aboard. The Democrat alternative in 1956, Adlai Stevenson, a scion of a wealthy Chicago-area family, was too liberal. Mainstream conservatives, like Buckley, recognized the futility in advocating a hopeless cause and voted for Ike.

Other conservatives pushed a third party gambit, which failed miserably. T. Coleman Andrews, a former commissioner of the Internal Revenue Service, became the standard-bearer of the Constitution Party. Andrews was on the ballot in fifteen states, getting 483 votes in North Dakota and two in South Carolina. In some states he was listed as head of the Constitution Party, in others as the candidate of the For America Party, and in the South as a states' rights candidate. Andrews called for the abolition of the income tax and for a clear constitutional acceptance of state sovereignty. Given the paucity of his ultimate support, Andrews surprisingly gave several radio addresses on national networks like ABC. He claimed in one address, "I represent a movement—a spontaneous movement rising from the hearts and minds of Americans—whose members believe that the Constitution properly provides for a federal government of strictly limited powers."[5] He spoke out against continued foreign aid, the violation of America's constitutional treaty powers, and states' rights.

Andrews was a bit disingenuous to claim that his movement was rooted in the spontaneous uprising of the people. For America, a conservative political action committee formed by Robert Wood, Clarence Manion, and other conservatives in 1954 was the power behind the scenes of the Andrews candidacy. A day after Andrews was nominated as the candidate for the Constitution Party, Bonner Fellers, a brigadier general who was national director of For America, contacted Andrews with a list of names and offer of funds to back his candidacy. "I would like to offer our office and services here to handle contributions and expenditures for your campaign effort," Fellers wrote.[6] Andrews accepted the assistance and Clarence Manion, for one, proved important in drafting speeches and advising Andrews on the campaign.

In the end, not surprisingly, the campaign went nowhere. In a letter to William F. Buckley Sr., who had given $4,000 to the campaign, Andrews wrote, "I cannot help but wonder how long it will take the American people to realize that they no longer control their elections, that our international involvement have [*sic*] now become such that their officials can be chosen for them by international politicians abroad. What a sad mess we have gotten ourselves into."[7]

The frustration of grassroots conservatives operating outside of the Republican Party was best explained by hostility to "one-worlders" and their lackeys in government who continued to influence many on the postwar Right. The controversy over the Bricker Amendment, a constitutional amendment proposed by Senator John Bricker (R-Ohio), to limit the treaty-making power of the presidency, was a case in point. The Bricker Amendment stipulated that no treaty could be ratified that contradicted the Constitution; the most controversial clause gave Congress the power to regulate all executive agreements and international arrangements, ostensibly to prevent another Yalta. Eisenhower, Democrats, and Republican internationalists all fought the treaty and when it came up for a vote in 1954, only fifty senators voted for it, short of the two-thirds required for ratification.

In the beginning For America conservatives like Robert Wood and Clarence Manion hoped to parlay the surprisingly strong grassroots support behind the amendment into an effective political vehicle. Manion was the former dean of Notre Dame Law School, who had been appointed to the chairmanship of the Intergovernmental Relations Committee, a committee enjoined to investigate unconstitutional programs. He was relieved of his chairmanship in 1954, and thought this not a coincidence, telling a television interviewer that "some of the Left-wing communists, who have had an unfortunate effectiveness in this administration, served notice on me that I was to be fired because of my advocacy of the Bricker amendment."[8]

Manion established himself as a noteworthy conservative radio host operating out of South Bend, Indiana. In October 1954, he began a syndicated program known as *The Manion Forum* over selected radio stations, including Chicago's powerhouse WGN (owned by the *Chicago Tribune*). Manion would pronounce on various topics in his half-hour broadcast, ranging from foreign affairs to politics. In the 1960s the program would host various conservatives, including Barry Goldwater, Robert Welch, members of the student group Young Americans for Freedom, and others. Like many disaffected conservatives who believed the GOP was too liberal, Manion became a board member of the John Birch Society in 1958, although he was careful to disassociate himself from the wilder allegations of Birch founder Robert Welch. Conservative radio programs became a vital means of distributing news and information outside the confines of the parties and the national press. There were a surprising variety of radio programs, ranging from the broadcasts of evangelical preachers to opinion forums. John T. Flynn delivered radio commentary in the late 1940s and early 1950s, memorably telling his audience at one point: "God Bless Joe McCarthy." Fulton Lewis Jr. delivered radio commentary and became a popular conservative "grumbler" as two pioneers of conservative media have called such radio fare. *The Dan Smoot Report* aired on many channels; in the early 1960s, Phyllis Schlafly provided commentary on communism through a program *America, Wake Up!* The number of listeners such programs had is unknown, but eventually conservative commentators, like Paul Harvey, did obtain a substantial audience in the 1950s and afterward; Ronald Reagan did radio commentary in the 1970s, delivering short analyses on specific issues.[9]

Other conservatives were becoming interested in political solutions as well in the mid to late 1950s. Young people led the charge in organizations like the Intercollegiate Society of Individualists (ISI), founded by Frank Chodorov. Throughout the decade ISI distributed conservative literature to students, including books like Hayek's *Road to Serfdom* and Ludwig Van Mises's *Human Action*. ISI also helped students form conservative clubs on campus. The organization supported student publications, some of which became impressive journals in their own right, such as the University of Chicago's *New Individualist Review* and the University of Wisconsin's *Insight and Outlook*.

The man most responsible for campus organizing was Victor Milione, the son of Italian immigrants who attended St. Joseph's College in Philadelphia after serving in the army in World War II. He began work as an employee of a public affairs organization funded by J. Howard Pew and Philadelphia banker Charles Hoeflich. The Pew family became important donors to ISI, convinced by Chodorov that such an organization could do much to "educate for liberty." Milione was the natural person to be the campus recruiter and made connections with students on many campuses.

ISI not only contributed, as far as conservatives were concerned, to a healthier intellectual dynamic on campus, but it also developed key relationships with conservative organizations and magazines. In 1957, ISI offered a summer journalism fellowship through *Human Events* and *National Review*. The first three journalism fellows, David Franke, Douglas Caddy, and William Schulz, would play crucial roles in moving conservatism toward political power, later organizing the student group Young Americans for Freedom. Eventually, ISI would support the creation of the National Journalism Center in Washington, headed by M. Stanton Evans, a young editor of *The Indianapolis News*, to train and help get jobs for conservative-oriented journalists.[10]

Unlike some of their elders in the conservative movement then taking shape, young conservatives mobilized by ISI tended to be interested in political power. Not content to simply stand by waiting for the liberal shoe to drop, young conservatives formed connections with each other, used the resources that conservatives had developed to their advantage, and sought to foment a political revolution.

Conservative clubs flourished in the late 1950s on many college campuses. At Williams College, students put out alternative reading lists to challenge the liberal views of their professors. They even started a radio station, Radio Free Williams, to broadcast conservative viewpoints and host speakers, like Buckley, who became a hero on campus with youthful conservatives. Young people also set out to influence elections and to win offices in the Young Republicans (YRs), a student offshoot of the national party, and to combat liberal and radical students in the National Student Association (NSA), an organization long dominated by liberals.[11]

The battles within the Young Republicans became legendary. In 1957, John Ashbrook, a conservative from Ohio, was elected president of the Young Republican National Federation. Ashbrook would later be elected to Congress from Ohio and served as a political conservative until his death in 1980. He was helped in his effort by William Rusher, an attorney for the Senate Select Committee on Investigations, and F. Clifton White, a New York political strategist. All of these men would play crucial roles in the political ascendancy of conservatism, helping take over the YRs before doing the same in the GOP.

Rusher was born in Chicago in 1924, attended Princeton University, and while at Princeton was a confirmed internationalist who supported GOP presidential candidate Wendell Willkie in 1940. He converted to conservatism over the communist issue and became a key supporter of Senator Barry Goldwater (R-Ariz.). In 1957 he began a long career as publisher of *National Review* and, with White, Ashbrook, and other acquaintances from the YRs, played a crucial role in organizing the draft of Goldwater as a candidate for president in 1964.[12]

AUH$_2$0

Goldwater was seen by Rusher and others as the most capable individual to lead the political revolution conservatives sought. Goldwater was a Phoenix department store heir, born in 1909, who was not particularly interested in politics growing up in the deserts of Arizona. His family heritage went back to the original settlement of the Arizona Territory in the 1870s, with Barry's grandfather Mike Goldwasser (the name was Anglicized) establishing a dry goods store and selling his goods to miners. The store eventually became the Goldwater Department Store in the early 1900s, and as Arizona developed as a state celebrated for its weather and beautiful scenery, the store (and Phoenix) prospered.

Goldwater grew up in economic privilege, attended Staunton Military Academy in Virginia and then the University of Arizona, which he left in 1929 after one year. He was bored with formal education but possessed a sharp mind. He spent the 1930s learning the department store business, becoming active in social concerns in Arizona, and flying planes, tinkering with mechanical gadgets, and exploring and photographing Arizona's mountains and desert countryside. He also joined the army reserve and was always a passionate believer in strong military power.

Like many conservatives, he opposed the New Deal, even though New Deal programs, particularly water projects, did much to help develop the arid West. "I think the foundations of my political philosophy were rooted in my resentment against the New Deal," Goldwater wrote in his memoirs.[13] In his family's department store, he had direct experience with the New Deal's National Recovery Administration code writing authority and came to detest the distant bureaucracy imposing its will on private ownership. He admired Herbert Hoover and was always a traditional Republican. Unlike Ronald Reagan, who began his career as a Democrat and a Roosevelt supporter, Goldwater never was anything but a conservative Republican, which made his views as strong as the desert rock in the state he loved.

During World War II, as an experienced pilot, Goldwater received a commission as a captain and ferried planes to North Africa, as well as to the China-Burma-India theater of operations. He made dangerous flights over "the Hump," the name for the Himalaya Mountains that were traversed to supply and equip Chiang Kai-shek's armies fighting against Japan. After returning from the war he was determined to enter politics and ran for a seat on the Phoenix city council. An effective and popular councilman, he decided to challenge popular New Deal Democrat Ernest MacFarland for a Senate seat in 1952. Goldwater, according to his biographer Robert Alan Goldberg, had matured after the war, finding purpose in defending what he thought was right about America: private enterprise, an active internationalism, and an end to statism. He was influenced by his reading of Hayek's *Road to Serfdom* as well as by his general business philosophy of free enterprise. He supported right-to-work laws in Arizona and applauded the Taft-Hartley Act. He was also a supporter of equality for African Americans and was a member of the NAACP.

Surprising all observers, Goldwater defeated MacFarland easily, helped by the Eisenhower landslide and by the fact that Joseph McCarthy, at the peak of his power, had campaigned against MacFarland (all four Democrats McCarthy targeted were defeated for reelection in 1952, including his nemesis Millard Tydings). Goldwater began a lengthy tenure on the Senate Armed Services Committee, and focused as well on labor unions and the corruption within them (he helped secure passage of the Landrum-Griffith Act in 1958). Goldwater was a key conservative voice in the 1950s, voting for the Bricker Amendment in 1954, against McCarthy's condemnation in 1955, and heading up investigations into corruption within labor unions. He did not write much legislation, but he became a rising star among conservatives.[14]

Like many conservatives he had become increasingly critical of Eisenhower and sought to make the GOP a more conservative vehicle. Easily reelected in 1958, a year in which the GOP lost seats in Congress, Goldwater was selected as head of the Republican Senatorial Campaign Committee, which gave him more national exposure, traveling the country in support of Republican candidates for Congress. He also started writing a nationally syndicated column distributed in hundreds of papers throughout the country, expressing his conservative views on any number of issues. It was through this column and in his many speeches that conservatives would begin to consider Goldwater as presidential material.

Events accelerated the general discouragement with consensus in the late 1950s. Eisenhower had allowed the Soviet invasion of Hungary, which he realized he could do nothing to thwart. In October 1957 America experienced a stunning shock with the launching of the Soviet space satellite *Sputnik*. The satellite was alarming, proving that the Soviets possessed missile strength that could allow them to attack America. Eisenhower knew better, from U-2 spy plane missions that revealed the Soviets possessed only a few rockets. Still, the Democrats urged action and Ike signed the National Defense Education Act that provided federal aid for scientific education, the first such appropriation by the federal government for secondary education.

One component of the act caused controversy—the presence of a loyalty oath that grant and scholarship recipients would be required to sign. Politicians, seeking to put the McCarthy period behind them, wanted to remove the oath from the act, but young conservatives Doug Caddy and David Franke urged that it remain, arguing that why should students receive federal money to study science to be used for defense purposes, if they were disloyal? They began the Student Committee for the Loyalty Oath and petitioned politicians, wrote letters, met with conservative congressmen and senators, and used their connections to student conservative groups to begin a forty-four-campus organization that did similar things. The pressure worked and the loyalty oath remained in the act.[15]

The next year Soviet leader Nikita Khrushchev visited the United States. Buckley urged conservatives to protest the visit, saying the East River in New York should be dyed red to reflect the "butcher of the Ukraine's" murder of innocents. Buckley entertained suggestions from readers about how to protest the visit. One said "kill the bastard" while others more constructively offered ideas like "let the kinsmen of the patriots of the captive nations parade flag-draped coffins down the streets of New York day after day."[16] *National Review* editors chose to protest, along with thousands of others, wearing black armbands and silently standing along the route Khrushchev's motorcade took in New York.

Many of the protests were organized by conservatism's own impresario, Marvin Liebman. A former communist and Zionist, Liebman moved to the Right in the early 1950s and became active as a fund-raiser and public relations guru for a variety of conservative organizations. He was especially important in public relations for the Committee of One Million and close to many in the emerging movement, especially Buckley. Liebman was a master at using communist techniques against the Left. Liebman organized Hungarian movie star protests outside the Soviet embassy in 1956 and even talked about getting together a student liberation army that would go to Hungary after final exams to support the freedom fighters in that central European nation. Luckily for the students, such an army never developed.[17]

THE OTHER SIXTIES

The intersection of all these various streams came to fruition with the effort to get Goldwater nominated as vice president at the 1960 GOP convention. The effort began with the publication of Goldwater's *The Conscience of a Conservative*, a slim 120-page book that was culled from speeches by the senator into publishable form by L. Brent Bozell, Buckley's brother-in-law and an editor at *National Review*. It was a powerful testament of the beliefs of the Arizona senator. The brain behind the project was Clarence Manion, who organized the Victor Publishing Company in Shepherdsville, Kentucky, to publish and distribute the book. It was a smash success, selling over 3.5 million copies and going through over twenty-three printings to become one of the seminal books in the conservative lexicon.[18]

It was not just a campaign book; indeed, Goldwater was indifferent, yet flattered, by any campaign to make him a vice presidential candidate. Rather, it reflected an accurate statement of the principles upon which conservatism developed in the postwar period. As Goldwater wrote, "conservatism is not an economic theory, though it has economic implications. . . . The Conservative is the first to understand that the practice of freedom requires the establishment of order: it is impossible for one man to be free if another is to deny him the exercise of his freedom."[19] Goldwater offered a definition of conservatism quite consistent with the reigning fusionist sentiments expressed by conservatives like Frank Meyer in the early 1960s.

Most of the book was dedicated to domestic issues, such as freedom for the farmer, states' rights and civil rights, and freedom for the laborer. On states' rights Goldwater made an argument similar to Kilpatrick's in *The Sovereign States* and one quite consistent with the views of conservatives as a whole: "The Constitution draws a sharp and clear line between federal jurisdiction and state jurisdiction. The federal government's failure to recognize that line has been a crushing blow to limited government. . . . Nothing could so far advance the cause of freedom as for state officials throughout the land to assert their rightful claims to lost state power; and for the federal government to withdraw promptly and totally from every jurisdiction which the Constitution reserved to the states."[20]

This was radical stuff, and was entirely within the sphere of argument advanced by Southern governors when dealing with the federal government and "outside agitators" in the civil rights movement. Goldwater could not have been unaware of the radical impact of such statements at a time when blacks were in revolt against the Southern state governments that were denying their equality. Principles of states' rights did not matter to those who fell under the jackboot of state governments in Alabama and Mississippi where the blatant exercise of violence against blacks was being employed.

Goldwater discussed civil rights, concluding "there can be no conflict between states rights—properly defined—and civil rights—properly defined." But social movements are not built on definitions and it was patently unfair for Goldwater to insist on a definitional reality when the real truth of racial unrest was reaching the majority of the nation through media and television. Still, his discussion of civil rights is catalogued under the Constitutional doctrines conservatives embraced at the time. Goldwater admitted the quandary for a principled conservative: "I am in agreement with the *objectives* of the Supreme Court as stated in the *Brown* decision. . . . I am not prepared, however, to impose that judgment of mine on the people of Mississippi or South Carolina. . . . That is their business, not mine. I believe that the problem of race relations, like all social or cultural problems, is best handled by the people directly concerned. . . . Any other course enthrones tyrants and dooms freedom."[21]

To the Cold War Goldwater dedicated one of the book's longest chapters, calling it the "Soviet Menace." Goldwater stated bluntly that "the Communists' aim is to conquer the world." Our struggle, Goldwater related, was not simply "to wage a war against communists, but to win it."[22] He then recommended offensive action against communism, following strategic theories to determine the moment and time when *we* would take action against communism and capture the momentum from the communists themselves.

Goldwater's book was a beacon for many conservatives. Pat Buchanan, a conservative commentator, then a student in college, called it "our new testament; it contained the core beliefs of our political faith, it told us why we had failed and what we must do."[23] Newspapers and magazines praised the book, while columnist Westbrook Pegler, a long distinguished and vitriolic conservative newspaper columnist, annointed Goldwater "the successor to Senator Taft of Ohio as the protector of the Constitution and freedom."[24]

The book's impact on students was especially profound. In the spring of 1960, Bob Croll, a Northwestern University student who had been active in the loyalty oath committee, started the Youth for Goldwater for Vice President. At the same moment when thousands of black students in the South were sitting in at lunch counters demanding equal service, young conservatives experienced what many of them would label "the thrill of treason," contemplating getting Goldwater on the Republican ticket in the fall as the candidate running alongside the certain nominee, Richard Nixon.

It was not to be. When the GOP met that August in Chicago, Nixon had already made arrangements—in what Goldwater later called a "domestic Munich"—with New York Governor Nelson Rockefeller, the liberal kingmaker in the party, to nominate Massachusetts Senator Henry Cabot Lodge Jr. as his vice presidential candidate. Nixon, who was seen as a conservative by many commentators, had deliberately sacrificed the vice presidency to a member of the eastern establishment, the well-connected Lodge. Young conservatives who had attended to show their support for Goldwater were dispirited. When Goldwater spoke to the convention, and when boos rang out after he pledged his delegates to Nixon, the senator lectured the crowd sternly, "Let's grow up, Conservatives! We want to take this party back and I think one day we can. Let's get to work!"[25]

The young people in the audience proceeded to do just that. Within a month of the convention, on the weekend of September 9–11, 1960, more than ninety young people, as well as conservative luminaries Buckley, Frank Meyer, James Burnham, and Marvin Liebman, met at Buckley's mother's home in Sharon, Connecticut, to form an organization known as Young Americans for Freedom (YAF). The students ratified a short statement of principles known as The Sharon Statement, which was drafted en route by M. Stanton Evans and articulated, similar to Goldwater's book, a fusionist conception of conservatism.

Buckley covered the event in *National Review*, telling readers that "what is so striking in the students who met at Sharon is their appetite for power. Ten years ago the struggle seemed so long, so endless, even, that we did not dream of victory."[26] But, as Buckley argued, "the difference in psychological attitude" between YAFers and the older conservative generation "is tremendous." The Sharon Statement revealed how much influence *National Review* had on conservatism. Evans was a fusionist who believed in the principle of ordered liberty and the statement revealed this clearly, arguing for a free market economy right alongside of demands for social order and tradition. Classical liberals served on YAF's National Advisory Board alongside traditionalists like Russell Kirk without any contradiction. Like Goldwater, the young conservatives in YAF believed in principle but they also were interested in political power and fights over what principles to enact were not important at the Sharon conference. The only real significant debate at the meeting was whether to place "God" in the statement—it was, by a vote of forty-four to forty.[27]

YAF established its headquarters in the New York office of Marvin Liebman. In its first few years in operation it dedicated itself to recruiting members on campus, developing a magazine (*The New Guard*, first published in March 1961), and working to push the nomination of Barry Goldwater for president in 1964. YAF also dedicated its time to protests against communism. It organized two rallies against communism, the second one drawing more than 20,000 people to Madison Square Garden in New York to hear Goldwater, Brent Bozell, and a variety of other speakers discuss the communist threat. According to Liebman, YAF claimed 25,000 members after one year in operation.[28]

But the harmony present at YAF's founding meeting did not last. The organization was beset by factional difficulties throughout most of its history. Early on these factional fights revolved around power, who had it and who did not. Caddy proved to be a key infighter, seeking to centralize power in the national office. But there were other ideological fights. Scott Stanley, a John Birch supporter, was accused of trying to move the organization toward Welch's control. William Cotter, a New Yorker, was accused of trying to connect the organization with Nelson Rockefeller, a nemesis to young conservatives. Within a few years all of these infighters left the organization. Like any student organization in the sixties, YAF experienced ups and downs in terms of membership and leadership.

William Rusher, who understood youth politics well from his days in the Young Republicans, worked to bring stability to YAF's national board. He hired Richard Vigeurie as executive director of the organization. Viguerie was from Houston, Texas, and became an activist through his involvement in Harris County Republican politics. He had volunteered in the successful campaign of John Tower to the Senate from Texas, the first Republican elected from Texas since Reconstruction. Viguerie was motivated, had experience with campaigns, and was a Goldwater conservative. He straightened out many of the problems within YAF's office and was an avid student of direct mail fund-raising, which Liebman had helped develop. Within a few years YAF had a premier fund-raising list and had become a significant influence in conservative politics.[29]

In the early 1960s it was conservative activity that drew significant, often negative, media attention. The John Birch Society was profiled in many news stories and the Anti-defamation League's Arnold Forster and Benjamin Epstein published *Danger on the Right* (1963), a book showcasing the extremism of various Rightist groups. Movies also portrayed the Right negatively. For example, *Seven Days in May*, starring Burt Lancaster as an anticommunist general who plans a coup against the president (played by Frederic March), was a popular smash. It was based loosely on the views expressed by General Edwin Walker, who resigned from the military after it was discovered he had distributed JBS pamphlets to the troops under his command, a violation of the Hatch Act (which made it illegal for federal employees to advocate political views).

Walker became a hero to many on the Right. A native Texan, he ran for governor on the Democratic ticket in 1962 and lost; that same fall he traveled to Oxford, Mississippi, to speak against the federal government securing the entry of James Meredith, a black student, into the University of Mississippi. Whites rioted at Oxford, and two people were killed in the melee. Walker was charged with conspiracy, incitement of riot, and insurrection for his role in the protests and the Kennedy administration confined him to a mental institution in Missouri. Politicians, like South Carolina senator Strom Thurmond, protested his confinement. He was released within a year and, ironically, was the first victim of Kennedy assassin Lee Harvey Oswald, who shot Walker through a window in Dallas in 1963.[30]

Not only did groups like YAF point to a political awakening on college campuses (ironic given what the campuses would look like by the late 1960s), but extremist groups like the Minutemen and the John Birch Society became targets of governmental action. The Kennedy administration was concerned about the nexus between anticommunist activism and civil rights. But it was also concerned about the growing radicalism of anticommunist groups who continued to call for the overthrow of Fidel Castro on Cuba (even after the failure of an American-backed invasion in April 1961) and for an aggressive war against the Soviet Union.

In response to the JBS and Walker, the Kennedy administration began covert operations against the Right wing. In December 1961, brothers and labor leaders Walter and Victor Reuther, as well as Americans for Democratic

Action attorney Joseph Rauh Jr., authored the Reuther Memorandum that
warned Attorney General Robert Kennedy to avoid confrontations with "the
radical Right" and instead to minimize their organizational, financial, and political influence. How? By using government agencies like the Internal Revenue Service, to investigate the tax-exempt status of organizations like the
Birch Society and the Christian Anti-Communist Crusade (and ten others).

The Ideological Organizations Project, as the IRS project was known, investigated Left-wing groups as well, but its main focus, as historian John Andrew has written, "remained on right-wing organizations." Eventually, before
the project was ended in 1967, the IRS removed the tax-exempt status from
seven Right-wing organizations. Not only that, but through audits and the
threat of audits, the IRS and the Kennedy administration blatantly attacked
and harassed ideological organizations. Not since the Roosevelt administration's efforts to harass America First had government tried to harass legitimate political and ideological groups.[31]

Many conservatives realized that the taint of association with radical
groups like the Birch Society would be detrimental if Goldwater were to ever
be a serious nominee for the presidency. William F. Buckley led the way in
the pages of *National Review*, raising "The Question of Robert Welch" in the
February 13, 1962, issue. He did not do so without first deliberating with
Goldwater, William Rusher, and other editors about the position he was to
take; but he did so with the intention of divorcing the "Vital Center conservatism" of *NR* from the extremist views of Welch.

The question Buckley asked was quite simple: "how can the John Birch Society be an effective political instrument while it is led by a man whose views
on current affairs are, at so many critical points, so critically different from their
own, and, for that matter, so far removed from common sense?" Buckley concluded that "Robert Welch is damaging the cause of anti-communism." Buckley then laid out a bill of charges against Welch, careful to disassociate the
Birch National Council and the thousands of Birch members from their leader.
He discussed the Eisenhower book, the comments Welch made after the Bay of
Pigs invasion of Cuba, which he blamed on officials in the U.S. government "to
make Castro stronger throughout Latin America." He criticized Welch's "finding" that "the government of the United States is under operational control of
the Communist Party." This, Buckley argued, was nonsense. "Mr. Welch has re-
vived in many men the spirit of patriotism, and that same spirit calls now for
rejecting, out of a love of truth and country, his false counsels."[32]

Buckley's decision was not made capriciously. In the end a few hundred individuals cancelled their subscriptions to *National Review* and there was dissent
from publisher Rusher, Frank Meyer, and others on the staff. But the editorial
proved important as an assurance that conservatism and anticommunism were

not represented by Welch. It did little to assure liberals, however, that conservatives were not extremists, but it was a sign of political maturity for the movement that the first step was taken in disassociating conservatism from the radical elements who claimed its moniker.

DRAFT GOLDWATER!

The reason for Buckley's condemnation of Welch had everything to do with politics and especially with the decision, made by a committee of conservatives headed by F. Clifton White, to draft Goldwater for the presidential nomination in 1964. Goldwater was an unwilling participant in any discussion of a run for the White House. But his prominence after 1960 made him the only feasible conservative choice. In December 1962, fifty-five conservatives, including Rusher, Ashbrook, White, and many others from YR ranks, met in Chicago to discuss a Goldwater candidacy. White was given the task of approaching Goldwater, who knew about the secret meeting due to leaks in the media and disapproved, lecturing White about going behind his back. He absolutely refused to have his name put into nomination.

At a February 1963 meeting, again in Chicago, the group met to discuss their options. After going around in a circle for awhile, someone interjected, "Why not draft the son of a bitch?" "What if he won't let us draft him?" someone asked. "Then let's draft him anyway!" It was decided to proceed with a draft of an unwilling candidate. A month later, the National Draft Goldwater Committee was formed, headed up by Peter O'Donnell, the GOP chairman from Texas, and Clif White, who ran operations from Suite 3505 in the Chanin Building in New York City. The committee was remarkably effective and, in coordination with groups like YAF, Goldwater support mushroomed over the course of the year. A rally held in midsummer in Washington, D.C., drew 15,000 Goldwater supporters to the unair-conditioned Armory building on an incredibly hot day. The depth of Goldwater support helped convince the senator that his candidacy was possible.[33]

Goldwater had nothing to do with the committee and continued to insist he was not a candidate. By autumn, however, he was convinced and even relished the thought of campaigning against his old Senate colleague John F. Kennedy. But the young president's assassination in November took the wind out of Goldwater's sails. He declared his candidacy officially in January 1964 but understood that it would be a difficult, if not impossible, task to defeat Lyndon Johnson.

The decision to draft Goldwater was made primarily to prevent another liberal Republican from securing the nomination in 1964. Nelson Rockefeller, the liberal governor of New York, was the most likely nominee, and it was to detour a Rockefeller nomination that conservatives acted. Rockefeller proved more important for rallying conservatives in the early 1960s than even liberals. He was detested by conservatives, considered a sellout and an example of "me-too" Republicanism by his support for expanded welfare state programs in New York and for high taxes to fund them. In 1962 New York conservatives founded the New York Conservative Party, headed by Daniel Mahoney, which ran a Senate candidate against the liberal Republican Jacob Javits. In 1970, the New York Conservative Party would nominate and New Yorkers would elect James Buckley, brother of William F. Buckley, to the Senate from New York.

But there were also political considerations of far greater weight behind conservative interest in a Goldwater candidacy. Both Rusher and White seemed to realize that the civil rights revolution pointed to trouble for the Democratic Party in the South. Southern whites tended to be more conservative on a wide variety of issues and were strongly anticommunist as well. If this vote could be tapped then the South might be poised for realignment behind the banner of a conservative candidate like Goldwater. Rusher wrote about this in a February 12, 1963, *National Review* article, "Crossroads for the GOP." Rusher argued that any Republican candidate could take "the GOP's Midwestern heartland, and such peripheral fiefs as northern New England and certain of the Mountain states, amounting in all to perhaps 140 electoral votes (with 270 needed to win)." But, as Rusher stated, "Goldwater, and Goldwater alone . . . can carry enough southern and border states to offset the inevitable Kennedy conquests in the big industrial states of the North and still stand a serious chance of winning the election."[34]

Conservatives had not typically thought this way before. This was electoral calculating, the type that parties and ideas with a chance to win typically engage in, something lacking in conservative strategizing to that time. Rusher was delineating an early Southern strategy, showcasing how an appealing conservative could tap into voter resentment against liberalism in the South and the West. He was also showing that such resentment existed and that, unlike in decades past, the GOP—the party of Abraham Lincoln—could compete in the South.

Rusher was not predicting anything more than the political calculus of 1963. The civil rights movement, and Kennedy's support for it, had engendered bitterness in the South against liberalism. Southern racial populists, like Alabama Governor George Wallace, tapped into this resentment, but Wallace did not appeal to many conservatives. He remained a liberal, offering high taxes and big spending alongside a racially divisive message. Wallace spoke in the urban north in 1964 and his message resonated there as well, especially as racial rioting became prevalent in northern cities.

Other Southern Democrats became convinced that Goldwater was the answer in 1964 and shifted parties as a result. Strom Thurmond, the South Carolina senator who had run as a Dixiecrat presidential candidate in 1948, for much of his career a racial moderate, switched to the GOP and supported Goldwater over Johnson. "My fellow extremists," Thurmond would say during speeches in support of Goldwater, "I did not leave the Democratic Party. It left me!"[35]

The majority of Democrats stayed in the party that year. The 1964 election has been referred to as "the last liberal election," which would have surprised any observer who did not live beyond that year. Liberalism was at its high point. Johnson doggedly sought to outdo FDR in his pursuit of federal aid for education (secured with the Elementary and Secondary Education Act as well as student loan programs and Head Start for preschool children); health care (Medicare and Medicaid were passed); a federally funded War on Poverty that greatly expanded federal money for welfare, food stamps, and other assistance for the poor; environmental legislation; and aid for urban areas. The Great Society was the name for Johnson's programs, and it proved extremely popular in 1964.

Johnson also did his predecessor one better. Using Kennedy's death to his advantage, Johnson was able to play on public sympathy to secure passage of the Civil Rights Act that ended racial discrimination in facilities and hiring. As a Southerner, Johnson had more advantages than Kennedy in gaining Southern support in his own party. But there was a filibuster nonetheless and the Civil Rights Act passed only with the assistance of Republicans like Senate Minority Leader Everett Dirksen (R-Ill.). A year later, after more protests and further violence and deaths, Johnson signed the Voting Rights Act into law.[36]

Goldwater opposed all of the Great Society legislation and voted against the Civil Rights Act. After Goldwater won the Republican nomination he campaigned against popular programs like Social Security, telling an audience of senior citizens he favored privatizing the program. In Tennessee, he told audiences that he favored selling the government-owned New Deal–era power project the Tennessee Valley Authority. Goldwater also attacked Great Society spending and urged cuts in government. All of this was applauded by conservatives who loved Goldwater's edge and sharp criticism of government, but it was not politically expedient, and Goldwater, who at times was irascible and stubborn, proved the wrong man to deliver conservatism's message.

The right man was waiting in the wings, as it turned out. One of the key events in the Goldwater campaign came when Ronald Reagan, a former movie actor turned television spokesman for General Electric, gave a superb address on national television a few days before the election. Reagan had delivered variations of "the speech," as it became known, hundreds of times before in his role as corporate spokesman for GE. In it Reagan articulated the real cost of the welfare state to taxpayers, laying out in detail what specific government programs cost, discussing how much money went to the taxman each year ("37 cents on the dollar") and broaching the idea that communism could not be dealt with in halfway measures. He spoke calmly, with a reassuring manner, was easy to understand, and was a superb spokesman for the conservative message, befitting his acting experience. He was good-looking and charming and his audience responded to what he had to say. It was an electric moment, perhaps the only one in a campaign that had been poorly organized and ineffective.[37]

The results were hardly surprising. Depicted as an extremist, warmonger, racist, nutcase, kook, and just about every other negative epithet the media could employ, the Arizona senator was slaughtered by Johnson. The Republican won only 27 million votes to Johnson's 43 million. Goldwater won six states, five of them in the Deep South, a sign of things to come for the GOP. Johnson won 61 percent of the popular vote, the greatest popular vote landslide in history to that time. Not only that, but Goldwater's inept campaign was bad for the GOP in Congress. Johnson possessed huge majorities, enough it was thought, to secure his Great Society programs and to fight communism in Vietnam. He had a 295–140 majority in the House and a 68–32 majority in the Senate. James Reston of the *New York Times* was half right when he argued in his election postmortem: "Barry Goldwater not only lost the presidential election yesterday but the conservative cause as well."[38]

Of the former there was no doubt; of the latter, it certainly appeared so on November 4, 1964. But there were several issues percolating beneath the surface of American life that exploded into the nation's consciousness after Johnson's reelection. By 1966, Republicans made tremendous gains in Congress and blocked the extension of further liberal programs. Reagan was elected governor of California, the start of a path that would take him to the White House in 1980. But most importantly, liberalism was cracking up, victimized by the war in Vietnam, race problems at home, and an economy struggling to maintain the "grand expectations" that had been delivered in the previous twenty years.

LIBERTARIANS AND TRADITIONALISTS

After the Goldwater debacle conservatives continued to organize as well. Rather than leading to the dire fate predicted by Reston, conservative journals like *National Review* and *Human Events* showed marked increases in subscriptions. Organizations like YAF also experienced growth in the late 1960s as young conservatives supported the Vietnam War (and urged victory in the war against communism) and battled the New Left antiwar radicals, best exemplified by the Students for a Democratic Society (SDS), on campus. By 1969, at the height of campus radicalism, YAF would claim 80,000 members, surviving another factional fight and continuing to develop cadres for conservatism.[39]

Other conservative organizations were born in 1964. The Philadelphia Society, a conservative intellectual group, was formed that year by Don Lipsett, a Michigan native who wanted to continue to provide a place where conservatives of different views could meet and discuss their ideas respectfully. Funded by start-up money from Buckley (a $100 check), the Philadelphia Society grew over the next two decades, providing conservative intellectuals a forum for the articulation of their ideas. The meetings were often productive and respectful of differences between conservatives, but sometimes the fireworks over rival interpretations of conservatism could prove disruptive.[40]

The American Conservative Union (ACU), a form of "graduate YAF" was also created in the wake of the Goldwater campaign. Its purpose was "to mobilize and consolidate the intellectual resources of the conservative movement"; "to provide leadership . . . for existing conservative-oriented organizations, magazines and political figures"; "to influence American public opinion toward the acceptance of conservative principles of economics and government"; and "to stimulate and direct responsible citizen action on social and economic problems and matters of legislation, public policy and in behalf of conservative candidates for public office."[41] Explicitly, the ACU combined the political and intellectual resources of the movement and was led in its early years by Indiana congressman Donald Bruce. Like YAF, factions almost ripped the organization apart, but due to prodding from its founders (including Frank Meyer, Liebman, Buckley, Rusher, and others), the ACU stabilized, and within a decade claimed over 40,000 members.

The Goldwater campaign represented fusionist conservatism best associated with *National Review* and YAF. But there were other conservative traditions that reawakened during the decade. Libertarianism was one of these traditions. While many conservative young people could trace their involvement in politics and their interest in conservative ideas back to Russell Kirk or *National Review*, for a whole different generation of activists, intellectuals like Ayn Rand and Murray Rothbard were more important in the construction of their ideals. An undercurrent of postwar conservatism, by the late 1960s, libertarians separated from the conservative movement and formed their own organizations, magazines, and think tanks.

Libertarianism had always been a key component of the conservative revival. Economists like F. A. Hayek, Ludwig von Mises, Milton Friedman, George Stigler, and Ronald Coase had laid the foundation for a revival in free market economic thinking. Most of these economists and intellectuals encouraged the development of free market, classical liberal thought within groups like ISI and YAF. By the early 1960s Friedman, a University of Chicago economist, had become one of the leading exponents of the doctrine of free markets, articulated in *Capitalism and Freedom* (1961), which pointedly depicted the linkages between economic and political freedom. In the late 1960s Friedman became a columnist for *Newsweek* and in the late 1970s hosted a Public Broadcasting series with his wife Rose (also a trained economist) called *Free to Choose*.[42]

Radical libertarians had long contributed to the growing challenge to state power in the twentieth century. In 1943 three important libertarian books were published, all written by women. All three of them contributed to the growth of libertarian ideas. The three books were Ayn Rand's *The Fountainhead*, Isabel Paterson's *The God of the Machine*, and Rose Wilder Lane's *The Discovery of Freedom: Man's Struggle Against Authority*.[43]

Rand's book is a novel about extreme individualism, her first hints of a philosophy that she would call objectivism. Howard Roark is the protagonist, an architect who refuses to make compromises with his work and who, at the end of the novel, blows up a government housing project he designed because of meddling with his scheme. Later made into a movie starring Gary Cooper, *The Fountainhead* and Rand's later novel *Atlas Shrugged* (where her philosophy was worked out) have sold millions of copies. Whittaker Chambers reviewed *Atlas Shrugged* in *National Review* and said: "Out of a lifetime of reading, I can recall no other book in which the tone of overriding arrogance was so implacably sustained. Its shrillness is without reprieve. Its dogmatism is without appeal. . . . From almost any page of *Atlas Shrugged*, a voice can be heard, from painful necessity, commanding: "To a gas chamber, go!""[44] Rand never spoke with Buckley again after the review appeared.

Paterson's and Lane's works are much less widely known. Paterson was a novelist and columnist for the New York *Telegraph-Herald*. She espoused a doctrine of individual rights and free market capitalism and was deeply influenced by Garet Garrett. She was appalled at the turn toward statism in the 1930s and defended American development, both economic and political, in her book. Lane was the daughter of Laura Ingalls Wilder, the author of the *Little House* series of children's books, which, in fact, daughter Rose, a much more talented writer, finished. Lane lived in rural New Hampshire and wrote essays for a variety of journals. Her *The Twilight of Authority*, much like Paterson's book, is an analysis of the American tradition of self-government and self-reliance.[45]

Yet it was the Russian-born Rand, a Jewish refugee from communism and former Hollywood scriptwriter, who had the most influence on young people turning toward libertarianism by the 1950s. Rand's books, her philosophy of objectivism, her powerful intellect, and her attractiveness as a model individualist all served to compel many individualist-leaning young people to her workshops, speeches, and some into the world of Rand herself. Her objectivist philosophy was a philosophy of extreme selfishness, that altruistic behavior and caring about anyone beside yourself was evil. Rand seemed to offer an extreme individualism that became, as Jerome Tuccille, a young devotee of Rand who soon moved on to other libertarian ideas, called it, a "new form of Marxism of the Right." "To be in disagreement with the ideas of Ayn Rand," Tuccille wrote, "was to be, by definition, irrational and immoral. There was no allowable deviation under the tenets of Objectivism. . . . Curiously, for a woman who started out as a champion of the independent mind, she began to consider her own ideas as natural corollaries of truth and objectivity."[46]

With Rand so unappealing for many libertarians and with the wider conservative movement promulgating a "global war against communism," libertarians constructed their own movement in sympathy with the antiwar students on campus. The Vietnam War disrupted American society and the Cold War consensus during the 1960s. The American decision to enter the war was taken in stages, with the Tonkin Gulf Resolution of August 1964 representing the first commitment of American military power to the area (up until that time the United States had advisors seeking to build a South Vietnamese army but had no official combat role). The resolution passed the Senate overwhelmingly and even Goldwater, battling Johnson for the presidency, voted for it. In February 1965 the United States began a bombing campaign against communist targets; known as Rolling Thunder, American planes pulverized the Vietnamese countryside, seeking to hinder the infiltration of communists to the South. Finally, in March 1965 Johnson committed combat troops into Vietnam, to protect American air bases and to engage in "search and destroy" missions against the communists. By the end of 1965, more than 200,000 American troops were in Vietnam.

Almost immediately young people on campuses organized against the war. Teach-ins critical of American policy were held at the University of Michigan. SDS, a radical group that floundered in terms of membership and influence, suddenly found relevance in the antiwar cause, sponsoring Easter protests in Washington that drew 20,000 people. New Left students mobilized thousands of other like-minded compatriots on campus and off into a formidable radical movement, transforming not only campus life but also national life as well. Not only did white middle-class students organize against the war, but the civil rights movement did as well. In 1966 Martin Luther King, against the wishes of his advisors, spoke out against the war. That same year the Black Power movement came to national consciousness, as African American radicals demanded not simply equality, but economic and political power. The Oakland-based Black Panther Party had a Marxist-based ideology and, eventually, as it found itself at war with the U.S. government, it made alliances with communists like Fidel Castro and Mao Zedong. Founder Huey Newton's memoir *Revolutionary Suicide* reveals the intention of race-based revolution and what it portended for American society.

Conservatives fought these trends. Instead of halfway measures against the communists, conservatives urged a "protracted conflict" involving the commitment of American military and economic power "based upon the premise that we cannot tolerate the survival of a political system which has both the growing capability and the ruthless will to destroy us."[47] Foreign policy think tanks began to flourish on the Right and included the Foreign Policy Research Institute at the University of Pennsylvania, headed up by Robert Strausz-Hupe, an Austrian émigré, who wrote the above words, as well as outposts at Georgetown and the Hoover Institution at Stanford University. More and more conservative academics became experts on foreign and strategic policy, including Notre Dame's Gerhart Niemeyer, and Georgetown's Richard Allen, Stefan Possony, and David Nelson Rowe (among many others). They all advocated a hard line toward the communists and an end to peaceful coexistence with the Soviet Union.

Young conservatives were deeply imbued with antipathy toward communism and with the advocacy of a victory strategy over the Soviets. Young conservatives supported the Vietnam War, with YAF protesting in favor of the war, holding teach-ins designed to educate students about communism, supporting wounded veterans, and combating the antiwar students on campus. When radical students began occupying campus buildings routinely in the late 1960s, YAF members seized the buildings of radical organizations, waved South Vietnamese flags, made declarations against communism, and then left the building. Former Maoist Philip Abbot Luce became a key advisor to YAF on how to confront the New Left and wrote many articles about the New Left's tactics and its communist influence for YAF's magazine *The New Guard*.[48]

But for many libertarian members of YAF, support for Vietnam was vitiated by the fact that in their view America's war was immoral and imperialistic. They also worried about the draft, which they considered illegal and increased the power of the state over individual lives. One of the more important libertarian critics was Murray Rothbard. Born in New York in 1926, Rothbard was the chief apostle of what would become radical libertarianism. Opposed to American intervention before World War II, Rothbard was a critic of the power of the state and was heavily influenced by the Austrian economist Ludwig von Mises. During the 1950s, he attended Rand's seminars but found her too extreme for his tastes, reading instead the nineteenth-century anarchist thought of Lysander Spooner and Benjamin Tucker. Rothbard believed "the United States was solely at fault in the Cold War, and that Russia was the aggrieved party."[49] New Left historians were coming to similar conclusions, producing a series of revisionist works that blamed the conflict on American demand for markets and on capitalism's rapacious quest for profit.

The linkage between the radical libertarianism of Rothbard, and the New Left critique of American foreign policy, came to fruition in 1965 when Rothbard and Leonard Liggio, a revisionist historian himself, founded the journal *Left and Right: A Journal of Libertarian Thought*. In the first issue, Rothbard wrote, "our justification is a deep commitment to the liberty of man." "Our title, *Left and Right*," he continued, "reflects our concern . . . with the ideological; and it also highlights the conviction that the present-day categories of left and right have become misleading and obsolete." "In particular, we hoped to be able to detach individualist-libertarians from their thralldom to a Conservative Movement that had become the major enemy of their own ideals and principles."[50]

But in his embrace of the New Left, Rothbard's effort to bring about a Left/Right alliance took a puzzling turn. Rothbard saw much to admire in SDS, the main organization of the New Left. In "SDS: The New Turn," he argued that, "in the broadest sense, the idea of participatory democracy [the main idea in SDS's Port Huron Statement] is profoundly individualist and libertarian."[51] As historian John Kelley points out, while, "the Port Huron Statement certainly included bits of libertarian rhetoric, its economic statements fundamentally clashed with the principles of *laissez-faire* economics."[52] Yet, Rothbard persisted, seeing great things in SDS's views on marijuana legalization, the military draft, and the Cold War. He appeared before the SDS National Council in Clear Lake, Iowa, in 1966 to speak against the draft. In a June 1968 article published in the New Left journal *Ramparts*, Rothbard attacked the New Right *National Review*'s "ex-fellow travelers and ex-communist" editors and spoke on how the Right had embraced those crusaders who wanted to fight a global war against Reds and destroy blacks and other minorities and political dissidents at home.

Karl Hess, a former speechwriter for Barry Goldwater and a contributor to *Newsweek*, became a convert to Rothbard's crusade. In 1969 he helped establish a new journal, *The Libertarian Forum*, which replaced *Left and Right*. Hess had always leaned to the libertarian side, more interested in such questions than in traditionalist concerns prominent in the conservative movement. Henry Regnery was a bit surprised by Hess's conversion, telling Felix Morley, "I have known Karl Hess for years. . . . Karl is an attractive, bright and very likeable man, but I don't think he is a person of much substance or stability. At one time, he had dreams of getting Admiral Doenitz out of jail and proclaiming him the legitimate ruler of Germany. . . . Romantics of his type can easily accept such aberrations."[53]

Vietnam led Hess to put aside his earlier juvenile views and to question the Cold War and the conservative defense of the war against communism. In 1968, in a very public way, he broke with the Right. Headlines screamed: "Ex Goldwater Aide Joins New Left." He spent the next several years lecturing to YAF groups, where libertarian influence was expanding, and attempting to get that organization to move in a libertarian direction.

This became necessary because by 1969, SDS imploded into factionalism, making a mockery of any suggestion that the organization was even mildly libertarian. The Weatherman, a Marxist faction, took over the organization, as did the Maoist group Progressive Labor, through what it called the Revolutionary Youth Movement. SDS's embrace of communist rhetoric and ideology had deeper roots in the organization than its libertarianism. Now only YAF existed as a student group that could become the vehicle for radical libertarianism.

The showdown between mainstream conservatives and libertarians occurred at the 1969 YAF convention in St. Louis. YAF had remained wedded to the conservatism of Goldwater and Buckley, but by 1967 several libertarians from Penn State University, including Don Ernsberger, made their way onto the board. At some campuses, like the University of Kansas, the campus head of YAF also served as the campus head of SDS. There were a small number of libertarians who were determined to force an issue at the 1969 convention, either taking over the organization or leaving it to establish their own.

In the *Libertarian Forum*, Rothbard published an inflammatory piece, "Listen YAF," calling YAF a fascist organization and urging libertarians in YAF to "get out, form your own organization, and breathe the clean air of freedom." Few listened and Ernsberger, for one, thought Rothbard's intervention made his task more difficult. At the convention itself, despite the theatrics of Karl Hess leading fifty anarchists to the St. Louis Arch to protest, and despite a ritual draft card burning by one libertarian—who was denounced as a communist and attacked by some delegates—the mainstream conservatives hung onto power. YAF remained wedded to the Cold War, passing resolutions to widen the war in Vietnam if the communists did not surrender within a year. Libertarians were attacked as "laissez-fairies" and some were expelled from the organization.[54]

That same year, any remaining libertarian influence in the conservative movement withdrew. Not only did the *Libertarian Forum* give them a journal to work out their philosophy, but a new magazine, *Reason*, was established as well. California libertarians founded the California Libertarian Alliance and, prodded by Hess, continued to seek alliances with the New Left. Rothbard gave up on the idea, recognizing that it was a "largely Stalinoid" group and that its only lasting feature was the counterculture, which possessed, Rothbard wrote, a "contempt for reason, logic, clarity, systematic thought," and through its drug use engaged in the politics of escape and "hallucination." While Rothbard by no means came back to the fold, he gave up on the idea of bringing about a Right-Left alliance and worked to build the libertarian movement through the 1970s and 1980s.

Conservatism had not only survived the tumultuous 1960s, but flourished as other ideological movements, like the New Left, floundered. Politically, although few could predict it then, conservatism was poised for a revolution, the capture of the GOP, the creation of policy institutions and think tanks, and the victory of Reagan in the 1980 presidential election. Not all was rosy, however. The libertarian revolt suggested that fusionism could break down. Conservative ideas seemed moribund, reflective of the concerns of proselytizers and pundits of the recent past, rather than being innovative and cutting edge for the present and future. There were a lot of question marks as conservatives faced the prospect of the 1970s, not least of which was whether conservatism could achieve political power and influence and whether such political power would be beneficial or detrimental for the movement.

NOTES

1. Barry Goldwater, Acceptance Speech at 1964 Republican Convention, reprinted in Schneider, ed., *Conservatism in America since 1930: A Reader* (New York: New York University Press, 2003), 238–46.

2. Theodore H. White, *The Making of the President: 1964* (New York: Atheneum, 1965), 217.

3. *National Review* (October 20, 1956), cited in Jeffrey Hart, *The Making of the American Conservative Mind: National Review and Its Times* (Wilmington, Del.: Intercollegiate Studies Institute, 2006), 71.

4. Gordon H. Chang, *Friends and Enemies: The United States, China, and the Soviet Union, 1948–1972* (Stanford, Calif.: Stanford University Press, 1990).

5. T. Coleman Andrews, October 27, 1956, Address over ABC Radio, Andrews Papers, Box 17, University of Oregon Division of Special Collections, Eugene, Ore.

6. Bonner Fellers to T. Coleman Andrews, August 31, 1956 and Sept. 12, 1956, Box 17 (Fellers), Andrews Papers.

7. Letter from Andrews to William F. Buckley Sr., Box 17 (Folder Bo–Bz), Andrews Papers.

8. Rick Perlstein, *Before the Storm: Barry Goldwater and the Unmaking of the American Consensus* (New York: Hill and Wang, 2001), 10.

9. Richard Viguerie and David Franke, *America's Right Turn: How Conservatives Used New and Alternative Media to Take Power* (Chicago: Bonus Books, 2004).

10. Lee Edwards, *Educating for Liberty: The First Half-Century of the Intercollegiate Studies Institute* (Washington, D.C.: Regnery Publishing, 2003), 17–28 (on Milione), 34–37 (on journalism fellows).

11. Gregory L. Schneider, *Cadres for Conservatism: Young Americans for Freedom and the Rise of the Contemporary Right* (New York: New York University Press, 1998), 17; John A. Andrew, *The Other Side of the Sixties: Young Americans for Freedom and the Rise of Conservative Politics* (New Brunswick, N.J.: Rutgers University Press, 1997), 24–31.

12. William A. Rusher, *Rise of the Right* (New York: Morrow, 1984); see also J. William Middendorf II, *A Glorious Disaster: Barry Goldwater's Presidential Campaign and the Origins of the Conservative Movement* (New York: Basic, 2006).

13. Barry M. Goldwater, *With No Apologies: The Personal and Political Memoirs of Barry Goldwater* (New York: William Morrow, 1979), 37.

14. Robert Alan Goldberg, *Barry Goldwater* (New Haven, Conn.: Yale University Press, 1995), and Lee Edwards, *Goldwater: The Man Who Made a Revolution* (Washington, D.C.: Regnery, 1995), are two fine biographies.

15. Schneider, *Cadres for Conservatism*, 20–23.

16. William F. Buckley Jr., "What to Do When Nikita Khrushchev Comes to New York," *National Review* (October 30, 1958): 152.

17. Marvin Liebman, *Coming out Conservative: An Autobiography* (San Francisco: Chronicle, 1992).

18. Perlstein, *Before the Storm*, 61–68, provides a useful discussion of the efforts to get the book published.

19. Barry Goldwater, *The Conscience of a Conservative* (Shepherdsville, Ky.: Victor, 1960), 10–11.

20. Goldwater, *Conscience of a Conservative*, 29, 30.

21. Goldwater, *Conscience of a Conservative*, 31, 37.

22. Goldwater, *Conscience of a Conservative*, 89, 118.

23. Pat Buchanan quoted in Lee Edwards, "The Other Sixties: A Flag-Waver's Memoir," *Policy Review* (Fall 1988): 61.

24. Buchanan in Edwards, "The Other Sixties."

25. Mary C. Brennan, *Turning Right in the Sixties: The Conservative Capture of the GOP* (Chapel Hill: University of North Carolina Press, 1995), 36.

26. *National Review* (September 24, 1960): 171.

27. Schneider, *Cadres for Conservatism*, 36.

28. Schneider, *Cadres for Conservatism*, 40–41.

29. Schneider, *Cadres for Conservatism*, 41–54.

30. Jonathon Schoenwald, *A Time For Choosing: The Rise of Modern American Conservatism* (New York: Oxford University Press, 2001), 100–23.

31. Andrew, *Other Side of the Sixties*, 151–68; John A. Andrew, *Power to Destroy: The Political Uses of the IRS from Kennedy to Nixon* (Chicago: Ivan R. Dee, 2002).

32. William F. Buckley Jr., "The Question of Robert Welch," *National Review* (February 13, 1962): 83–88.

33. There is a large literature on Draft Goldwater, including Middendorf, *Glorious Disaster*; Rusher, *Rise of the Right*; F. Clifton White, with William J. Gill, *Suite 3505: The Story of the Draft Goldwater Movement* (New Rochelle, N.Y.: Arlington House, 1967); and Perlstein, *Before the Storm*.

34. William Rusher, "Crossroads for the GOP," *National Review* (February 12, 1963): 110.

35. On Thurmond and his change to GOP see Earl Black and Merle Black, *The Rise of Southern Republicans* (Cambridge: Belknap Press, 2003).

36. On Great Society and its political impact, Gareth Davies, *From Opportunity to Entitlement: The Transformation and Decline of Great Society Liberalism* (Lawrence: University Press of Kansas, 1996), remains the best study; see also, Steven F. Hayward, *The Age of Reagan: The Fall of the Old Liberal Order* (New York: Prima Lifestyles, 2001), which is an exceptional conservative study. For a good political overview, see Allen J. Matusow, *The Unraveling of America: A History of Liberalism in the 1960s* (New York: Perennial, 1985).

37. On Reagan's move from liberalism to conservatism, see Thomas W. Evans, *The Education of Ronald Reagan: The General Electric Years and the Untold Story of His Conversion to Conservatism* (New York: Columbia University Press, 2006); and Matthew Dallek, *The Right Moment: Ronald Reagan's First Victory and the Decisive Turning Point in American Politics* (New York: Free Press, 2000).

38. James A. Reston, *New York Times* (November 4, 1964): 23.

39. Schneider, *Cadres for Conservatism*, 123–26.

40. Lee Edwards, *History of the Philadelphia Society*, (Jerome, Mich.: Philadelphia Society, 2004), published by The Philadelphia Society to commemorate 40th anniversary, copy in author's possession.

41. "The American Conservative Union" (Background of ACU: meetings of 12/1 and 12/19/1964), Box 57, Marvin Liebman Papers, Hoover Institution, Stanford University.

42. Milton Friedman and Rose D. Friedman, *Two Lucky People: Memoirs* (Chicago: University of Chicago Press, 1999).

43. Brian Doherty, *Radicals for Capitalism: A Freewheeling History of the Modern American Libertarian Movement* (New York: PublicAffairs, 2007), 113–47.

44. Whittaker Chambers, "Big Sister is Watching You," *National Review* (December 28, 1957): 596.

45. William Holtz, *Ghost in the Little House: A Biography of Rose Wilder Lane* (Columbia: University of Missouri Press, 1995).

46. Jerome Tuccille, *It Usually Begins with Ayn Rand* (New York: Stein and Day, 1971).

47. Robert Strausz-Hupe, William R. Kinter, and Stefan T. Possony, *A Forward Strategy for America* (New York: Harper, 1961).

48. Schneider, *Cadres for Conservatism*, 110–26.

49. Justin Ramaindo, *An Enemy of the State: The Life of Murray N. Rothbard* (Amherst, N.Y.: Prometheus, 2000).

50. Editorial: The General Line, *Left and Right: A Journal of Libertarian Thought* 1, no. 1 (Spring 1965): 3.

51. Murray Rothbard, "SDS: The New Turn," *Left and Right* 3, no. 1 (Winter 1967): 9–17.

52. John Kelley, *Bringing the Market Back In: The Political Revitalization of Market Liberalism* (New York: New York University Press, 1997), 97.

53. Letter from Henry Regnery to Felix Morley, October 10, 1969, Box 53, Folder 1 (Morley Corr.), Regnery Papers, Hoover Institution.

54. Schneider, *Cadres for Conservatism*, 134–41; Murray Rothbard, "Listen YAF," *Libertarian Forum* (August 15, 1969): 1–2.

Chapter Five

Revolution . . .

In this present crisis, government is not the solution to our problem; government is the problem. . . . It is my intention to curb the size and influence of the Federal Establishment. . . . Government can and must provide opportunity, not smother it; foster productivity, not stifle it.

—Ronald Reagan, First Inaugural Address

On January 20, 1981, on a cold but clear Washington afternoon, Ronald Reagan, an actor turned politician, was inaugurated as the fortieth president of the United States. What had begun as a dream of a few hundred conservative intellectuals and young people some twenty years earlier when they attempted to get Barry Goldwater nominated for vice president at the 1960 Republican National Convention (RNC), had come to fruition: a movement conservative was now president of the United States.

Conservatives were elated, believing that Reagan would live up to the rhetoric he had campaigned on, slashing and cutting the size of a bloated federal government, lowering taxes, rebuilding America's military, and renewing the nation's resolve in the face of an expansionist Soviet Union. Conservatives called it the Reagan Revolution and hoped it marked a departure from the liberal policies that had guided American domestic and foreign policy since the end of World War II.

Conservatives were ready to assume responsibility for governing the nation. Reagan's victory signaled the end of a period when conservatism had been building institutions like think tanks, many of them located in Washington. There were not only the beginnings of a political realignment, as the once Democratic "solid South" switched to the GOP, but a social and intellectual one. The emergence of the religious Right was one sign of a shift of Protestant evangelicals and traditionalist Catholics to conservatism. Former liberal

119

intellectuals, many of them Jewish and culturally modern—lumped together under the rubric neoconservative—switched to the conservative viewpoint on social and foreign policy. Reagan capitalized on this sea change in American politics in order to win election in 1980. It would be up to him to keep these diverse groups together and lead the nation toward his goal of representing, once again, "a shining city on a hill."[1]

THE DECLINE OF LIBERALISM

By the end of the 1960s liberalism was in decline. Lyndon Johnson had won a landslide election in 1964, but his pursuit of a war in Vietnam and a Great Society at home led to deep divisions among liberals within the Democratic Party. After 1966 his Great Society was all but dead, with a GOP–Southern Democrat coalition blocking further reforms. Johnson refused to raise taxes to fund his expansive governmental programs, fearing that tax increases would undo political support for the programs and undermine support for the war in Vietnam, which by 1968 was costing $2 billion per month. That year he was forced to increase taxes. The result was inflation and a devastated economy.[2]

Liberals also faced the problem of a fractured Cold War consensus as student and radical protesters drove a wedge between the Democrats over the Vietnam War. Johnson's decision to commit combat troops into southeast Asia and to bomb targets in Vietnam awakened an antiwar sentiment not seen in America since the America First movement before World War II. The antiwar movement dominated the campus, especially in groups like Students for a Democratic Society, whose membership exploded because of the war. At the University of California, beginning in the autumn of 1964, student radicals demanded free speech and barricaded themselves in Sproul Hall, the main administration building on the Berkeley campus. The radicals eventually gave up the building, but they were arrested and expelled, further inciting students who may have only marginally agreed with such tactics.[3]

The antiwar movement spread to Congress as J. William Fulbright (D-Ark.), chairman of the Senate Foreign Relations Committee, conducted public hearings on the war. Fulbright grew quite critical of the war as a result and was vocal in expressing outrage at administration claims that the United States was winning in Vietnam. Eventually, even Secretary of Defense Robert McNamara, one of the engineers of the war under John F. Kennedy, would turn against the conflict. Senator Eugene McCarthy (D-Minn.) would challenge Johnson in the presidential primaries in 1968, nearly defeating the president in the New Hampshire primary, contributing to Johnson's decision not to seek reelection that year.[4]

The troubled New Deal coalition split apart over numerous issues in the late 1960s. Taxes played a big role as inflation began to drive up the cost of living and as government began to take a larger share of middle-class wages. With many Americans paying higher taxes, they naturally embraced the idea that government spending was to blame and many social programs meant to help the poor (welfare, Medicaid, food stamps, housing allowances) were seen as wasteful. If the poor received support from government, why should they work? Why should they alter their behavior? More and more Americans began to see the futility of Johnson's War on Poverty.

Inextricably linked to this was the issue of race. Black Americans were among the poorest of all racial groups in the country. Both in the rural South and the urban north, blacks faced problems of joblessness, poor education, declining opportunities, racial segregation in housing, discrimination, and high rates of out-of-wedlock births. Daniel Patrick Moynihan, a Harvard social scientist, diagnosed the latter problem and how it contributed to poverty in a 1966 study about the black family. Black families were struggling because about 27 percent of all black children were born into single-parent homes. Moynihan's report caused a stir; he was "blaming the victim" (single mothers) for the problem of poverty. What was needed instead, many social scientists argued, were more programs to help the poor, especially as African Americans had been denied economic opportunity. Welfare, as a result, became a hot issue for social scientists and government officials after the 1960s.[5]

Racial problems manifested themselves in northern cities with rioting. The first riot was in Watts, a poor black neighborhood in Los Angeles in 1964. Rioting became a normal summertime event thereafter. There were major riots in Newark, Washington, D.C., Chicago, and in Detroit, where over thirty people were killed in rioting that lasted a week in the summer of 1967. Johnson was particularly confused by the rioting, as many of the Great Society's urban programs were designed to ease the plight of poor neighborhoods. A government-backed inquiry into the causes of urban rioting blamed the riots on the lack of opportunity and on racism; white middle-class ethnics had a different explanation and blamed it on blacks themselves. Neither answer was sufficient; both contributed to further divisions within the Democratic Party.

The nexus of white working-class backlash against the Great Society was based not on any new developments within American life but rather, as historian Kenneth Durr argues, because the "white working-class . . . was a harbor of social and cultural conservatism that the New Deal Democratic order contained for a time but never substantially altered."[6] Whites in northern urban areas were concerned with their homes, their neighborhoods, their churches, and their jobs. When intrusions into these domains began to occur in the 1950s, as blacks moved into white ethnic neighborhoods—and into jobs at local factories—whites reacted. In almost every northern urban area studied by historians, the pattern of white backlash was not a result so much of civil rights, but an ongoing development tied into deeper traditions and concerns with "place."[7] When liberals tried to excuse the actions of rioting blacks, the white New Dealers revolted against liberalism and formed the core for Richard Nixon's "silent majority" and, later, for the so-called Reagan Democrats.[8]

The emergence of a more permissive society, embodied by the sexual revolution, the counterculture, the drug and rock culture of the 1960s, and of feminism, all served to further divide the New Deal coalition. New Deal ethnics, labor union members, the white working class and middle-class, and Southern whites tended to be cultural conservatives. The onset of the permissive society shocked them. Who was responsible? Permissive parents were blamed for coddling youngsters and giving them everything they wanted (the baby boom generation was raised on a steady diet of indulgence, critics said). Government, especially the Supreme Court, was blamed for the rise of permissiveness. Court decisions took prayer out of public schools, ruled school dress codes unconstitutional, and declared a right to privacy existed in a 1966 case, *Griswold v. Connecticut,* which served as the basis for the Court's ruling on abortion in the 1973 case *Roe v. Wade.* Rising crime rates, especially violent crimes like armed robbery, murder, and rape, the number of which exploded during the 1960s, beginning three decades in the ascendancy, also contributed to anxiety among middle-class Americans.[9]

By the end of the decade there was a potent brew of issues that contributed to the election of Republican Richard Nixon in 1968, as well as the equally stunning success of the independent candidate George Wallace (who won 12.5 percent of the vote). Wallace polled better in the urban north than anywhere else and he campaigned to the Right of Nixon. Nixon relied on his vice presidential selection, Spiro Agnew, to attack liberals. A former Rockefeller Republican who became nationally known when he chided black clergymen in Maryland for not speaking out against riots in the wake of the April 1968 assassination of Martin Luther King, Agnew became a Populist conservative hero whose rise to the vice presidency bears comparison to that of Calvin Coolidge in 1920. Famous for his invective language and attacks on the "nattering nabobs of negativism" and the media, whom he called "an effete corps of impudent snobs," Agnew was incredibly popular with young conservatives. A former YAF National Chairman, David Keene, served in Agnew's White House office as a liaison to conservative organizations. One of Agnew's speechwriters was Patrick Buchanan, a young journalist and aide to Nixon beginning a long career in conservative politics.[10]

THE LURE OF PUBLIC POLICY

The Great Society and the expansion of the welfare state, which it brought to fruition, served one important function for conservatism. It forced conservatives into the realm of public policy. Up until the 1960s, conservatives had made arguments about programs like Social Security based on allegory and anecdote. Barry Goldwater had campaigned saying he would make Social Security a voluntary system, but he lacked hard evidence and statistics regarding how such a voluntary program could be achieved. Conservatives had not proven very adept at the study of policy to that time and lacked the institutes and think tanks that would have allowed them to challenge more objectively, and with hard evidence to support their assertions, the claims of poverty warriors and liberal economists.[11]

Nixon dealt with policy issues. He proposed a welfare reform program, the Family Assistance Plan (FAP), which many conservatives initially supported but later backed away from, which would have reduced bureaucracy and provided a government payment of $1,600 annually to poor families. Too little, argued the National Welfare Rights Organization and many Democrats, who pushed for a $5,000 payment. FAP failed to gain support and Nixon let the initiative die. Nixon signed into law government regulatory agencies such as the Environmental Protection Agency (EPA) and the Occupational Safety and Health Administration (OSHA) to regulate business. He created Amtrak, the national passenger railroad corporation, to relieve the expensive burden of passenger service from the ailing railroads. On the domestic front, the Nixon presidency contributed to the growth of government and to the growing tax burden the middle class bore to pay for it. Nixon, in this regard, may have been the last liberal president. By the end of his term in the White House, the percentage of budgetary spending on social programs grew to 40 percent of the budget (up from 25 percent when he took over).[12]

The Nixon years reminded conservatives that policy mattered. In an age of expanded government intervention in the economy and in social programs and policies, to simply criticize liberal policy was not enough. To have detailed policies of one's own, showing how the free market could solve social problems and pointing out the flaws in government programs, was crucial for political success. Barry Goldwater's failures to address in any concrete way during the 1964 campaign how Social Security privatization could be achieved, or how the Tennessee Valley Authority could be privatized, necessitated a plunge into policy as well as politics.

In this sense, the Nixon years marked the emergence of a conservatism concerned about politics and policy; principles mattered less than they had during the Goldwater campaign. Historian Jonathon Schoenwald has written that the post-Goldwater years marked a conservative move toward moderation.[13] This was explicitly the case as conservatives now saw political opportunities by embracing positions that were politically palatable. If "politics is the art of the possible" as Russell Kirk consistently stated, then the Nixon years marked the first possibility for the emergence of a conservative politics.

Initially conservatives delved into the policy views emanating from the political Left. *The Public Interest*, a quarterly journal first published in Fall 1965 spelled out its intention "to know a little better what we are talking about . . . when we discuss issues of public policy."[14] Edited by Daniel Bell, a Democratic Socialist, and former Trotskyite Irving Kristol, *The Public Interest* contributed to the emergence of the "policy intellectual," academics and politicians dedicated to the study and shaping of public policy. Throughout the 1960s and 1970s, as James Q. Wilson argued, policy intellectuals "provided the conceptual language, the ruling paradigms, the empirical examples . . . that became the accepted assumptions for those in charge of making policy."[15] Policy intellectuals surrounding *The Public Interest* were not interested in turning back the clock on state power in America or even eliminating the social welfare state and its programs, as many conservatives had advocated. Instead, as Irving Kristol described their beliefs: "all of us had ideas on how to improve, even reconstruct, the welfare state—we were meliorists, not opponents, and only measured critics. It was when the Great Society programs were launched that we began to distance ourselves, slowly and reluctantly, from the newest version of official liberalism."[16]

About the only conservative think tank in existence had been founded in 1943. Named the American Enterprise Association (later renamed the American Enterprise Institute), the money for AEA came from the Johns Manville Corporation and it was explicitly founded to advance the principles of free enterprise. Through its first decade in existence AEI was wedded to a strategy of hosting conferences and discussion groups with businessmen and politicians. It was not until William Baroody Sr. the son of Lebanese immigrants, and W. Glenn Campbell, both economists, took over the direction of AEI that the institute became a policy think tank, not simply one that hosted conferences and symposia. Baroody attracted donations and grants and built up, by the early 1970s, a conservative think tank that attempted to impact policy decisions on Capitol Hill.[17]

Baroody was fond of an axiom that he routinely cited in speeches. "A free society," he said, "can tolerate some degree of concentration in the manufacture of widgets. But the day it approaches a monopoly in idea formation, that is its death knell."[18] Baroody had built a policy institution around economists Campbell and Milton Friedman (both would eventually leave for the Hoover Institution on War, Revolution, and Peace at Stanford). During the Goldwater campaign Baroody served as an important policy advisor, cutting conservatives like William F. Buckley out of Goldwater's inner circle. After Goldwater's defeat, Baroody retreated back to policy, receiving substantial sums from industrialists such as J. Howard Pew and from a fund-raising campaign spearheaded by Nixon Secretary of Defense Melvin Laird.

By the early 1970s AEI had little to show for its policy advocacy. AEI fellows produced studies that sat on the shelves of congressional offices. The institute was too scholarly and their research was not timely. One study on the virtues of the Supersonic Transport aircraft was released after Congress voted to kill the plane. "Great study," Colorado Republican Senator Gordon Allott's staffer Paul Weyrich told Baroody, "why didn't we get it sooner?" "We didn't want to affect the outcome of the vote," Baroody replied. It was obvious to Weyrich that some other policy venue was needed in order to influence the direction of conservative politics.[19]

Timing is everything in politics and Weyrich's dissatisfaction with AEI proved fortuitous. Patrick Buchanan, a young staffer in the Nixon White House, realized that a policy institution was necessary in order to advance conservative causes. In a November 1972 memo to Nixon on "How to Make Permanent the New Majority," Buchanan specified, among other things, the necessity for a conservative policy institute that could be "the repository of its political beliefs" as well as a "communications center" for conservatives throughout the country. Weyrich and Edwin Feulner, an administrative assistant to Representative Phil Crane (R-Ill.), were discussing the same idea. As historian Lee Edwards wrote, "they envisioned an activist think tank but separate from Congress and not officially connected to any political party."[20]

Such an idea had been in the works for some time. Joseph Coors, the Colorado brewer, had been looking to invest money in a public policy institute in Washington for several years. A libertarian on most issues, Coors funded the Analysis and Research Association (ARA), founded in 1969 with an $80,000 budget, which in 1971 became the Robert M. Schuchman Memorial Foundation, named after the first national director of YAF and endowed by Coors with an operating budget of $250,000. Weyrich, Feulner, and Coors served on the board, but there were differences between the directors over how to effect change and how to address policy issues. In 1973, the foundation split and a new tax-exempt foundation, named the Heritage Foundation, was formed.

For the first several years Heritage struggled to define its mission. In the aftermath of Watergate, conservative causes were damaged by their association with Nixon. Weyrich had resigned as president of Heritage to form his own Committee for the Survival of a Free Congress, which he still heads (now called the Free Congress Foundation). Weyrich wanted to influence politics and especially, in the aftermath of Watergate, the 1974 midterm elections, which proved disastrous for the GOP. The new president of Heritage was Frank Walton, a California businessman and supporter of Ronald Reagan. Walton raised the Heritage profile and also secured funds for the organization. By 1976 Heritage had secured over $1 million in contributions, most of which came from direct mail solicitations. Feulner took over as president in 1977, a role he has held since, and has guided Heritage into an enviable position among Washington think tanks, with even the Soviet newspaper *Pravda* conceding in 1985 that it was a crucial vehicle for American politics.[21]

POLITICAL STRATEGIES

The formation of think tanks marked a concerted effort to influence policy, a departure for conservatives who had been somewhat wary in their approach to politics since the Goldwater defeat in 1964. But American politics was changing. Nixon had secured a large percentage of his 1972 electoral victory from a coalition of groups that he had earlier called the "silent majority." Comprising union members, white ethnics, Southern whites, suburbanites, and other groups hostile to liberalism, Nixon constructed a new coalition, "an emerging Republican majority," as Nixon aide Kevin Phillips described it in a book of the same name. Nixon's political strategy, the "Southern strategy" was predicated on attracting Southerners resentful at liberal support for civil rights and new suburbanites angry at increased taxes.[22]

The shift in Southern politics was already well under way by the time Nixon won the White House. Nixon's efforts could be seen not as a Southern strategy, but as a suburban strategy. Support for the GOP in the South came from suburbs and from middle-class whites hostile to liberalism. These New South denizens were not the old segregationists who had dominated Southern politics since Reconstruction; rather, those groups still reliably supported Democrat candidates into the 1980s.[23] The growing bifurcation between once loyal Democratic bastions in the South and liberalism lay in the emergence of the social issues and growing concerns with taxes and inflation in the wider economy. Nixon capitalized on this, seeking to build a political coalition around elements of disaffected Democrats.

He succeeded tremendously, winning a huge electoral majority in the 1972 presidential election. But his strategy, cynical, cunning, and devious, contained within it the seeds of its own destruction. Growing paranoia within the administration concerning political enemies drove the president and his advisors to take action against such threats, including domestic spying operations and harassment of antiwar groups and Black Power organizations. None of this was new in American politics, but the sophomoric handling of the break-in of the Democratic National Committee headquarters at the Watergate hotel, a "third rate burglary" in the words of Nixon press secretary Ron Ziegler, and the ensuing cover-up ordered by Nixon himself, undermined efforts to build a new majority. After a lengthy and divisive investigation, Nixon was forced to resign the presidency on August 9, 1974. His replacement was not Spiro Agnew, a hero to many on the Right, but Gerald Ford, who assumed the vice presidency when Agnew resigned his office in 1973 after pleading nolo contendere to charges of income tax evasion.

Conservatives had always been wary of Nixon. Some, like Phyllis Schlafly, had supported him in 1968 over the last-minute effort to get Californian governor Ronald Reagan the nomination, but Schlafly had second thoughts herself by 1972.[24] Those conservatives associated with *National Review* and with YAF found less about which to be enthusiastic with Nixon. It was not so much Nixon's domestic policy with which they disagreed, but rather his foreign policy strategy of détente with the Soviet Union and of his visit to communist China in 1972. A variety of conservative organizations sent representatives to a meeting in Manhattan to plan for open opposition to Nixon. The Manhattan Twelve, as the group was named, included *National Review* publisher William Rusher, YAF members, editors of *Human Events*, and a variety of other prominent conservatives.[25] They protested Nixon's foreign policy and urged John Ashbrook, a congressman from Ohio, to challenge Nixon in the presidential primaries. The Ashbrook candidacy went nowhere, with the congressman withdrawing from the race after the New Hampshire primary.

Conservative dissatisfaction with the GOP was intense in the 1970s. It reached visceral levels when Gerald Ford nominated New York governor Nelson Rockefeller to be vice president. Richard Viguerie recalled how he "turned on my television to watch our brand new president Gerald Ford announce he was picking Nelson Rockefeller to be his vice-president. Nelson Rockefeller . . . as a conservative I could hardly have been more upset if Ford had selected Teddy Kennedy."[26] Viguerie held a meeting of fourteen conservatives in Washington to try to stop the Rockefeller nomination, but the regular Republicans had no stomach for a fight so soon after the Nixon resignation.

The result was the formation of the New Right. Generally, historians have treated the New Right in its political manifestations, studying the shift in regional voter support for the Republican Party in areas like the South and the Sunbelt West. Suburbanization, white backlash against civil rights, and the rise of tax revolts have been the benchmarks historians have examined in their treatments of the shift of former New Deal Democrats to the Right in the 1970s. Historian Kevin Kruse, in a study of Atlanta, discussed how white flight from the city caused tax revolts and suburban secession after the civil rights movement had transformed the South.[27] The roots of Newt Gingrich and his suburban conservatism allegedly lie in the backlash against civil rights, many historians have claimed.

Such a categorization, as conservative author Samuel Francis argued, was, in part, correct. However, as he wrote, "the New Right is not merely an electoral coalition concerned with winning elections and roll calls; it is the political expression of a relatively new social movement that regards itself as a depository of traditional American values and as the exploited victim of an alliance between an entrenched elite and a ravenous proletariat." "The New Right is not a conservative force," he continued, "but a radical or revolutionary one [that] seeks the displacement of the entrenched elite, the discarding of its ideology of liberalism and cosmopolitanism, and its own victory as a governing class in America." Using the social base of the Sunbelt and the New South, Francis claimed nothing less than the dissolution of the old elites (which he defined as liberalism) and their replacement by the new dynamism of what he termed "Middle American Radicalism."[28]

The emergence of such a radical dispensation within conservatism reflected a marked shift toward a more populist orientation on the Right. Less an intellectual force than in previous years, conservatives were more interested in and consumed with political power. Liberalism had become an ideology of elites; conservatism had become home for the amorphous "people." Some conservatives looked with some disdain on such a shift. Historian Stephen Tonsor wrote, "a number of conservatives have argued for an alliance with populism—have argued that there is room for hardhats and rednecks under the big tent of a broadly defined conservatism. I understand the temptation for these groups are of great political importance. I do not believe . . . that such an alliance can be formed. And the fact of its impossibility will save conservatism from the temptation of a politics that is reactionary rather than progressive."[29]

Tonsor's concerns reflected those movement conservatives who looked more toward the intellectual life of the campus rather than the activist life of inside-the-beltway politicking. Yet increasingly during the 1970s policy prescriptions and political organizing took center stage. Conservatives combated liberalism in the political system and left efforts at self-definition behind. By the mid-1970s, the possibility of political power was looming and conservatives seized the opportunities, reflecting the new reality of postliberal American politics. For the remainder of the century, political influence would determine the conservative dispensation; intellectual debates on what constituted conservatism in America would never entirely go away, and indeed would intensify as the century ended, but intellectual conservatives found themselves on the margins of a movement they had helped create, a reflection of the political turn conservatism had taken.

DÉTENTE AND ITS DISCONTENTS

Expanding their political power became the focal point of conservatism in general and of the New Right in particular during the 1970s. Events helped accelerate this shift to politics. Watergate was just one symptom of the political crisis gripping not only America but Western democracies as a whole through the 1970s. The collapse of American resolve in Vietnam ended with the communist takeover there as well as with communist victories in neighboring Cambodia and Laos. Nixon's policy of détente allowed Soviet leaders to expand their influence in the Third World, emboldening communists to support revolutions in the Middle East, Africa, and Asia. Western European governments looked to improve relations with their eastern counterparts with West German Chancellor Willy Brandt practicing a politics of *Ostpolitik* designed to improve relations between the divided Germanys.[30]

The Ford administration presided not only over the endgame in Vietnam, but also over a rapid diminishing of American military and diplomatic influence in the world. Ford continued the détente policies of Nixon, seeking arms control agreements with the Soviets, as well as improving trade and cultural exchanges with the Russians. He met with Leonid Brezhnev in Vladivostok and, in 1975, signed the Helsinki Accords, which recognized the "permanent" boundaries of European governments and legitimized Soviet control over the Baltic states of Lithuania, Latvia, and Estonia (states taken by Stalin in the 1939 Nazi-Soviet Pact).

Meanwhile, under the cloak of improved relations between the Soviets and the United States, communists expanded their influence throughout the Third World. Cuban troops aided revolutionary movements in Angola and Southwest Africa. Soviet military support for radical liberation groups, like the Palestinian Liberation Organization (PLO) and for communist regimes in the Middle East pressured the American-backed government of Israel and assisted in the rise of terrorist tactics against capitalist targets. The 1972 Munich Olympic Games, where Palestinian radicals kidnapped and murdered eleven Israeli athletes, the hijacking of aircraft, and the revolutionary activities of sundry Marxist and Maoist terrorist groups in Europe became the pattern; most of these groups—from Basque separatists in Spain to Italy's Red Brigades to West Germany's Bader Meinhof Gang—were sponsored amply with "Moscow gold."

Ronald Reagan, who had recently left political life after two terms as governor of California, attacked the détente strategy in radio addresses, syndicated on over one hundred stations throughout the country. In one address Reagan reported on a secret speech given by Soviet leader Leonid Brezhnev in 1973 that mocked the goals of détente. Brezhnev said, "we are achieving with détente what our predecessors have been unable to achieve using the mailed fist. We have been able to accomplish more in a short time with détente than was done for years pursuing a confrontation strategy with NATO. . . . Trust us comrades . . . a decisive shift in the correlation of forces will be such that come 1985, we will be able to extend our will wherever we need to."[31]

For the Soviets this meant not only support for revolutionary movements abroad but also the buildup of both their nuclear and conventional forces. Nixon had, with Soviet leader Brezhnev, signed the Strategic Arms Limitation Treaty (SALT) and the Anti-ballistic Missile Treaty (ABM) in 1972, limiting Soviet and American ICBM missiles to 1,054 for the U.S. and 1,518 for the Soviets. But the treaty did nothing about payloads and allowed the Soviets to keep a distinct advantage. Phyllis Schlafly attacked the treaty, calling it "the obituary of the United States strategic power."[32] Senator Henry Jackson (D-Wash.) concurred, arguing, "simply put, the agreement gives the Soviets more of everything; more light ICBMs, more heavy ICBMs, more submarine launched missiles, more submarines, more payload, even more ABM radars. In no area covered by the agreement is the U.S. permitted to maintain parity with the Soviet Union."[33] The treaty, nevertheless, was ratified by the Senate.

Schlafly was keenly interested in issues related to defense, particularly nuclear issues. She had authored several books with Admiral Chester Ward during the 1960s, including *The Gravediggers* (1964), *Strike from Space* (1965), and *The Betrayers* (1968). *Gravediggers* alone sold 2 million copies. In the mid-1970s, the pair added *Kissinger on the Couch* (1975), at 846 pages in length, and *Ambush at Vladivostok* (1976). Schlafly's main view, shared by Ward, who provided the technical expertise in defense matters, was that America was vulnerable to communist attack and that the Soviet Union was building superiority in nuclear weapons, a superiority that treaties like SALT only enshrined. "America will never have peace and security in the world until our people, especially our leaders, face the awful truth about the hideous cruelty, inhumanity and immorality of the Communists." On nuclear and security matters, Schlafly was blunt: "America has been deceived."

Conservatives found they had allies among Democrats discontented with détente. Henry Jackson, a senator from Washington, was one such Democrat. A hawk on foreign policy and defense, Jackson was nicknamed "the senator from Boeing" for his efforts on behalf of the aircraft manufacturer and defense contractor. A New Deal liberal on social and economic issues, he was a Cold Warrior who disliked détente and sought to rebuild America's defenses.

He was also instrumental in placing human rights on the agenda of conservatism and for being a propagator of a viewpoint that would come to be called neoconservatism. A strong supporter of the state of Israel, Jackson was concerned about the internal plight of Soviet Jews, who, after Israel's defeat of the Arab states in the October 1967 Six-Day War, yearned to emigrate to Israel but were denied the privilege by Soviet officials. The Soviets cracked down on Jewish emigration, placing an education tax on those citizens who had college degrees, prohibiting such people from freely leaving the Soviet state. Jews were the main casualties of such a tax and Jackson, along with Representative Charles Vanik, placed an amendment on a Nixon trade bill. The Jackson-Vanik amendment refused to grant Most Favored Nation trade status to the Soviet Union. "We proposed to deny the benefits of our abundant economy . . . to any nonmarket economy that denies its citizens the right of opportunity to emigrate."[34] The amendment easily passed Congress; both Kissinger and Nixon had attempted to kill it unsuccessfully. In the end, as Soviet dissident Anatoly (now known as Natan) Sharansky later argued, "Jackson understood that you cannot deal with the Soviet Union by ignoring the issue of human rights. You cannot trust the nature of the Soviet Union."[35] It is no small surprise that Sharansky, one of the first Jewish "refuseniks" freed from Soviet prison and allowed to emigrate to Israel, would later credit Jackson with being a key architect of the Soviet Union's collapse.[36]

One episode that galvanized the forces of opposition to détente involved Ford's refusal to meet with exiled Soviet author Alexander Solzhenitsyn, whose masterpiece, *The Gulag Archipelago*, described in grim reality the Soviet prison system and the human rights abuses under communist rule. Convinced by Henry Kissinger that a meeting with Solzhenitsyn would be a stumbling block in U.S.-Soviet relations, Ford refused to meet with the author. Jackson helped organize a congressional meeting with Solzhenitsyn, helped by conservative Republican senator Jesse Helms (R-N.C.) and Clifford Case (R-N.J.). At the meeting Solzhenitsyn criticized détente, saying "the tender dawn of détente was precisely the time when the starvation rations in the prisons and concentration camps in the U.S.S.R. were even skimpier." Solzhenitsyn attacked Western governments who bought Soviet promises about détente and ended with a climactic argument that if freedom were to triumph over slavery, America "will have need not only of exceptional men, but of great men."[37]

RISE OF REAGAN

One of the great men of conservatism was waiting in the wings. Convinced that Ford's foreign and economic policies were disastrous, Ronald Reagan threw himself into the Republican campaign for president, challenging Ford for the GOP nomination. Reagan brought his conservative views on economics and his criticism of détente to the race, hoping to convince the GOP that bold leadership was needed.

Ford possessed the advantage of incumbency, but little else. Only two years after Watergate and his pardon of Richard Nixon, Ford was unpopular with the majority of Americans. Conservatives had organized against him and were mobilizing to take over the direction of the party. Ford inherited tremendous economic difficulties, especially inflation. His response was not to cut taxes or end governmental regulations but rather to treat the psychological impact of inflation by having administration officials and staff wear WIN buttons, "Whip Inflation Now." The buttons did not do the trick and by 1975 the American economy was in a recession.[38]

Reagan promoted bold reforms. In a speech to businessmen in Chicago in September 1975, Reagan proposed decentralizing governmental programs by returning authority over such programs to the states. "What I propose is nothing less than the systematic transfer of authority and resources to the states," Reagan said. "This collectivist, centralizing approach, whatever name or party label it wears, has created our economic problems. By taxing and consuming an ever-greater share of the national wealth, it has imposed an intolerable burden of taxation of American citizens. By spending above and beyond even this level of taxation, it has created the horrendous inflation of the past decade."[39] Reagan recommended the transfer of $90 billion in federal responsibilities to the states; not controversial after he gave the speech, the proposal would have increased taxes at the state level and would come to doom him in the early primary states like New Hampshire when media scrutiny (and Ford attacks) forced Reagan to back away from the plan.

By mid-March 1976 the Reagan campaign effort appeared paralyzed, short of money, and short of the spark necessary to challenge a sitting president. Ford had prevailed in crucial primaries in New Hampshire, Illinois, and Florida. Reagan's campaign appeared spent but the candidate decided to stay in the race, giving it his all in North Carolina, a key barometer for the primaries to come. Conservative organization in the state proved crucial, as did radio and newspaper advertisements funded by the American Conservative Union, led by M. Stanton Evans, which attacked Ford and showed the stark comparison between the candidates: "Gerald Ford appointed Nelson Rockefeller as Vice President. . . . He appointed Henry Kissinger as Secretary of State and fired a Secretary of Defense [James Schlesinger] who disagreed with Kissinger's 'détente'. . . . The choice for North Carolina Republicans is clear: continued deficits and the weakness of 'détente' or Ronald Reagan's new initiatives in freedom."[40] The ads helped Reagan tremendously, as did the organization of Senator Jesse Helms and the strong voter turnout in favor of Reagan in the primary. But the candidate's attacks on Ford proved crucial, particularly on the weaknesses of détente and on the administration's decision to go along with the unpopular Panama Canal treaties, which would return the

Canal, built by America in the first decade of the century, back to the Panamanians. Reagan's line on the canal was incendiary: "It's ours! We built it! We paid for it! And we should keep it!" Reagan won the primary; journalist Lou Cannon observed, "North Carolina was the turning point of Reagan's political career. It kept him in the race to Kansas City, and it made him the presumptive Presidential nominee in 1980. At all times after North Carolina, Reagan was a legitimate candidate."[41]

The rest of the primary season seesawed between the two candidates, resulting in a virtual dead heat by the time the candidates reached the GOP convention in Kansas City in July. Hoping to draw support from moderate Republicans convinced that Reagan was an "extremist," Reagan had selected Pennsylvania Governor Richard Schweiker as his running mate, considered a liberal, but on defense and support for the Cold War, he was a hawk similar to Reagan. The gambit was desperate, with the campaign hoping to secure delegate support in order to have a brokered convention. Reagan urged Ford to adopt a similar strategy and select a running mate before the balloting, but Ford resisted. In the end, the Reagan campaign could not prevail at the convention and Ford wrested the nomination away from Reagan when the Mississippi delegation was persuaded to back the president.

In an unprecedented and magnanimous gesture, Ford invited Reagan and his wife Nancy to the stage after he accepted the nomination. The uproar in Kemper Arena was greater than that accorded Ford. "We Want Ron! We want Ron!" was the refrain as Reagan took the podium and spoke to the delegates. Delivering a speech he had given many times, Reagan told the story of how he was asked to write a letter for a time capsule to be opened in Los Angeles in 2076. He discussed the problems facing the country and then he spoke from his heart about the threat of nuclear weapons. "We live in a world in which the great powers have poised and aimed at each other horrible missiles of destruction. . . . And suddenly it dawned on me, those who would read this letter a hundred years from now will know whether those missiles were fired. . . . Will they look back with appreciation and say, thank God for those people in 1976 who headed off that loss of freedom; who kept us now a hundred years later free; who kept our world from nuclear destruction. . . . That is our challenge."[42] The 1980 campaign had begun.

RELIGION AND CONSERVATISM

In the fall Georgia Democrat Jimmy Carter was elected president. Crucial to his election was the support of Protestant evangelicals. Carter was a born-again Christian, a phrase few Americans outside of the South had heard of before

Carter employed it during the primaries. Evangelical Protestants from a number of churches, including Pentecostals, Southern Baptists, Nazarenes, and Assemblies of God, entered presidential politics somewhat warily. While mainstream Protestant churches had always involved themselves in political affairs, evangelicals participated less overtly in politics. While some were involved in anticommunist groups like the Christian Anti-Communist Crusade, when it came to working on behalf of political candidates for office, evangelicals typically did not participate. Usually confined in membership to the backwaters of Southern states or Appalachia, the evangelicals were not a crucial constituency in either party.

But as the number of members in mainstream churches began a precipitous decline in the 1970s, evangelical Protestant churches grew tremendously. According to British author Godfrey Hodgson, membership in the United Methodist Church fell from 11 million in 1965 to 9.5 million by 1980. Membership in the Presbyterian Church fell by a third in the decade, as did membership in the Episcopal Church. Meanwhile, the Southern Baptist Convention went from 10.8 million members in 1965 to 13.6 million in 1980. The most explosive growth came in the Assembly of God, which almost doubled in the same span of years, from 570,000 to 1.1 million members.[43]

Traditionally associated with reform movements throughout American history, including abolitionism, temperance, and prohibition, evangelical moralism had lain dormant since the Scopes Trial. In the 1930s novelist John Steinbeck's *The Grapes of Wrath* showed the struggle of the Pentecostal Joad family to survive the Great Depression, yet sublimated the Joad's religious radicalism to class-based radicalism instead, reflecting the left-liberalism of Steinbeck himself. With explosive growth due to World War II and Cold War military spending, evangelicals—now prosperous and middle-class—became more active in politics, especially in Southern California. Public evangelical Protestantism emerged on the radar screen in the 1950s with the ministry of Billy Graham, who employed television and radio to reach millions, a tactic mimicked later by televangelists like Pat Robertson, whose *700 Club* reached millions, and Jerry Falwell, whose *Old Time Gospel Hour* had similar audiences.

The main concern of Protestant evangelicals was the issue of communism. Many found common cause with conservative anticommunists and supported organizations like Fred Schwarz's Christian Anti-Communism Crusade. In Orange County, California Christian anticommunist women proved especially active in defending the home and community from communist intrusion. Many became activists in the John Birch Society, organizing coffee klatches to educate fellow middle-class women on the dangers of communism. By the end of the 1960s, the same women would become instrumental in advancing their religious concerns about the moral decline they witnessed in American society, proving especially concerned about the social issues, from abortion to sex education in public schools.[44]

It was this latter issue, as well as what it portended for the relationship between man and wife in the traditional family, that pushed evangelicals into political action. Frustrated evangelical Christians battled school boards in Anaheim, California, in 1969 and in West Virginia during the 1970s to keep sex education out of public schools. The sexual revolution of the 1960s, helped both by cultural changes in the 1950s—the evolution of values regarding sexual behavior advanced by Indiana University biologist Alfred Kinsey and *Playboy* magazine publisher Hugh Hefner—and technological changes like the birth control pill, helped shatter the older predispositions toward sexual behavior. By the early 1960s groups like the Sex Information and Education Council of the U.S. (SIECUS) were arguing for the instruction in schools of programs that "rais[ed] the consciousness of people about the value of human sexuality as an integral part of personality development and an important source of either marital health or disharmony."[45]

Parents in Anaheim, California, fought against such efforts to get sex education introduced into the public schools there. While the majority of parents in the district supported sex education, religious activists gained control of the school board, fired the superintendent, and opposed any introduction of curricula published from SIECUS. One of the heroes of the fight gained national attention in conservative circles. John Steinbacher became a national speaker on sex education after publishing *The Child Seducers*, a book that argued that communists were behind sex education. Popular among John Birch Society members, the book featured a jacket with a blond-haired schoolgirl tied to a chair beneath a light bulb with pictures of Hitler, Marx, Lenin, Trotsky, and Castro (for good measure) on the wall behind her. "A factual EXPOSE of America's Sexploitation conspiracy," appeared under the book's title.[46]

In Kanawha County, West Virginia, a similar grassroots effort to prevent sex education textbooks from being assigned in schools ignited national attention to the awakening of evangelical Christians. Alice Moore, a housewife, fundamentalist Christian, and newcomer to the area, was elected to the local school board in 1970. In 1974 the school board sought to adopt new textbooks that contained, according to Moore, anti-Christian themes. But she also objected to the prevalence of black authors in literature textbooks that opponents castigated as racist. Most of her charge was that the more realistic literature of black authors like Amiri Baraka—famous for his poem "Up Against the Wall, Motherfucker"—contained too much profanity, not something she wished on her children. Unable to prevail on the school board, Moore organized a boycott of the schools, which succeeded after the United Mine Workers in the county supported her boycott and kept their children at home. A week later, the board capitulated and recommended a Textbook Review Committee look into controversial books. Protests continued through the fall and violence erupted on both sides of the issue as Kanawha's culture war drew national media attention. The Heritage Foundation intervened on behalf of Kanawha County parents, beginning a process of unification between the New Right and what would soon be labeled the "religious Right."[47]

Throughout the country traditional religious conservatives were on the march, organizing boycotts and challenging the control of state and local authorities. Galvanized initially by what they perceived to be the communistic inclinations of modernist liberalism, they also fought to defend and sustain their own traditional viewpoints, challenged by the sexual revolution, Supreme Court decisions, and governmental bureaucrats.

One area of increased attention for social conservatives and religious traditionalists was the feminist movement. In 1972 the issue of feminism versus traditionalism exploded when Congress passed the Equal Rights Amendment (ERA). A simple statement of gender equality—"equality of rights under the law shall not be denied or abridged by the United States or by any State on account of sex"—the ERA passed in a climate when equality and social justice for African Americans had galvanized a powerful rights revolution among other aggrieved groups, among them women. The ERA easily passed Congress and within a few months thirty-five states had ratified the amendment; only three more states were needed for it to become a constitutional amendment. Then Phyllis Schlafly entered the debate.

Schlafly was not interested in the feminist movement before she published an essay entitled "What's Wrong with 'Equal Rights' for Women" in the February 1972 issue of the *Phyllis Schlafly Report*, a monthly newsletter that reached thousands of homes. Schlafly argued that ERA threatened the family, "the basic unit of society, which is ingrained in the laws and customs of our Judeo-Christian civilization [and] is the greatest single achievement in the history of women's rights." She described the threat of feminism to the traditional role of woman as a mother, mocking feminist Betty Friedan's contention, made in the 1962 book *The Feminine Mystique* that the home was a "comfortable concentration camp." Instead, Schlafly insisted that women had never had it better and that what the feminist agenda argued for was a world that was "anti-family, anti-children, and pro-abortion." While feminists stood for important issues of equality in opportunity and pay—both of which Schlafly supported—"women libbers view the home as a prison, and the wife and mother as a slave. . . . The women libbers don't understand that most women want to be a wife, mother and homemaker—and are happy in that role."[48]

Schlafly's essay lit a grassroots firestorm that eventually culminated in the defeat of ERA in 1980 when Illinois refused to ratify the amendment. Schlafly's influence was paramount; persuaded by one of her supporters to lead the effort against ERA, she formed STOP-ERA in July 1972; within a year there were twenty-six "loosely organized" state chapters. Schlafly drew on her own network of conservative women in the GOP's National Federation of Republican Women. But she also drew most of her support from religious women. STOP-ERA and feminist groups were remarkably similar in every demographic but one: "a remarkable 98 percent of anti-ERA supporters claimed church membership, while only 31 to 48 percent of pro-ERA supporters did," according to historian Don Critchlow. Schlafly's organization proved dedicated to their one cause, while the various feminist organizations, including ERAmerica and the National Organization for Women (NOW) competed against each other for funds and differed on objectives.[49]

Schlafly was articulate, fearless—despite constant threats—and a capable spokesperson, especially powerful in debate with leading feminists. "I'd like to burn you at the stake," feminist Friedan, frustrated at her inability to disrupt her opponent, shrieked at Schlafly during one debate. Her favorite opening line in speeches was to thank her husband for allowing her to speak tonight, a witty repartee designed to break the heart of any feminist in the audience. With constant pressure and with her dedicated army of supporters, STOP-ERA prevailed and the ERA was dealt a deathblow when the Illinois legislature voted against ratification.[50]

During the mid-1970s grassroots Christians did not reliably support conservative Republicans for high office. Jimmy Carter, a born-again Christian himself, secured the support of evangelicals in the 1976 election. Gerald Ford was pro-abortion, as was the majority of the Republican Party; the GOP would not have a pro-life platform until the 1980 convention. Betty Ford spoke out in favor of ERA. Carter was the more socially conservative candidate that year, but he was head of a party that no longer drew support from social traditionalists but rather represented the liberationist ideas of the feminists and the counterculture. In the November 1976 issue of *Playboy* Carter spoke about lust in his heart for women; evangelicals wondered why he was speaking to *Playboy* at all. During his presidency, Carter supported a conference on the family that endorsed an expansionist definition of family that included gay and lesbian families and nonmarried parents as well.[51]

Carter also did nothing about an Internal Revenue Service investigation into the tax-exempt status of Christian schools in the South. Many of these schools were all-white and had been formed after the passage of the Civil Rights Act in 1964. The IRS was worried that they were segregation academies, deliberately using their religious status to avoid federal taxes. Paul Weyrich helped Bob Billings, an evangelical minister, form Christian School Action to protest the investigation. Jerry Falwell, a fundamentalist minister from Lynchburg, Virginia, used his television and radio broadcasts to attack the IRS. Falwell said, "it is easier in some states to open a massage parlor than to open a Christian school."[52] James Dobson, a child psychiatrist who had distributed books, pamphlets, and films on traditional child-rearing techniques, also got involved in the fight.

Through a network of churches, with leadership from Billings and Dobson, and with support from conservative foundations, half a million letters flowed into Washington offices. The IRS dropped its plans for an investigation. Weyrich later said that the threat of IRS investigation into their churches and their schools "enraged the Christian community and they looked upon it as interference from government. . . . It was at that moment that conservatives made the linkage between their opposition to government interference and the interests of the evangelical movement, which now saw itself on the defensive and under attack by the government."[53]

The attack on Christian schools and the challenges to "family values" pushed evangelical Christians further away from the president. During a 1979 breakfast meeting with leading evangelical ministers, including Jim Bakker, D. James Kennedy, Oral Roberts, and Jerry Falwell, Carter was vague about his position on abortion and why he had not appointed evangelicals to his cabinet. Frustrated, Tim LaHaye came to one conclusion: "Christians have to vote for the candidate most deeply committed to moral values."[54]

The end result of growing Christian conservatism was the formation of Moral Majority in 1979. Organized at a Lynchburg Holiday Inn with Falwell, Weyrich, Billings, Howard Phillips, and Ed McAteer in attendance, the ministers and New Right activists agreed that, as Weyrich stated, "out there is what one might call a moral majority—people who would agree on principles based on the Decalogue for example—but they have been separated by geographical and denominational differences. . . . The key to any kind of political impact is to get these people united in some way." Falwell pounced on the name *moral majority* for the organization; the rest of the meeting centered on what issues the organization would focus its attention, with abortion most significant to the ministers.[55]

Falwell described the organization as "pro-life, pro-family, pro-moral and pro-American"; he described its purpose as to "mobilize the grassroots of moral Americans in one clear and effective voice" and to "lobby intensively in Congress to defeat left-wing, social-welfare bills that will further erode our precious freedom."[56] The concerns of conservative Republicans and conservative Christians had meshed by the end of the Carter administration. Moral Majority would play a crucial role mobilizing Christians for Ronald Reagan in 1980.

Evangelical Christians were hardly alone in their aversion to postsixties culture. The Catholic Church had actually taken the lead in condemning the sexual revolution and abortion. Pope Paul VI's encyclical *Humanae Vitae* (1968) reaffirmed the Church's position on the sacredness of reproduction, challenging Catholics to remain committed to a doctrine that stipulated that life began at conception and that the only justifiable sexual unions were for procreation, not pleasure. Yet the Church had also engaged in substantive reforms in the 1960s—the Vatican II Council—which, while not part of what the bishops and cardinals wished, contributed greatly to the liberalization of the Church. American Catholic participation at Sunday Mass would never be as high as it was in the decades before Vatican II, vocations to religious orders dropped precipitously, especially in convents as women shirked religious orders in favor of liberation. Parish priests routinely challenged their bishops, who routinely challenged Rome's authority to speak for all Catholics.

Yet on certain issues, Catholics in the United States remained quite conservative, especially in their attitude toward abortion. Catholics who attended church weekly and were dedicated to their faith believed that the liberationist agenda of the 1960s, with its release from moral constraints and its emphasis on "if it feels good, do it" threatened the very social order of American society. There was a growing rupture between Christians who attended church regularly and those who did not on issues like abortion. Political scientist Geoffrey Layman, who has studied the voting records of strongly religious Christians, has concluded that a "great divide" was erupting in American politics, one which would contribute to the growing culture war in America.[57]

The *Roe v. Wade* decision was one sign of this, greeted with alarm by churchgoing Catholics, but not so much by those who rarely attended Church. In 1976, and again in 1980, the Catholic vote was hotly contested by both political parties. Carter won Catholic support in 1976 only after Ford made a gaffe in the debate between the candidates concerning communist occupation of Poland. In 1980, Ronald Reagan won a substantive Catholic vote. On social issues, at least, but not yet on many others, Catholics were willing to suspend their long support for Democrats in favor of conservative candidates like Reagan.

ECONOMICS 101

Social issues were far from the only problems Carter faced in the late 1970s. The economy proved a continuing source of trouble for the nation. The main problem was inflation, which continued to inundate the economy, weakening business and contributing to the view expressed by a *Time* magazine cover story in 1977: "Is Capitalism Dead?" Carter sought to fight inflation by jawboning it; the Democratic Congress sought a jobs bill that would have assured full employment by creating jobs if unemployment reached certain levels. The bill passed but was watered down substantially, signifying another death-blow for the postwar liberal order. Nothing Carter did slowed inflation's course, which continued its rapacious assault on the economy, growing from around 7 percent in 1977 to over 12 percent by 1979. *National Review* opined, "nobody is even talking, anymore, about getting inflation below 6 or 7 percent." In opinion polls in 1978, a midterm election year, Americans rated inflation as the most severe problem facing the economy.[58]

Part of the problem for liberalism in the 1970s was that few liberals any longer seemed to believe that economic growth was a solution to the problems facing the nation. Prompted by the environmentalist movement and the stagnant industrial economy, liberal economists now urged policies that sought to limit growth. They were joined in this view by the influential Club of Rome, founded by Italian businessman Aurelio Peccei, which published *The Limits to Growth* (1972), arguing that natural resource depletion and pollution threatened life on earth unless Western nations limited their consumption of fossil fuels and other commodities. The energy crisis of the early 1970s, during which Middle East oil producers and their cartel OPEC (Oil Producing and Exporting Countries) boycotted oil shipments to Western powers for their support of Israel, accelerated concerns about the growing problem of fossil fuel dependency.

There were other concerns as well. Paul Ehrlich, a Stanford biology professor, wrote *The Population Bomb* (1968) and advocated strict controls on the population of countries like China and the United States. He was a regular guest on Johnny Carson's *Tonight Show*, appearing twenty-five times in the 1970s and 1980s. Concern over the sustainability of food supplies and a growing world population made policies like abortion rights favored alternatives in the decade; China would implement a one-child policy, rigorously enforced by forced abortions and forced sterilization. Ehrlich preached population control and predicted a world where famine and shortages were endemic if nothing was done about world population. But Ehrlich's predictions were dealt a severe blow when economist Julian Simon, a critic of the environmental movement, made a famous bet with Ehrlich in 1980. Ehrlich could pick five commodities and Simon bet that they would be lower in price—thus less scarce—than they were in 1980. Ehrlich took the bet, selecting copper, tin, tungsten, chrome, and nickel. All five commodities were substantially lower in price, regardless of adjustments for inflation, in 1990; Ehrlich dutifully paid the bet.[59]

Carter was trapped by his own party on the issue of economic stagnation. Carter tended to blame the problem of inflation on Americans themselves, on a "preoccupation with the self" and by an unwillingness of Americans to "sacrifice for the common good."[60] As liberals like Carter became rather dour and pessimistic about the economy, conservatives became optimists, a rather sudden reversal of ideological schadenfreude. Rather than accept what liberals were calling the limits to growth, conservatives discussed policy changes that would lead to more explosive economic growth.

What historian Robert Collins labeled an "intellectual revolution" in economic thinking began in the 1970s over concerns about inflation's disastrous impact on tax rates.[61] As government budgets took more of what Americans earned, tax rates rose accordingly; at the same time wages lagged and did not keep up with rising taxes. The phenomenon of "bracket creep," of taxpayers being pushed into higher tax brackets while their wages did not keep pace with inflation, began to enter public discussion. The middle class, many of whom had supported New Deal programs and liberal politicians, now felt themselves squeezed. They received little relief from Democratic politicians.

The economic theory of Keynesianism, which had guided policy makers since World War II, was collapsing. Keynes had predicated economic growth on the premise that if the economy was weak, government spending could be used to "prime the pump"; when the economy improved, taxes could be raised to balance the budget. The Phillips Curve, named after Australian economist A. W. Phillips, stipulated that fiscal and monetary policy could be employed to "fine tune" the economy, allowing for a trade-off between unemployment and inflation, keeping both to a minimum. Throughout the 1960s, where Keynesian growth stimuli were employed effectively by both John F. Kennedy and Lyndon Johnson, the economy grew strongly (Kennedy even went so far as to recommend tax cuts, enacted after his death). But in the 1970s, this trade-off broke down and Keynesian economists had no answer for why this occurred.[62]

Economist Milton Friedman of the University of Chicago had an answer. The Phillips Curve was predicated on a trade-off between unemployment and inflation. Friedman argued that a trade-off was impossible, for there existed a "natural rate of unemployment" that government intervention could not redress. Friedman predicted that governmental efforts to alter this would result in the very conditions plaguing the economy of the 1970s: high unemployment and high inflation. Friedman recommended instead minimizing governmental intervention in the economy through spending reductions, the reduction of regulation, and tax cuts and monetary policies not focused on the Keynesian trade-off. In 1976, Friedman won the Nobel Prize; in 1978 PBS ran his televised series, "Free to Choose," which further contributed to the challenge of the most basic assumptions of government spending and economic prosperity. He wrote a syndicated column in *Newsweek* and became one of the more celebrated and recognized economists in the world. Most importantly, he privately advised Ronald Reagan on economic policy during his 1980 campaign.[63]

A second important change in economic thinking was put forth by Friedman's Chicago colleague Robert Lucas (for which he was eventually awarded the Nobel Prize as well). Known as "rational expectations," Lucas's theory was that "predictable government intervention was destined to be futile and ineffectual because economic actors would anticipate it" and change their economic behavior. If one knew a tax or interest rate increase was on the horizon, one would take action to prevent it from affecting them. Both Friedman and Lucas had contributed to make Keynesianism a moribund doctrine.

The intellectual revolution also contributed to a policy revolution as well. Economists set out to advance new solutions to the economic problems facing the country. Arthur Laffer, an economist at the University of Southern California, devised the Laffer Curve—basically an updated classical economics principle known as Say's Law—which argued that supply creates its own demand. The Laffer Curve was deceptively simple. When government cut marginal tax rates across the board, government revenue actually increased. Why? Wealthier tax payers, who paid the bulk of federal taxes, hid their income and assets in tax shelters. When government raised taxes on the wealthy, government revenue actually declined.

Laffer, along with the long-haired Columbia University economist Robert Mundell, ran a weekly meeting at a posh Wall Street area restaurant known as Michael I. Attendees at the meetings included Irving Kristol, Jude Wanniski, and Robert Bartley from the *Wall Street Journal*, who soon dedicated the editorial page to the theory. Wanniski would popularize the theory in a book entitled *The Way the World Works* (1978). Kristol devoted attention to the theory in his journal *The Public Interest*. Former Nixon budget advisor Herbert Stein gave the theory a name when he tagged it "supply-side economics." Meanwhile, the theory permeated among staff members on Capital Hill, including Paul Craig Roberts, who worked in the office of Representative Jack Kemp (R-N.Y.), a former quarterback for the Buffalo Bills turned policy wonk congressman.[64]

Kemp advanced the supply-side tax cut mantra in Congress, introducing legislation with Senator William Roth (R-Del.), known as Kemp-Roth, which proposed a 30 percent reduction in income tax rates in 1978. William Steiger (R-Wis.) proposed halving the capital gains tax rate in the same House session, from 49 to 25 percent. Neither bill was expected to advance very far, as Democrats controlled the House and Speaker Thomas "Tip" O'Neill (D-Mass.) sought to kill Kemp-Roth before the midterm elections.

But popular momentum was on the side of tax cuts. California led the way with Proposition 13, a ballot initiative credited to the activism of Howard Jarvis, passed by a margin of two to one in June 1978. California had been home to tax revolts since the 1950s, when high property tax rates to fund construction of schools and public services in the state led many taxpayers to protest high tax bills. A variety of antitax groups had existed in the 1960s but had failed to secure property tax reforms. Activist Lewis Uhler had secured a spending cap initiative, Proposition 1, on the California ballot in 1970, but it was defeated as well. But by the mid-1970s, property tax relief in California was a significant issue due to inflation, expanded government spending, and the failure of politicians in either party to provide tax relief. When Proposition 13 passed, there was an immediate 57 percent reduction in property taxes and a cap on the growth of taxes on homes purchased before 1975.[65]

The tax revolt spread nationwide, with Tennessee passing tax relief and Massachusetts voters passing Proposition 2 ½, a cap on property taxes. Various other states followed suit, with many placing spending caps on state legislatures. The tax revolts were a mixture of populism, antigovernment libertarianism, and conservatism. While Kemp-Roth failed to pass Congress in the fall, Steiger's bill to cut capital gains did; ignoring the tea leaves, Carter actually proposed an increase in capital gains taxes that was defeated.

In the midterm election, voters sent Congress a message by electing conservative Republicans in crucial elections that year. The GOP gained three seats in the Senate but the newcomers were all conservative: Roger Jepsen defeated liberal Democrat Dick Clark in Iowa; Allegheny Airlines pilot Gordon Humphrey won in New Hampshire, defeating a liberal incumbent. In the House, the GOP gained fifteen seats, with most new members dedicated to conservative principles and policies, including a former history professor from Georgia named Newt Gingrich. This marked a major change in American politics. *Newsweek* analyzed the election and editorialized that "the real message of the election returns was the ratification of a new and no longer partisan agenda for the nation—a consensus on inflation as the priority target and tax-and-spend government as the primary villain."[66]

CARTER'S FOIBLES

While the economy played a strong role in the midterm election results in 1978, foreign policy proved especially important in galvanizing voters to support conservative candidates. The main issue was the Senate ratification of the Panama Canal Treaties that were to turn the canal back to the nation of Panama. The treaties were negotiated over several presidencies and Carter supported the ratification of the treaties, as did the Republican Party. The majority of the American people, according to some polls, did not, with close to 70 percent saying the United States should continue to control the canal. Richard Viguerie and other New Right operatives used the issue to mobilize the electorate, raise money, and elect conservatives. Columnist Pat Buchanan recognized the issue's importance when he wrote, "a political war to the death over the canal treaty could realign American politics, reinvigorate a weakened spirit of nationalism, and if lost, do for those who surrendered the Canal what Yalta did for the Democratic Party."[67] Direct mail letters were mailed out to conservatives, raising thousands of dollars (typically in ten- and twenty-dollar denominations) and a "Truth Squad" of New Right leaders, including Viguerie, traveled the country discussing the canal issue. Millions of postcards flooded Capital Hill congressional offices, yet the Senate voted to ratify the treaties.[68]

The Carter administration was proving to be conservatism's best friend when it came to foreign policy. Carter had begun his administration criticizing America's role in the Cold War. At the University of Notre Dame in May 1977, Carter declared that "our inordinate fear of communism" was the cause of the Cold War and that "the unifying threat of conflict with the Soviet Union has become less intensive."[69] He supported cuts in the defense budget at the same time the Soviets were spending increased amounts of their gross national product on weaponry. He promoted human rights but rather than confront the Soviets' dismal record on human rights, he attacked American allies instead, especially Iran and Nicaragua. However odious their human rights records, Carter's feckless criticism of strong anticommunist regimes in both Iran and Nicaragua came as both governments faced mounting dissension, much of it backed by Moscow. In 1979 both regimes fell, with Muslim clerics taking over Iran and the Marxist Sandinistas taking over Nicaragua. Meanwhile, Carter was silent on the treatment of Soviet dissidents, fearing that criticism would jeopardize Carter's desire to secure ratification of SALT-II.

Democrat Jeane Kirkpatrick wrote a prominent critique, "Dictatorships and Double Standards" in *Commentary*, assaulting Carter's foreign policy. "Democratic governments have come into being slowly," she wrote, "after extended prior experience with more limited forms of participation. . . . Hurried efforts to force complex and unfamiliar political practices on societies lacking the requisite political culture . . . not only fail to produce desired outcomes; if they are undertaken at a time when the traditional regime is under attack, they actually facilitate the job of the insurgents." Kirkpatrick was arguing that while certain authoritarian regimes were odious to American traditions of democratic government, it would be years before these governments could be converted to democracies. Meanwhile totalitarian governments supported by the Soviets were not criticized by the administration; such governments were immune from liberalization. Carter was uninterested in criticizing communist governments, allowing the administration "to participate actively in toppling of non-communist autocracies while remaining passive in the face of communist expansion."[70]

Kirkpatrick's essay was a major contribution to conservative criticism of Carter's foreign policy failures. Much of this criticism came from Democrats themselves, such as Henry Jackson and Kirkpatrick, as well as from former Leftists who were moving to the political Right by the end of the 1970s. Dubbed the "neoconservatives" by socialist Michael Harrington, the former radicals were finding much to defend about American society as it came under assault by the Left and the threat of communist expansion. Two of the most prominent neoconservatives were Norman Podhoretz, editor of *Commentary* magazine, and Irving Kristol, editor of *The Public Interest*, who was one of the few to accept the label *neoconservative* to define his changing political and social views.[71]

Both were men of the Left. Kristol was a Trotskyite who had famously battled Stalinist students when in college "in the alcoves" at the City College of New York, where many intelligent Jewish students—a group who would be labeled New York intellectuals—matriculated due to quotas on Jewish enrollment at the Ivy League schools. After service in World War II, Kristol became an editor for *Commentary*, a publication of the American Jewish Committee, and a founding editor of *Encounter*, the magazine of the American Committee for Cultural Freedom, an organization dedicated to challenging communism and promoting Western culture. It was secretly funded by the CIA, a point that gave New Left critics of Vietnam a field day when uncovered in 1966.

Kristol wound up editing several publications before becoming an editor at Basic Books and founding *The Public Interest*. He was not a conservative in the classical sense of opposing government; he wanted to make the Great Society function better. But he soon became disenchanted with liberalism and began a marked turn toward the political Right. During the 1970s he became a regular contributor to the editorial pages of *The Wall Street Journal* and a defender of capitalism and big business. He was, perhaps, a tepid supporter of capitalism, offering, in a book of the same name, "two cheers for capitalism" instead of three (or more), yet he saw the prosperity of America threatened by government regulation, and by a "new class" of highly educated bureaucrats hostile to corporate interests and the acquisitiveness that was the basis of American prosperity. Kristol's critique of the "new class" fit very well with the growing perception that the new class permeated the Democratic Party.[72]

Norman Podhoretz was a decade younger than Kristol. Born in Brooklyn, he became editor of *Commentary* in 1960 at age thirty. He turned the publication into a journal dedicated to New Left causes, publishing authors like Norman Mailer and civil rights advocates such as Bayard Rustin. But increasingly Podhoretz was bothered by the growing anti-Americanism of the

New Left and their support for communist North Vietnam. He also objected to the radical turn toward Black Power in the civil rights movement of the late 1960s. Podhoretz was an incendiary stylist and he angered many of his allies on the Left after he published "My Negro Problem and Ours," in which he described his youth growing up in Brooklyn, being attacked by black young people, seemingly implying that blacks were dangerous and that the problems of crime and poverty in black neighborhoods were due to their own refusal to accept responsibility for their own actions; it was not due to racism.[73]

By the 1970s, Podhoretz had moved *Commentary* far away from sixties radicalism. Even *National Review* editorialized, "Welcome In, the Water's Fine," and praised the intellectual contributions of the magazine. Such a welcome was not initially greeted warmly by neoconservatives. Kristol viewed William F. Buckley as likeable but "crackpotty." But increasingly conservative views became more and more amenable to them. Podhoretz wrote on the growing isolationism and "appeasement culture" he saw developing in America after Vietnam, criticizing Carter and liberal intellectuals in 1977 for not taking seriously Soviet efforts to build up their nuclear and conventional forces. He worried that America's growing isolationism, according to historian Gary Dorrien, "was making America not only unwilling, but literally incapable of fighting the Soviet enemy."[74] Such positions sounded very similar to the foreign policy writing of conservative intellectuals in the decade.

In 1976 Podhoretz joined the Committee on the Present Danger (CPD), an organization that grew out of a moderate Democratic effort to gain the presidential nomination for Henry Jackson. Jackson helped bring together Paul Nitze, Walt Rostow, former Defense Secretary James Schlesinger, and many future Reagan administration officials, including Paul Wolfowitz, Elliot Abrams, and Jeane Kirkpatrick. Throughout the late 1970s CPD alerted the nation to the growing Soviet threat, including their ability to launch a first strike against American missiles, thereby undermining deterrence. Arms control agreements with the Soviets were the culprit, and as Carter attempted to conclude the SALT-II treaty, Jackson and the CPD hammered away at the fallacies of the treaty. Only when the Soviets invaded Afghanistan on Christmas Day 1979 did Carter pull the treaty from consideration, greatly expanding defense spending and allowing for the development of a new missile, the MX missile, which CPD had advocated for three years.[75]

The focus on Carter's handling of the nation's foreign policy reached a fever pitch in the fall of 1979. In November fifty-two Americans were taken hostage in Iran by the new government headed by cleric Ayatollah Khomeini. Carter was unable to free the hostages over the course of the next year, failing to negotiate their release and failing to rescue them—one effort was aborted when two Marine helicopters collided in the Iranian desert, killing all the Marines on board. In December, the Soviets invaded Afghanistan, prompting Carter to get tough with the Soviets. Conservative critics of détente were saying that Soviet expansion had been going on for years; now they had the definitive proof they needed.[76]

Carter's economic problems reached a trough in 1979; inflation rates hovered around 12 percent. In part to end inflation in the economy, Carter appointed anti-inflation hawk Paul Volcker as chairman of the Federal Reserve Board. Volcker raised interest rates drastically; by the summer and fall, interest rates on bank loans were as high as 18 percent, rates most Americans paid on credit cards. The economy reeled. High energy prices that same year due to yet another OPEC oil crunch, pushed the economy into recession. During an election year, that was the last thing the Democrats needed.

Ronald Reagan had been waiting in the wings as the presumptive Republican nominee after his strong showing in the challenge to Ford four years earlier. Reagan had written a syndicated column and had given radio addresses, broadcast throughout the country, in which he criticized détente, spoke about the need for fiscal conservatism in Washington, and urged reforms such as tax cuts.[77] But Reagan was not someone all conservatives favored; initially, as the primary season began, Reagan was challenged by conservative congressman Phil Crane, who had the support of groups like the American Conservative Union and New Right activists Weyrich, Viguerie, and Phillips. George H. W. Bush, former chairman of the RNC, also challenged him, hoping to draw moderate support away from Reagan. John Connally, the former Johnson Democrat turned Republican, also drew some conservative support. Moderate congressman John Anderson entered the race as well, staying in as an independent and taking about 8 percent of the vote in the general election.

Reagan's age was a factor for many conservatives. When he stumbled out of the box in Iowa, Reagan looked beatable, but he regained initiative in New Hampshire and coasted to the Republican nomination, choosing Bush as his running mate. During the general election, Reagan swept aside concerns about his "extreme" positions and his age. Yet Reagan was a great campaigner, humorous, serious, and capable on the issues. He was relentless in his criticism of Carter and détente. Carter, haggard and tired from his efforts to solve the hostage crisis, was no match. After a debate between the two candidates in the election's final week, Reagan showed most Americans that he was trustworthy and not the extremist as presented by the media. He won 51 percent of the vote in November while taking 489 electoral votes, a stunning victory. The GOP also won control of the Senate.[78]

Ronald Reagan, who had been a Democrat but had left the party due to its position on taxes and on government spending, was now president. A movement conservative, one whose favorite magazine was *Human Events*, one who was on speaking terms with William F. Buckley, one who had embraced the classical liberalism of Hayek and Friedman, was now president. The constituencies that got him to the White House—evangelical Christians, Catholics, blue-collar workers, ethnics—and the conservative movement that had shaped his rise to power since the 1960s, all expected something from the new executive, a revolution in the way government worked and in the way America conducted itself abroad. As Reagan said in an election eve broadcast, "the question before us tonight [is] does history still have a place for America, for her people and for her great ideals?" For Reagan, the answer would always be yes; but increasingly conservatives began to answer differently. Lacking the faith and confidence that helped bring conservatives to power in 1980, the movement began to fracture once again.

NOTES

1. John Patrick Diggins, *Ronald Reagan: Fate, Freedom, and the Making of History* (New York: Norton, 2007), xviii–xix, provides an extended discussion of how Thomas Paine's words influenced Reagan. Diggins contends that Reagan's optimism about America's future was shaped more by his liberal upbringing than by his conservative beliefs, a dubious argument.

2. For the economic failures at the end of the 1960s, see Robert M. Collins, *More: The Politics of Economic Growth in Postwar America* (New York: Oxford University Press, 2000); and Collins, "Growth Liberalism: Great Societies at Home and Grand Designs Abroad," in Farber, ed., *The Sixties: From Memory to History* (Chapel Hill: University of North Carolina Press, 1995), 11–44.

3. For the antiwar movement in the 1960s see William Rorabaugh, *Berkeley at War: The 1960s* (New York: Oxford University Press, 1990); Kenneth Heineman, *Campus Wars: The Peace Movement at American State Universities in the Vietnam Era* (New York: New York University Press, 1994); Tom Wells, *The War Within: America's Battle over Vietnam* (Berkeley: University of California Press, 1994); and Adam Garfinkle, *Telltale Hearts: The Origins and Impact of the Vietnam Anti-War Movement* (New York: Palgrave Macmillan, 1997).

4. See Dominic Sandbrook, *Eugene McCarthy and the Rise and Fall of Postwar American Liberalism* (New York: Knopf, 2004), for a thorough study of the complexities of McCarthy, who in many ways possessed conservative instincts. See, for 1968, David Farber, *Chicago '68* (Chicago: University of Chicago Press, 1994).

5. On the Great Society, race, and welfare, Gareth Davies, *From Opportunity to Entitlement: The Transformation and Decline of Great Society Liberalism* (Lawrence: University Press of Kansas, 1996), remains the best academic analysis of the Great Society.

6. Kenneth Durr, *Behind the Backlash: White Working-Class Politics in Baltimore, 1940–1980* (Chapel Hill: University of North Carolina Press, 2003), 204.

7. The literature on race as a fundamental feature of the backlash against liberalism, and by extension, as an explanation for the rise of conservatism, is quite large at this point. It is also quite unsatisfactory as an explanatory tool for the rise of conservatism. For a sample of this literature, see Matthew D. Lassiter, *The Silent Majority: Suburban Politics in the Sunbelt South* (Princeton: Princeton University Press, 2005); Kevin M. Kruse, *White Flight: Atlanta and the Making of Modern Conservatism* (Princeton: Princeton University Press, 2005); Robert O. Self, *American Babylon: Race and the Struggle for Postwar Oakland* (Princeton: Princeton University Press, 2003); Joseph Crespino, *In Search of Another Country: Mississippi and the Conservative Counterrevolution* (Princeton: Princeton University Press, 2007); and the collection of essays in Robert J. Schulman and Julian E. Zelizer, eds., *Rightward Bound: Making America Conservative in the 1970s* (Cambridge, Mass.: Harvard University Press, 2008).

8. For a discussion of the connections between Nixon and contemporary American politics, see Rick Perlstein, *Nixonland: The Rise of a President and the Fracturing of America* (New York: Scribner, 2008). Conservative columnist George Will criticized the idea in his review of Perlstein's book: *New York Times Book Review* (May 11, 2008): 1, 10–11.

9. The best conservative statement on the Warren Court and its movement toward judicial legislating from the 1960s is L. Brent Bozell, *The Warren Revolution: Reflections on the Consensus Society* (Chicago: Crown, 1966); for a discussion of law and order impacting Nixon's election and liberalism, see Michael W. Flamm, *Law and Order: Street Crime, Civil Unrest, and the Crisis of Liberalism in the 1960s* (New York: Columbia University Press, 2005).

10. For Spiro Agnew, see Jules Witcover, *Strange Bedfellows: The Short and Unhappy Marriage of Richard Nixon and Spiro Agnew* (New York: PublicAffairs, 2007).

11. For a good general history of think tanks and the policy process, see James A. Smith, *The Idea Brokers: Think Tanks and the Rise of the New Policy Elite* (New York: Free Press, 1990).

12. Melvin Small, *The Presidency of Richard M. Nixon* (Lawrence: University Press of Kansas, 2003), is a useful starting point for the history of the Nixon presidency.

13. Jonathon Schoenwald, *A Time for Choosing: The Rise of American Conservatism* (New York: Oxford University Press, 2001).

14. Irving Kristol, "What Is the Public Interest?" *The Public Interest* (Fall 1965): 3–5.

15. James Q. Wilson, "'Policy Intellectuals' and Public Policy," *The Public Interest* (Summer 1981): 31–45.

16. Irving Kristol, *Neoconservatism: The Autobiography of an Idea: Selected Essays, 1949–1995* (New York: Free Press, 1995), 31.

17. Smith, *Idea Brokers*, 174–80; see also Carlin Bowman, "American Enterprise Institute," in Frohnen et al., eds., *American Conservatism: An Encyclopedia* (Wilmington, Del.: Intercollegiate Studies Institute, 2006), 25–27.

18. See Smith, *Idea Brokers*, 178.

19. See Lee Edwards, *The Power of Ideas: The Heritage Foundation at 25 Years* (Ottawa, Ill.: Jameson, 1997), 4–5.

20. Edwards, *Power of Ideas*, 5.

21. Edwards, *Power of Ideas*, 6–13. See also, Donald T. Critchlow, *The Conservative Ascendancy: How the GOP Right Made Political History* (Cambridge, Mass.: Harvard University Press, 2007), 116–22.

22. Kevin Phillips, *The Emerging Republican Majority* (New Rochelle, N.Y.: Arlington House, 1969).

23. Byron E. Shafer and Richard Johnston, *The End of Southern Exceptionalism: Class, Race, and Partisan Change in the Postwar South* (Cambridge, Mass.: Harvard University Press, 2006).

24. Donald T. Critchlow, *Phyllis Schlafly and Grassroots Conservatism: A Woman's Crusade* (Princeton: Princeton University Press, 2005), 207–9.

25. Manhattan Twelve Meeting, Memo to William F. Buckley, Stan Evans, Tom Winter, and Ronald Docksai from Randall Teague, William Rusher, John Jones, and Allan Ryskind, April 16, 1971, Box 284, Folder 2492, William F. Buckley Jr. Papers, Sterling Library, Yale University.

26. Richard Viguerie, *The New Right: We're Ready to Lead* (Falls Church, Va.: Viguerie, 1980), 51.

27. Kruse, *White Flight*.

28. Samuel T. Francis, "Message from MARS: The Social Politics of the New Right," in Whitaker, ed., *The New Right Papers* (New York: St. Martin's, 1982), 64–83.

29. Stephen J. Tonsor, "The Second Spring of American Conservatism," *National Review* (September 30, 1977): 1106.

30. The traditional narrative of détente can be found in Raymond Garthoff, *Détente and Confrontation: American–Soviet Relations from Nixon to Reagan*, rev. ed. (Washington, D.C.: Brookings Institution, 1994). For an interesting perspective concerning how student protests in the sixties impacted détente and foreign affairs (absent student conservatives of that decade), see Jeremi Suri, *Power and Protest: Global Revolution and the Rise of Détente* (Cambridge, Mass.: Harvard University Press, 2003).

31. Kiron K. Skinner, Annelise Anderson, and Martin Anderson, eds., *Reagan in His Own Hand* (New York: Free Press, 2001), 117–19. The radio address is dated March 23, 1977, and Reagan credited British intelligence for the secret speech from which he cited.

32. Critchlow, *Phyllis Schlafly*, 207.

33. Critchlow, *Phyllis Schlafly*, 207.

34. Robert G. Kaufman, *Henry M. Jackson: A Life in Politics* (Seattle: University of Washington Press, 2000), 267.

35. Kaufman, *Henry M. Jackson*, 294.

36. Author conversation with Natan Scharansky, Office of Senator Sam Brownback (R-Kans.), Washington, D.C., May 2005.

37. Alexander Solzhenitsyn, "The Strangled Cry of Solzhenitsyn," *National Review* (August 29, 1975): 930–38; for coverage of the trip see William A. Link, *Righteous Warrior: Jesse Helms and the Rise of Modern Conservatism* (New York: St. Martin's, 2007), 141–44; and Kaufman, *Henry M. Jackson*, 291–92.

38. On Ford see John Robert Greene, *The Presidency of Gerald Ford* (Lawrence: University Press of Kansas, 1993); Sean Wilentz, *The Age of Reagan, 1974–2008* (New York: Harper, 2008), 49–72; for conservative views of Ford, see Steven Hayward, *The Age of Reagan: The Fall of the Old Liberal Order, 1964–1980* (New York: Prima Lifestyles, 2001), 395–446.

39. Craig Shirley, *Reagan's Revolution: The Untold Story of the Campaign that Started It All* (Nashville: Thomas Nelson, 2005), 80–81.

40. Ads quoted in Shirley, *Reagan's Revolution*, 167. For the role of the Helms machine in the North Carolina primary, see Link, *Righteous Warrior*, 150–57; and Adam Clymer, *Drawing the Line at the Big Ditch: The Panama Canal Treaties and the Rise of the Right* (Lawrence: University Press of Kansas, 2008), 28–33.

41. See Lou Cannon, *Reagan* (New York: Putnam, 1985), 218.

42. Discussion in the previous two paragraphs follows from Shirley, *Reagan's Revolution*, 297–331; for Reagan's remarks, see pp. 332–34.

43. Godfrey Hodgson, *The World Turned Right Side Up: A History of the Conservative Ascendancy in America* (New York: Houghton Mifflin, 1996), 165–66.

44. Lisa McGirr, *Suburban Warriors: The Origins of the New American Right* (Princeton: Princeton University Press, 2001), 21–75; Dan Morgan, *Rising in the West: The True Story of an Okie Family from the Great Depression through the Reagan Years* (New York: Knopf, 1992), is an excellent study of the Tatham family and their movement from liberalism to conservatism, from poverty to prosperity.

45. William Martin, *With God on Our Side: The Rise of the Religious Right in America* (New York: Broadway, 1996), 102.

46. Martin, *With God on Our Side*, 113.

47. Martin, *With God on Our Side*, 117–20.

48. Critchlow, *Phyllis Schlafly*, 218.

49. Critchlow, *Phyllis Schlafly*, 221.

50. Critchlow, *Phyllis Schlafly*, 12, 277–83.

51. Martin, *With God on Our Side*, 168–90; see also, Kenneth Heineman, *God Is a Conservative: Religion, Politics, and Morality in Contemporary America* (New York: New York University Press, 1998), 112–13.

52. Martin, *With God on Our Side*, 172.

53. Martin, *With God on Our Side*, 173.

54. Martin, *With God on Our Side*, 189–90.

55. Martin, *With God on Our Side*, 199–200.

56. Martin, *With God on Our Side*, 201.

57. Geoffrey Layman, *The Great Divide: Religious and Cultural Conflict in American Party Politics* (New York: Columbia University Press, 2001).

58. *National Review* (October 24, 1970), 1160.

59. For a discussion the Erlich-Simon wager, see Ed Regis, "The Doomslayer," *Wired*, available online at www.wired.com/wired/archive/5.02/ffsimon_pr.html (accessed July 27, 2007).

60. Carter quoted in Hayward, *Age of Reagan*, 520–21.

61. Collins, *More*, 179–91.

62. Daniel Yergin and Joseph Stanislaw, *The Commanding Heights: The Battle for the World Economy* (New York: Free Press, 2002).

63. Milton Friedman and Rose D. Friedman, *Two Lucky People: Memoirs* (Chicago: University of Chicago Press, 1999).

64. Robert Bartley, *The Seven Fat Years: And How to Do It Again* (New York: Free Press, 1995), 61–76.

65. Hodgson, *World Turned Right Side Up*, 203–11; Critchlow, *Conservative Ascendancy*, 164–66.

66. *Newsweek* (November 1978), 8; Clymer, *Drawing the Line*, attributes the results of the midterm election to the Panama Canal Treaties, but there was more than simply the canal at stake. See Critchlow, *Conservative Ascendancy*, 162–66.

67. Buchanan cited in Viguerie, *New Right*, 84–85.

68. Clymer, *Drawing the Line*, 58–60.

69. Speech at the University of Notre Dame, May 22, 1977, *Public Papers of the Presidents: Jimmy Carter: 1977* (Washington, D.C., 1978), 956–57.

70. Jeane Kirkpatrick, "Dictatorships and Double Standards," *Commentary* (November 1979): 34–45.

71. On the origins of neoconservatism see Murray Friedman, *The Neoconservative Revolution: Jewish Intellectuals and the Shaping of Public Policy* (Cambridge: Cambridge University Press, 2005); Peter Steinfels, *The Neoconservatives: The Men Who Are Changing America's Politics* (New York: Touchstone, 1980); John Ehrman, *The Rise of Neoconservatism: Intellectuals and Foreign Affairs, 1945–1994* (New Haven, Conn.: Yale University Press, 1995); and Gary J. Dorrien, *The Neoconservative Mind: Politics, Culture, and the War of Ideology* (Philadelphia: Temple University Press, 1993).

72. Kristol, *Neoconservatism*, 3–40.

73. Norman Podhoretz, *Making It* (New York: Random House, 1967), describes his ascent as a cultural radical; *Breaking Ranks: A Political Memoir* (New York: Harper & Row, 1979), describes his break from the Left.

74. Dorrien, *Neoconservative Mind,* 170.

75. Norman Podhoretz, "The Present Danger," *Commentary* (March 1980); Kaufman, *Henry M. Jackson*, 360–61, 364–65.

76. David Farber, *Taken Hostage: The Iran Hostage Crisis and America's First Encounter with Radical Islam* (Princeton: Princeton University Press, 2006), is a solid treatment of the hostage crisis.

77. Skinner et al., *Reagan in His Own Hand*, 92–99, provides a good sample of Reagan's criticism of détente.

78. See Andrew E. Busch, *Reagan's Victory: The Presidential Election of 1980 and the Rise of the Right* (Lawrence: University Press of Kansas, 2005).

Chapter Six

... And Its Discontents

To be "neo" is to live in danger. Mutant types in culture and in biology are, as any sophomore student of biology knows, nearly always fatally flawed and prone to an early and ugly demise.

—Stephen Tonsor

The Philadelphia Society is perhaps one of the least known conservative organizations. Founded in 1964, the society hosts annual meetings open by invitation to conservatives to speak on a variety of issues facing American society. Don Lipsett was the founder and the perpetually cash-poor organization was endowed with a $100 check from William F. Buckley Jr., "forever rupturing my relations with the bank, which used to be friendly to me, but now spent its time coping with the Society's overdrafts." When asked why the organization was named the Philadelphia Society, Wabash College professor Ben Rogge wrote, "because [our] annual meetings are always held in Chicago," a fact in the first twenty years of the organization's history, due, as Lee Edwards related, to "Chicago serving as the center of the conservative movement for much of the last forty years or more."[1]

During those early years the Society was known to have quite fractious meetings owing to the split between conservatives and libertarians. A *National Review* editorial described the tenor of the meetings: "an urge to save the world was near the surface; how to do it was the question that divided the house. One group argued for restoring the traditional values of Western civilization; another pleaded the case for freedom. Others, holding that liberty and tradition were compatible, steered the Society towards the reconciliation of values."[2] By the end of the 1970s things had settled down and older tensions had withered away, making for sometimes somnolent meetings.

It was met with some surprise when Philadelphia Society president M. E. "Mel" Bradford, a professor of literature at the University of Dallas, dedicated the April 1986 meeting to a discussion of neoconservatism. He invited Harvard political theorist William Kristol, Burton Pines from Heritage, Rockford College professor Paul Gottfried, and University of Michigan historian Stephen Tonsor to discuss the new dispensation in American conservatism.

Bradford had his reasons for sponsoring such a meeting. A candidate for the directorship of the National Endowment for the Humanities, Bradford's candidacy was derailed by Irving Kristol, columnist George Will, and Heritage Foundation president Ed Feulner, who believed his defense of Southern conservatism would harm the Reagan administration. Bradford had written critically about Abraham Lincoln and his introduction of the "Gnostic ideal of equality" into American discourse with Lincoln's Gettysburg Address. More harmful, he had labeled Lincoln a "war criminal" and had supported segregationist George Wallace during his 1972 Democratic primary campaign. In a *Washington Post* column, George Will labeled Bradford a part of a "nostalgic Confederate remnant within the conservative movement."[3] There was no doubt that his academic record was impressive; much of the anxiety over his candidacy centered on whether his views were beyond the pale of a politicized conservatism. "It's asking rather a lot," neoconservative David Frum wrote many years later, "to ask a newly elected president to wreck his political honeymoon to refight the Civil War."[4]

Initially Bradford had the support of Russell Kirk, William F. Buckley, and the Southern historian Eugene Genovese. His candidacy had the backing of North Carolina Senator John East, who had suggested the nomination to Reagan. Yet it was not enough. Neoconservatives backed the far more politically palatable Texas professor William Bennett and their pick prevailed after Buckley swung his support behind Bennett. The selection ignited a firestorm of controversy concerning the prominent role neoconservative intellectuals were playing in the Reagan administration, in both its foreign policy and in its cultural war.

Bradford was interested in highlighting the dispute at the Philadelphia Society meeting. The participants were willing to deliver. Tonsor delivered a fiery missive against the neoconservatives. "It is splendid when the town whore gets religion and joins the church," Tonsor said. "Now and then she makes a good choir director, but when she begins to tell the minister what he ought to say in his Sunday sermons matters have been carried too far." He also alluded to the communist background of many of the neoconservatives when he wrote, "it has always struck me as odd, even perverse, that former Marxists have been permitted, yes invited, to play such a leading role in the conservative movement of the twentieth century," surmising that if Trotsky were still alive he would be writing conservative tracts at the Hoover Institution.[5]

R. Emmett Tyrrell Jr., the Menckenesque editor of *The American Spectator*, a former "alternative" student publication published for years from an old farmhouse near the Bloomington campus of the University of Indiana, delivered a written riposte about the meeting, arguing against the "phony conservatives" who were dividing the movement. "Most of the paleos," Tyrrell later wrote, "were thoroughly dominated by the conservative temperament so much so that they were prisoners of their own private musings. A government fit for their participation would be one suspended somewhere in the vapors of yesteryear, far away in old Europe in a time when government ministers wore powdered wigs, tucked dainty handkerchiefs up silky sleeves, and walked with elegant walking sticks."[6]

Tyrrell was certainly correct in one regard: paleoconservatives, as they were coming to be called—their conservative views seemingly fossilized in the procrustean bedrock of prehistory—were not impressive politicians. They were far more concerned with "insights from a humanistic and religious heritage." As Russell Kirk wrote, "the most pressing need of the conservative movement in America is to quicken its own right reason and moral imagination. A political movement that fancies it can subsist by slogans and by an alleged 'pragmatism' presently is tumbled over by the next political carnival, shouting fresher slogans."[7] Kirk offered a prescient critique of the problem inherent in moving conservatism too closely to the inside-the-beltway politicking that had defined liberalism in America since the 1930s, but inside the beltway remained the place most conservatives wanted to be in the years of the Reagan revolution, a time when all seemed possible for conservatives and an era that would help redefine the conservative disposition into the twenty-first century.

REAGAN'S REVOLUTION

Ronald Reagan's election signified that conservatives had grown up. Barry Goldwater's defeat in 1964 had inspired conservatives to take control of the GOP and to move it in a conservative direction. They had organized think tanks, employed grassroots issues to great effect, raised money, and had benefited from the internal tumult that marked the liberal coalition within the Democratic Party since the 1960s.

Yet all was not well within the ranks of the conservative movement. Now that Reagan was president, conservatives expected him to act on their agenda. "Conservatives complained about Reagan's administrative style," political scientist John Sloan wrote, "because they felt that he was not using his time and resources as efficiently as he could to fulfill their agenda."[8] The New

Right carped about Reagan's seemingly glacial movement on social issues. Neoconservatives, especially in his second term, were visceral in their criticism of his foreign policy. And supply-side economists and tax cutters were frustrated by Reagan's signing of four tax increases in the 1980s, ostensibly undoing the benefits of his 1981 tax cut.

Reagan stood above the conservative fray. He turned out to be, in Lee Edwards's phrase, a "remarkable political fusionist" capable, as John Sloan has also observed, of "lead[ing] and personify[ing] the conservative movement while maintaining the broad support necessary to be an effective president."9 Reagan understood that while he came into office as perhaps one of the most ideological presidents in history—and in many ways stayed that way—he presided over a federal system that in many ways works against ideological coherence. Reagan had to govern, not simply address the concerns of the conservative movement that had helped in his quest for the presidency. This proved a more difficult task for conservatives than it did for Reagan, who knew what he wanted to accomplish: restore American resolve against the threat of the Soviet Union, build up the military to deal with the Soviets, and restore America's economic growth.

If conservatives had paid more attention to Reagan's career as governor of California they would have seen a remarkably similar pragmatism at work. Journalist Lou Cannon, who chronicled Reagan's entire political career, has written about how Reagan campaigned as a conservative, sincerely employing the support from anticommunist groups to help win the governorship, but then wound up governing as a pragmatist. Reagan was not an absolutist and believed in getting something when it came to legislation rather than getting everything all at once.10

In many ways, Reagan's presidency followed the same path. He campaigned and won as a conservative but advanced a rather different policy agenda once in office. His Chief of Staff James Baker argued that Reagan had three issues when he took office, "the economy, the economy and the economy."11 In his first year he sought to secure a massive tax cut. Reagan hated the progressive income tax and believed it came "directly from Karl Marx who designed it as the prime essential of a socialist state." As a well-paid Hollywood actor, Reagan had groaned under the weight of an income tax that took 90 percent of his income. During the 1950s as a spokesman for General Electric, Reagan became an advocate of tax cuts. But he was also well schooled in the conservative economic doctrines of Ludwig Van Mises, F. A. Hayek, Frank Chodorov, and Henry Hazlitt. Reagan knew all the conservative arguments against the income tax and had long employed them himself in his political career.12

As the grassroots rose up against taxes in the 1970s Reagan moved to make tax cuts a central feature of his economic agenda. Reagan emphasized how tax cuts would restore growth to the economy. "By cutting taxes," Reagan wrote, "I wanted not only to stimulate the economy but to curb the growth of government and reduce its intrusion into the economic life of the country."[13] In August 1981, after an assassination attempt on the president failed, Reagan secured the passage of the Economic Recovery Tax Act, which reduced personal income taxes by 23 percent over three years and lowered the top level marginal tax rate from 70 to 50 percent. There was indexing for inflation and favorable depreciation guidelines and investment tax credits for business.

Combined with the necessary but harsh anti-inflationary policies implemented by Paul Volcker, the chairman of the Federal Reserve Board, Reagan's economic reforms began to reverse a period of economic stagnation and contributed to economic growth. There were consequences. A severe recession, the worst since the 1930s, disrupted the economy and contributed to the collapse of once-vital American industries such as steel and railroads. Thousands lost their jobs in steel towns in Pennsylvania's Monongahela Valley and in the Motor City of Detroit. Unemployment reached over 10 percent in 1982 but Reagan stood the course and urged Americans to do the same. A second impact of Reagan's economic program was budget deficits. The growth rates predicted by the administration after the tax cuts were too rosy. Budget director David Stockman urged the administration to reduce its spending on the military in order to reduce the glaring deficits. Reagan refused. Reagan also proved unable to slash federal programs and reduce the spending in Washington. Reagan had run on a program of reducing the federal government's size, but in the end the size of government grew while deficits to pay for it expanded tremendously.[14]

The deficits forced Reagan to increase taxes four times during his presidency (although there was no increase in the federal income tax on individuals). Deficits and budget issues dominated politics in the 1980s and 1990s. Senator Daniel Patrick Moynihan (D-N.Y.) argued in *The New Republic* that the budget deficits had been deliberate, designed to squeeze the budget to reduce funding for social programs.[15] But such reductions never came; social programs expanded in size during the Reagan years and while smaller than in previous postwar presidencies, the budget expansion of government continued unabated.

Political compromise over Reaganomics left supply-siders angry at the administration's failure to pursue spending cuts. Despite his best instincts not to give in on the supply-side idea, Reagan refused to sacrifice spending on his military buildup for spending reductions domestically. Supply-siders like Paul Craig Roberts, the assistant secretary of the treasury for economic policy and the author of the Kemp-Roth tax bill, left the administration after Reagan raised taxes in 1982. Roberts wrote an insider history, *The Supply-Side Revolution,* which put much of the blame for failure on Budget Director David Stockman and on Reagan's "management style."[16] Stockman had secretly discussed administration budget details with *Rolling Stone* magazine reporter William Greider, resulting in a negative article in *The Atlantic Monthly* entitled "The Education of David Stockman." Under pressure to fire Stockman, Reagan chose to believe that the young staffer was loyal and was duped into his comments by the press. Roberts believed that Reagan's loyalty to people around him who were not entirely supportive of his vision was his biggest problem.[17]

The view that individual appointments were derailing the Reagan revolution was shared by the New Right, which was also unhappy with Reagan's personnel selections. When George H. W. Bush received the nomination for vice president at the 1980 Detroit Republican National Convention conservatives booed lustily. Bush was considered a liberal, country-club Republican, pro-choice on abortion (he subsequently changed this view), and during the primary campaign Bush had referred to Reagan's tax cutting ideas as "voodoo economics." The price of the Bush selection was high. Bush campaign manager James A. Baker, a powerful Houston lawyer, was named Reagan's chief of staff rather than California loyalists and Reagan confidants Ed Meese or Michael Deaver (Meese was named counsel to the president and Deaver was a special assistant). The White House operation was commandeered, conservatives believed, by a Bush appointee.

Only one month into Reagan's presidency, James Lofton, editor of the New Right *Conservative Digest*, recommended that Reagan fire director of White House personnel E. Pendleton James. Lofton wrote, "the success of your presidency depends directly on the views of those who hold the top jobs in your administration. People make policy. And if the key individuals in your government are not dedicated, demonstrated, energetic advocates of your positions on the issues, your views will not prevail. There will be no Reaganism without Reaganites."[18] The problem was that there were few experienced conservatives who had been in government before the Reagan years. That left Reagan staffers with few options but to appoint, as Lofton wrote, "former Nixon and Ford retreads." The *New York Times* reported that "in his first eight Cabinet-level appointments . . . Reagan has given a mainstream, establishment Republican cast to his administration that may please the business community but has left staunch conservatives of the New Right decidedly unhappy."[19]

Conservative columnist Robert Novak put it more bluntly: "no incoming president since Franklin D. Roosevelt has faced such an array of problems too long unconfronted. The overriding problem for the Reagan Presidency is whether to approach the current American crisis, both foreign and domestic, with moderate policies adding up to a Nixon-Ford restoration, or to follow his own more *radical* impulses."[20] *National Review* agreed, stating that Reagan had to provide "his administration with a sense of mission."[21]

In most cases Reagan did just this. But high-level appointments disappointed conservatives. Former Nixon chief of staff General Alexander Haig was named secretary of state (at least it was not Henry Kissinger, as many conservatives feared). Haig lasted until his resignation in 1982 and George Shultz, more conservative by temperament but still a pragmatist, was made secretary of state. Jeane Kirkpatrick, who had written the important "Dictatorships and Double Standards," was given the post of United Nations ambassador, a position that she delighted in using to advance the case of America around the world. She was a neoconservative, a Democrat and had voted for Reagan in 1980 only after some deliberation. One of the few "movement" conservatives—he had been a member of YAF and a longtime conservative activist in the American Conservative Union—who was appointed to a foreign policy position was Richard Allen, named Reagan's national security advisor. He was forced to resign in 1982 and a revolving door of advisors followed before stability was reached with the appointment of General Colin Powell to that position after the Iran-Contra scandal erupted in 1987.

Initially neoconservatives in foreign policy appointments were not a concern for conservatives. The neoconservatives shared the anticommunist views of the conservative movement, and many neoconservative intellectuals, such as Irving Kristol, pushed for supply-side economic thinking in the editorial pages of the *Wall Street Journal*. The New Right, which had organized around the social issues and emphasized religious and cultural issues, was more concerned about the one governmental body that had transformed the Constitution: the Supreme Court.

REVOLTS ON THE RIGHT

Conservatives had long seen the judicial activism of the Supreme Court as a major problem, a sea change since the 1930s, when they were supportive of the judicial activism of the Court in overturning New Deal programs. Since the Warren Revolution of the 1950s the Court had taken an activist tinge, often encouraged by the legal profession itself, a doctrine first developed in the early twentieth century known as "legal realism," designed to use the bench to solve social problems outside legislative inaction. Conservatives opposed this sort of judicial activism, especially when it impinged on the proper role of the judiciary under the Constitution.

Conservatives challenged the dominance and liberal tilt of the legal profession, especially when it came to legal education. During the 1970s conservatives had formed public interest legal institutes, such as the Pacific Legal Foundation, to litigate in favor of development and economic growth. They went further in the 1980s, developing their own legal society. Law students

Steven Calabresi at Yale and Lee Lieberman Otis and David McIntosh at the
University of Chicago formed the Federalist Society in 1982. Supported by
conservative law faculty such as Antonin Scalia at Chicago and Robert Bork
at Yale (both of them nominated by Reagan to the Supreme Court), the Federalist Society blossomed into a legal organization with representation at over
140 law schools and with 25,000 members. Reagan told a Federalist Society
audience in 1988 that "the Society is returning the values and concept of law
as our founders once understood them to scholarly dialogue. . . . You are insisting that our Constitution is not some elaborate ink-blot test in which liberals can find prescribed policies that the people have rejected."[22] It was in
this doctrine that Reagan set out to remake the judiciary.

Reagan made his first Supreme Court nomination in July 1981 after the retirement of Justice Potter Stewart. He had promised to name a woman to the
court when he had the chance, and in selecting Arizona Court of Appeals
Judge Sandra Day O'Connor, he fulfilled that promise. O'Connor was a longtime friend and supporter of Barry Goldwater and had served both on the
bench and as a state legislator. She was conservative, but was not pro-life on
the issue of abortion. When Reagan selected O'Connor he was praised by
Senator Edward Kennedy, the National Organization for Women, House
Speaker Thomas "Tip" O'Neill, and the American Civil Liberties Union, not
exactly the type of individuals and groups from which conservatives typically
received endorsements.

The New Right believed O'Connor's nomination was a disaster. *The New
Right Report* reported that "it appears President Reagan has been betrayed on
this matter . . . early research revealed that Judge O'Connor had supported
both the ERA and abortion while in the Arizona Senate."[23] Phyllis Schlafly
told CBS News that "some of the people who are praising Reagan's appointment of this judge are people who would never vote for him . . . who are not
his friends. And I hope he won't end up the way Jimmy Carter did—which is
to find out that he tried to curry favor with his enemies, but he lost out all the
way around."[24] *Human Events*—Reagan's favorite publication—editorialized
that "under a Reagan presidency, we expected to see a major transformation in
the High Court, a sea-change shift to the right. But that kind of alteration is not
likely to come about with O'Connor type appointments. Conservatives—no,
the country—have a right to expect better."[25]

Reagan was concerned enough about the reaction from the New Right that
he telephoned Moral Majority founder Jerry Falwell to assure him that
"[O'Connor] represents values that I campaigned on."[26] Nevertheless Cal
Thomas, then assistant communications director for the organization (now a
syndicated newspaper columnist), did release a statement expressing concerns over O'Connor's views on abortion. Thomas later lamented that Rea-

gan failed to appoint a more conservative justice. "At a time when you had a Republican Senate and pretty much a free ride for anybody Ronald Reagan would nominate there was really no excuse for not nominating someone with the convictions of Robert Bork."[27] Bork was later rejected by a Democratic-controlled Senate.

Although the O'Connor fight proved temporarily disruptive—Barry Goldwater said during the midst of the controversy that he would "like to kick Falwell in the ass"— Falwell and the religious Right continued to support Reagan. Secular leaders of the New Right, such as Viguerie, Paul Weyrich, and Howard Phillips openly criticized the administration. Feeling isolated from the administration, Viguerie came to embrace a "new populism" critical of political and business establishments. Sounding like the radical sociologist C. Wright Mills, Viguerie, in *The Establishment vs. The People* (1983), assaulted the "ruling elite in America," whom he defined as big business executives, television moguls, the National Council of Churches leadership, bankers, union officials, National Education Association officials, judges, lawyers, and social work counselors. Viguerie argued that conservatives should reach out to "disillusioned Americans" who resented this "unelected and elitist power structure."[28]

There were other reasons for disenchantment with Reagan. Reagan had relied on the social issues to mobilize grassroots religious organizations in the 1980 election. While Reagan never backed away from supporting an antiabortion policy in his administration, he placed the social issues on the back burner as he sought to confront the Soviets and rebuild the economy. He told the annual meeting of the Conservative Political Action Conference in 1981 that "we do not have a social agenda, separate economic agenda, and a separate foreign agenda. We have one agenda. . . . Just as surely as we seek to put our financial house in order and rebuild our Nation's defenses, so too we seek to protect the unborn."[29]

Action occurred in the Senate throughout 1982 as five separate amendments designed to limit abortion were put forth and debated that year. The most controversial was an amendment authored by Senator Jesse Helms (R-N.C.), who defined the fetus as a person protected by the Fourteenth Amendment. "The paramount right to life is vested in each human being from the moment of fertilization," Helms wrote, "without regard to age, health or condition of dependency."[30] Orrin Hatch (R-Utah) proposed an amendment to return the abortion issue to the states, and both amendments reached the Senate floor for debate. Oregon Republican Robert Packwood filibustered the Helms amendment, and social conservatives within the administration, such as Morton Blackwell, urged Reagan to intervene to obtain cloture on the Packwood filibuster. Blackwell argued, "we are at a critical moment in the relationship between the President and the prolife activists. . . . If the President fails to take specific steps to obtain cloture in the Senate . . . the failure will be read as betrayal."[31] Reagan negotiated with senators, but the cloture motion failed twice and the Helms amendment was tabled (Hatch had withdrawn his, putting an end to the matter).

In the end *National Review* argued pragmatically, "politically speaking, it is very doubtful that the President should lead a major move to enact a constitutional ban on abortion. No national consensus exists in favor of such a ban . . . there are social issues on which the administration could move . . . responsibly and with political effectiveness, there are others where effort might be premature and counterproductive. The art of politics involves making just those judgments."[32] If, as Russell Kirk was fond of saying, "politics is the art of the possible," Reagan was learning the art quite well, more than the conservatives he had relied upon to win the presidency.

Other fissures within conservatism were emerging over Reagan's foreign policy. Reagan had long combined a moralistic anticommunism, long a part of the conservative viewpoint, with a universalism regarding human rights and an abhorrence of nuclear weapons that held more in common with traditional twentieth-century liberalism. He believed that communism was not to be the world's fate and he liked to cite radical revolutionary Thomas Paine frequently: "We have it in our power to begin the world over again." Historian John Patrick Diggins claims that "Reagan's goal to end the cold war was closer to the hopes of liberals, who thought it feasible, than to the fears of conservatives, who thought it impossible."[33] Diggins raises an interesting point, asked many times since the Cold War ended. Did conservatives need a foreign enemy? Did their belief that communism was monolithic, expansionist, uncompromising bind them to a perspective that placed more credibility in the communist system than was warranted? Reagan seemed to believe otherwise but his viewpoint was hardly in keeping with the spirit of liberalism, especially as liberals had become too accommodating with totalitarian regimes—the point made by Kirkpatrick in her "Dictatorships and Double Standards." Reagan intended to win the Cold War, not simply contain communism. And he intended to do so, as Diggins himself makes clear, through diplomacy, not war.

Much of Reagan's success as president was rhetorical, and when it came to his view of the Soviets his rhetoric was heated. In 1981 at the University of Notre Dame, Reagan said, "the West won't contain communism, it will transcend communism. . . . It will dismiss it as some bizarre chapter in human history whose last pages are even now being written." In June 1982 in London he told the assembled Parliament, "we are witnessing today a great revolutionary crisis . . . where the demands of the economic order are conflicting directly with those of the political order. . . . From Stettin in the Baltic to Varna on the Black Sea, the regimes planted by totalitarianism have had more than 30 years to establish their legitimacy. But none—not one regime—has yet been able to risk free elections. Regimes planted by bayonets do not take root . . . the march of freedom and democracy . . . will leave Marxism-Leninism on the ash-heap of history." Finally, in March 1983 before an audience of evangelical ministers, he famously labeled the Soviet Union an evil empire. So long as communists "preach the supremacy of the state, declare its omnipotence over individual man, and predict its eventual domination of all peoples on Earth, they are the focus of evil in the modern world." He talked about the moral power Whittaker Chambers had testified to decades earlier, "the crisis of the Western world exists to the degree in which the West is indifferent to God, the degree to which it collaborates in communism's attempt to make man stand alone without God." Finally, Reagan believed that "the struggle now going on for the world will never be decided by bombs, rockets, by armies or military might. The real crisis we face today is a spiritual one; at root, it is a test of moral will and faith."[34]

Reagan believed the Soviets needed to be convinced, however. His rhetoric alone did not make the difference in combating the Soviets. He authorized a massive arms buildup; he placed IRBM missiles in western Europe after the Soviets had done the same in eastern Europe (his actions precipitated a worldwide protest against his policy that in part was funded by Soviet intelligence); he supported anticommunist wars in the Third World and used the CIA effectively to wage them. Finally, only a few weeks after his evil empire speech, Reagan did the unthinkable—he proposed a defensive missile shield, known as the Strategic Defense Initiative (SDI), given the name Star Wars by the press, which would make the deterrence equation obsolete by developing technologies that could conceivably defend America from nuclear attack.[35]

Reagan, as historian Paul Lettow has argued, was a nuclear abolitionist. Far from being a cowboy conservative with an itchy finger on the nuclear trigger, Reagan abhorred nuclear weapons and had consistently been opposed to them since Hiroshima. "Ronald Reagan, beginning in 1945 and extending throughout his public life," Lettow wrote, "loathed nuclear weapons and the threat of nuclear war. Long before he became president, Reagan desired to intervene in and solve the nuclear dilemma. He sought to abolish all nuclear weapons, and pursued that goal as a personal mission."[36] Reagan believed that SDI would end the arms race and eliminate nuclear weapons and he pursued it with zeal, defending it from trade-offs during later meetings with Soviet General Secretary

Mikhail Gorbachev (even when Gorbachev offered to eliminate all nuclear weapons in trade for the elimination of SDI). Reagan held firm and reached major agreements with the Soviets, who, under Gorbachev, began an effort to reform their moribund economic system.

Reagan began to move away from confrontation with the Soviets and toward détente with the regime. He did so as early as 1983, worried perhaps that his rhetoric was convincing the Soviets that he did have warlike ambitions.[37] After his reelection in 1984, convinced that his arms buildup had restored American strength, he spent the majority of his second term securing agreements with the Soviets (part of the problem for why this did not come sooner was because of the selection of octogenarian Soviet leaders who "kept dying on me," as Reagan wrote to his wife Nancy). It was not until the selection of reformer Mikhail Gorbachev as general secretary of the Communist Party of the Soviet Union (CPSU) in 1985 that Reagan had a worthy bargainer. It took the fifty-year-old Soviet apparatchik to deal with the "old man" in the White House.

Conservatives who had supported Reagan's confrontational approach against the communist world were horrified at the turn of events. Norman Podhoretz, the influential neoconservative and editor of *Commentary*, criticized Reagan. "In his first term," Podhoretz wrote, "Mr. Reagan proved unwilling to take the political risks and expend the political energy that a real break with the underlying assumptions of détente would have entailed . . . overwhelmed by the political present, and perhaps lured by seductive fantasies of what historians in the future might have to say of him as a peacemaker, Mr. Reagan seems ready to embrace the course of détente wholeheartedly as his own."[38] Podhoretz attacked Reagan's arms control initiatives and argued that Gorbachev's reformist mask was a pawn to trick the West into complacency regarding the Soviet threat, an argument conservatives had made after the Yalta conference—the Soviets can never be trusted to hold up to their agreements.

In retrospect, given the sudden and surprising end of the Soviet eastern European empire in the autumn of 1989 and the whimper by which the Soviet Union itself expired—the end came with, of all things, a televised announcement by Gorbachev on Christmas Day in 1991—Podhoretz's criticism does not hold up very well. British Prime Minister Margaret Thatcher was fond of the axiom—repeated at Reagan's funeral in 2005—that "Ronald Reagan won the Cold War without firing a shot."[39] He did so through diplomacy after restoring America's strength and resolve to combat the challenge of communist expansion. Podhoretz's claim that Reagan never did enough to "break the underlying assumptions of détente" misses a larger point. Détente under Presidents Richard Nixon, Gerald Ford, and Jimmy Carter was a foreign policy of limits and of weakness after the American failure in Vietnam. Détente under Reagan represented negotiations from strength. "Reagan convinced the Soviet leadership that time was working against it," John Gaddis wrote.[40] He optimistically believed communism would fail and he set out to quicken the process. In the end, Reagan—not the conservatives, who remained convinced that communism was a threat and, as George Will wrote in 1988, that "Reagan has forcefully licensed détente, and hence the moral disarmament of the West"—had a far better understanding of the nature of communism and of its limitations, and a greater faith in the freedom and strength of Western civilization.[41]

A NEW CONSERVATISM?

Conservative disappointment with Reagan was very much a byproduct of generational shifts within conservatism. For those conservatives who came of age with the founding of *National Review* or with the early years of YAF or with the Goldwater campaign of 1964, the Reagan administration was a disappointment. Much of the dissatisfaction with Reagan emanated from the disappointment among conservatives convinced that a revolution would follow Reagan's election to the presidency. They were let down, believing that Reagan would deliver on more of their agenda that he did.

Younger conservatives who entered the conservative movement during the 1970s and 1980s did not feel this way and worshipped Reagan. They felt the "thrill of treason" when they drank Coors beer and smoked cigars. They challenged their college professors and university administration, who bowed at the altar of a growing political correctness on campus. Not unlike their baby boomer conservative forebears in groups like YAF, young conservatives in the 1980s formed their own counterculture, fighting against the Left just as intensely as members of YAF did in the late 1960s. Young conservatives in the 1980s organized campus magazines, founded with the assistance of Washington-based think tanks. The most prominent and controversial was *The Dartmouth Review*, which attacked such campus props as affirmative action, political correctness, feminism, and other radical ideas on campus.[42] While groups like YAF declined in the 1980s, the College Republicans boomed, and conservative Reaganites dominated the organization.

Reagan's optimism and his hard line against the Soviets was one of the main reasons young people—those under twenty-one who voted for the first time in 1984—voted for Reagan. Young conservatives loved movies like *Red Dawn*

(1984), in which the Soviets take over America and a resistance is led by young "wolverines" who blow up Soviet tanks and kill Russians and their Cuban lackeys. Sylvester Stallone's *Rambo* (1985) and Chuck Norris's *Missing in Action* films, which portrayed the rescue of American prisoners of war held by the communists in Vietnam (whose existence was denied by the communist government and by liberal politicians in America in the film), were popular fare as well.

Some young conservatives took their anticommunist beliefs quite seriously and, like the Rambo character, went into the bush to fight alongside the mujahideen in Afghanistan or the forces of anticommunist Jonas Savimbi in Angola. Dana Rohrabacher, a congressman from California elected in 1988, claims that he "disappeared" to fight alongside Afghan freedom fighters in their war against the Soviets. He described this "as a rite of passage for a lot of conservative anticommunists."[43] The inspiration for this type of activism was Jack Wheeler, a PhD in philosophy, the "real-life Rambo" who worked with anticommunist groups in Cambodia and motivated young conservatives to do the same. An adventurer by trade—his exploits involved retracing Hannibal's route over the Alps, free-fall skydiving over the North Pole, as well as hunting tigers in Vietnam—Wheeler traveled widely to help support and fight for the Reagan doctrine. The Soviet newspaper *Izvestia* referred to him as "an ideological gangster." College Republicans loved him and many young conservatives went abroad to fight for anticommunist guerrilla groups. On campus the College Republicans produced an "Adopt a Contra" poster urging that "only 53 cents per day will support a Nicaraguan freedom fighter."[44]

Young politicians like Newt Gingrich (R-Ga.), a backbencher in the House who used new technology like C-Span effectively to get his message out over the heads of Republican moderate party leaders like House Minority Leader Robert Michel, were the heroes of this new generation of activists. Political reporter Nina Easton described these young "Reaganites" as confrontational: "they lived by a dictum that inverted [Carl von] Clausewitz's: politics is a continuation of war by other means, a way to smash your cultural and ideological enemies. Compromise, caution, negotiation, anything that blurred ideological differences risked obscuring the mission that had drawn them to Washington in the first place."[45]

Drawn them to Washington in the first place—that may have been the biggest problem facing conservatism in the Reagan years and afterward. Instead of looking to the campus, or to local communities, conservatives focused more and more of their attention on Washington. An old adage from the early 1970s went: "you could get all the conservatives in Washington to fit inside a phone booth." Ten years later that changed drastically. The Heritage Foundation, American Enterprise Institute, the CATO Institute, and hundreds of other smaller operations, think tanks, single-issue forums, and magazines were now deeply ensconced in the nation's power structure and became deeply embedded in focusing on solutions from the top down.

The grassroots never completely withered but they received more direction than previously from well-connected and well-funded think tanks and professional politicians. Liberal journalist Sidney Blumenthal referred to this as the "rise of a counter-establishment" that challenged liberalism and focused on conservative causes.[46] The conservative movement was now a political operation with money and influence going to think tanks to mobilize policy victories and support political candidates who could bring them about. The great majority of these individuals were less connected to the long sweep of conservative intellectual history than they were to the changing political coalition that brought conservatives to power.

REVOLT OF THE PALEOCONSERVATIVES

Of course, conservative intellectuals who had long espoused a different conception of what constituted conservatism hated the new "inside-the-beltway" politicking and believed it represented a betrayal of the humanistic principles on which conservatism should be based. In 1986 the Intercollegiate Studies Institute (ISI) organized a symposium entitled "The State of Conservatism" in their publication *The Intercollegiate Review,* featuring several scholars critical of the drift away from traditional conservatism. Many of the essays centered their criticism on the rise of neoconservatism. University of South Carolina historian Clyde Wilson wrote about how "our estate has been taken over by an imposter just as we were about to inherit." In cryptic language, Wilson described the neoconservative takeover: "the offensives of radicalism have driven vast herds of liberals across the border into our territories. These refugees now speak in our name, but the language they speak is the same one they always spoke. . . . It contains no words for the things that we value."[47]

Gerhart Niemeyer, a professor of political theory at Notre Dame, wondered "whether, in terms of ideas, there is such a thing as American conservatism." Paul Gottfried offered the most caustic commentary on the conservative plight. "Conservatives cannot prevail on policy issues in the long run unless they first win acceptance for their view of human nature." Gottfried then unleashed a bromide against neoconservatives and the New Right, arguing that "self-labeled conservatives have embraced the neoconservative caricature of the post-war conservative movement. Thus they maintain that the neoconservatives are giving respectability to what used to be a collection of nativist Neanderthals. . . . It is, to me, appalling that some of our most influential conservatives can no longer distinguish themselves from the advocates of welfare state and of global democratic revolution."[48] On the New Right Gottfried was equally caustic: "The New Right distresses me for being a lowbrow imitation of what the Old Right represents. Its spokesmen are well-meaning but often intellectually crude. . . . The New Right is also on the horns of a dilemma, trying to reconcile its biblically-based morality with populist majoritarian rhetoric. . . . New Rightists depict the American people as a God-fearing, hymn-singing nation. This is largely wishful thinking that takes no account of the influence of leftist media and educators upon one entire generation of Americans."[49]

Gottfried repeated much of this criticism in a history of conservatism published in 1988. Coauthored with Thomas Fleming, the editor of *Chronicles*, a publication of the Rockford Institute, *The Conservative Movement* (1988) presented a history that focused on the incredible flux and dynamism within American conservative history. "It is possible to regard conservatism as a series of trenches dug in defense of last year's revolution," the authors wrote. But the book also sought to look past the Cold War and to embrace instead the humanistic heritage of Western civilization rather than to continue to fight for democracy in the world. "The older conservative writings express hostility toward communism as the enemy of the western religious heritage," they wrote, "of historic nationalities, and of metaphysical as well as political freedoms. The recent anticommunist writings rest on the stated or implicit assumption that American democracy with its mixed economy is the supreme human good."[50] At its very denouement paleoconservatives were moving away from the Cold War and from their new conservative brethren who sought to continue to wage it no matter what.

The reaction from the neoconservatives was decidedly hostile. Dan Himmelfarb, reviewing the book (and the wider split between neocons and paleocons) in *Commentary*, suggested that "an implicit thesis [in the book] is that neoconservatism is not an authentic conservatism, that it is insufficiently indistinguishable from welfare-state liberalism."[51] Himmelfarb claimed the tradition of neoconservatism to be represented by individuals such as Montesquieu, Tocqueville, and Madison; paleoconservative views were rooted in Christian religious belief. In a symposium in *Commentary* magazine in 1976, Irving Kristol had argued that neoconservatives wished to revive the "political tradition associated with the birth of modern liberal society—a society distinguished from all others by representative government and a predominantly free-market economy."[52]

The underlying problem was that neoconservatives were claiming a mantle that had long been that claimed by conservatives in general. Neoconservatives had accepted the premise of the welfare state. They fought over its extension, certainly, and argued about whether specific policies were worthy of continuing, but they did not doubt its efficacy in the manner conservatives had. "Government is not the solution to our problems," Reagan said in his first inaugural address, "government is the problem."[53] Very few, if any, neoconservatives believed this.

But there was more to the growing bifurcation than simply a matter of interpreting the attitudes of neoconservatives regarding government. There was a growing and permanent divide between the two camps regarding foreign policy, culture, and ultimately power within the movement. Sinister conspiracies were raised on both sides regarding the influence of each camp. Neoconservatives charged anti-Semitism against the paleocons, insisting that individuals like Stephen Tonsor, who defined conservatism's world view as rooted in "Roman or Anglo-Catholic" religious belief and in the "culture of Christian humanism," seemed to exclude Jews and other non-Christian conservatives from conservatism.[54] In 1987 Norman Podhoretz wrote *National Review* senior editor Jeffrey Hart concerning his colleague editor Joseph Sobran, who had been increasingly critical of Israel in his syndicated columns. Podhoretz complained about one column in particular that criticized American policy in the Middle East and took issue with *National Review*'s strong support for Israel. Buckley responded to Podhoretz denying the charge of anti-Semitism, calling the column in question "contextually anti-Semitic" and defending Sobran from the charge made by Podhoretz. Podhortez replied, "for the record, I deemed Joe Sobran's columns anti-Semitic in themselves, and not merely 'contextually.'"[55]

Sobran would eventually be forced out of the magazine and Buckley dedicated the entirety of the December 1991 *National Review* to the issue. "In Search of Anti-Semitism," later published as a short book with the same title, detailed how uncomfortable Buckley was growing up in a home where his father expressed anti-Semitic views and how he, growing up Catholic in a privileged environment, had encountered anti-Semitism on many occasions.[56] Sobran responded viscerally in a self-published pamphlet entitled "How I Was Fired by Bill Buckley," accusing Buckley of acting "out of fear" and "selling out to his buddies" in the neoconservative camp. He also accused Buckley of turning *National Review* into a "neoconservative magazine."[57]

At the same time that Reagan was moving the country's politics in a more conservative direction, conservatives were fighting over definitions and over what it meant to be conservative in America. Power within the movement was central to this whole debate. One of Sobran's most pointed criticisms of Buckley in his essay relates to the fact that Buckley, desiring to protect the "vital center conservatism" represented by *National Review*, had moved far away from the conservatism represented by the magazine in its first three decades. "His conservatism," Sobran wrote, "is a conservatism of image, show business, public relations, stock mannerisms; big words, anfractuous grammar, repetitious Latinisms, implying a depth that isn't there."[58] That indeed expressed the problem Sobran and other paleocons faced: they were out of power within the new movement and they were facing a long twilight struggle to win back conservatism to their principles and ideas.

One of the leading architects of paleoconservative ideas, Samuel Francis, was, as David Frum described him, "a huge man, with a bright red face who puffs cigarettes below anachronistic black horm rim glasses."[59] Francis was born in North Carolina and was a member of Young Americans for Freedom during his college years in the late 1970s. He was a staff member for Senator John East (R-N.C.), and after leaving that position became an editorialist with the *Washington Times*, a conservative paper founded in the 1980s. Frum contended that Francis's hostility to neoconservatism emerged after Tod Lindberg, a roommate of John Podhoretz at the University of Chicago, became editorial page editor of the *Times* over him, "a coincidence that Francis and his friends imbued with sinister significance."[60] In the new culture of conservative Washington, Francis was passed over for the editorship, and eventually released from the paper, because of his increasingly unpopular views on civil rights and his concern with ethnic politics and identity.

Francis continued to write a syndicated column and he appeared regularly in the Rockford Institute's *Chronicles*. Edited by South Carolinian and classics scholar Thomas Fleming, *Chronicles of Culture*, as it was called at its founding in 1977, was a magazine dedicated to the paleoconservative worldview. Founded by Rockford College President John Howard and edited in its early years by Polish novelist Leopold Tyrmand, *Chronicles* originated as a protest against both the liberal state and the conservative economist and represented an effort to fight on the "battleground of culture."[61] Fleming joined the magazine as a managing editor in 1984, having founded the *Southern Partisan*, a largely apologetic magazine about the culture of the South. After Tyrmand's untimely death in 1985, Fleming became editor and guided *Chronicles* to its most important growth and influence by the early 1990s (it would peak at around 15,000 subscribers in 1992).[62]

In May 1991 *Chronicles* published a symposium featuring Francis's provocative article "Beautiful Losers: The Failure of American Conservatism." Francis argued that "the American right lost on such fundamental issues as the fusion of state and economy, the size and scope of government, the globalist course of American foreign policy, the transformation of the Constitution into a meaningless document that serves the special interests of whatever faction can grab it for a while, and the replacement of what is generally called 'traditional morality' by a dominant ethic of instant gratification."[63] Francis referred often to the work of James Burnham, one of the principal editors of *National*

Review until a stroke incapacitated him in 1979 (he died in 1987). Burnham wrote in 1972 that while neoconservatives had broken with "liberal doctrine," they still adhered to "the emotional gestalt of liberalism, the liberal sensitivity and temperament."[64] Neoconservatives, who were to blame for much of the failure of conservatism, were not much different in Francis's view from the progressives and New Dealers. "Much of what neoconservatives are concerned with," Francis wrote, "is merely process—strategy, tactics, how to win elections, how to broaden the base of the GOP, how to make the government run more effectively . . . not with the ultimate goals themselves."[65]

If that were true, then the whole conservative movement, including many who had once defined themselves under the parameters of the old Right doctrines Francis extolled, were tacticians, including Reagan himself, who famously said in his diary that "the press is trying to paint me as trying to undo the New Deal. I remind them that I voted for FDR four times. I'm trying to undo the Great Society. It was LBJ's War on Poverty that led us to our current mess."[66] One can fairly but gently criticize Reagan for his lack of understanding of historical continuity—it was the New Deal that made the Great Society possible, just as it was the progressive era that made the New Deal probable.

Francis recommended a rejection of "inside-the-beltway" strategizing and the creation of "middle American radicalism." "A new American right," he wrote, "must recognize that its values and goals lie outside and against the establishment and that its natural allies are not in Manhattan, New Haven and Washington but in the increasingly alienated and threatened strata of Middle America."[67] There was a bit of the romantic revolutionary in Francis's rhetoric. "The strategy of the Right should be to enhance the polarization of Middle Americans from the incumbent regime, not to build coalitions with the regime's defenders and beneficiaries," Francis wrote. "The main focus of the Middle American Right should be the reclamation of cultural power, the patient elaboration of an alternative culture within but against the regime—within the belly of the beast but indigestible by it." The only way to build a successful and conservative path to political power was from the ground up, without the necessity of building coalitions with the Left and "bargaining with the regime."[68]

BATTLE FOR CONSERVATISM AFTER REAGAN

The politician most influenced by Francis was the increasingly disaffected conservative journalist Patrick Buchanan. Buchanan had been a longtime fixture on the populist Right since coming to national attention as a speechwriter for Vice President Spiro Agnew. A gifted columnist and controversialist, Buchanan became Reagan's director of communications in 1986. A longtime dedicated anticommunist and Cold War hawk (Buchanan was a traditionalist Catholic), he supported a strong foreign policy and, for awhile, also supported the free trade doctrine beginning to dominate conservative thinking in the Reagan years.

When the Cold War ended, however, Buchanan began to have second thoughts about the continuing need for American military power throughout the world. He published an essay in *The National Interest* entitled "America First—and Second and Third" questioning the need for the continuation of a Cold War military presence in Europe. Buchanan also challenged the globalist free trade doctrine that had one time been the benchmark of liberalism but had become a key focus of both parties in the Reagan era. He was particularly incensed at the strong bipartisan support for the North American Free Trade Act (NAFTA) signed into law by President Bill Clinton with the support of all the living ex-presidents.[69]

Buchanan would tailor these concerns into an expression of dissatisfaction with the GOP as a whole and would challenge President George H. W. Bush in the 1992 primaries. Bush was never a conservative favorite. Too wimpy, too nonideological, too much the country-club Republican, Bush was the front-runner as much due to Reagan as anyone else. There were no real conservative challengers in the 1988 primaries, save for the entry of televangelist Pat Robertson, host of *The 700 Club*. Robertson was the son of U.S. Senator Willis Robertson (R-Va.) and had been a leading figure in the growth of the religious Right. The Bush forces mocked him initially, until he won the Iowa caucus and the Michigan primary. But then scandals associated with other televangelists unraveled the Robertson campaign. Bush supporter Jim Bakker, who headed up the PTL Club, was charged with evading some $56 million in federal taxes. When the press reported the scandal they also uncovered a sexual affair with a secretary, Jessica Hahn, who was paid $265,000 per year in salary. Later in the year Jimmy Swaggart, also a Bush supporter, admitted to his television audience that "he had sinned against God" when affairs with numerous prostitutes were uncovered by the press. Robertson's campaign never recovered.[70]

Promising he would not raise taxes—he later reversed himself owing to concerns about the budget deficit and costly bailout of the savings and loans—Bush won the GOP nomination and went on to defeat Massachusetts Governor Michael Dukakis in the fall campaign. Bush had selected the young senator Dan Quayle as his running mate and no one could really understand the choice. Quayle was depicted as a conservative by the press—he was the grandson of *Indianapolis Star* and *Arizona Republic* publisher Eugene Pulliam, a strong backer of Barry Goldwater's career. But he was not trusted by many on the Right who, as Illinois congressman Henry Hyde put it, were "under whelmed" by his selection. R. Emmett Tyrrell was less than pleased—he labeled him an ingrate—when Quayle announced that he favored the liberal *New Republic* to the conservative *American Spectator*.[71]

Bush did gain some support from the Right during his presidency, and that was from the neoconservatives, who positively welcomed him due to what they believed was Reagan's too-cozy relationship with Soviet leader Gorbachev (they took to calling the president "Reaganchev"). They believed Bush was giving a more realistic appraisal of the foreign policy situation. Conservatives also cheered when Bush authorized the invasion of Panama to oust the corrupt dictator Manuel Noriega. But Bush broke his pledge on taxes, prompting a short-lived recession, and he did little to advance the cause of religious conservatives.

Most controversially Bush sent troops into the Middle East after the Iraqi invasion of Kuwait in August 1990. Fearing that Saddam Hussein would dominate Persian Gulf oil fields and put pressure on neighboring Saudi Arabia, Bush condemned Iraq's invasion, secured four United Nations resolutions to intervene to protect Saudi Arabia from Iraqi aggression, and sent over 500,000 American military personnel to the deserts of Saudi Arabia in what was billed as Operation Desert Shield. Conservatives strongly supported Bush's action to defend the Saudis. Hungry for the recently concluded Cold War, conservatives agreed with Bush when he compared Saddam Hussein to Adolf Hitler.

In late January 1991 Bush unleashed a bombing campaign against Iraq followed by an invasion of Kuwait, known as Operation Desert Storm. The war lasted four days and the Iraqi armed forces were destroyed by the United Nations troops. Hussein launched Scud missiles against Israel, in part to disrupt the Arab-American alliance, but the nations involved in the liberation of Kuwait remained committed to their involvement in the war and supported the mandate in the resolution. Bush's popularity soared to over 80 percent in public opinion polls, and Americans strongly supported the quick and easy victory in the Gulf.[72]

Conservatives were mostly unified on the need to intervene to free Kuwait and secure oil supplies in the Middle East. The issue of Israel became one of the more divisive issues, which contributed to the charge made by Buckley of anti-Semitism against Sobran and Pat Buchanan. Russell Kirk criticized those neoconservatives who "mistook Tel Aviv for the capital of the United States."[73] Buchanan went further, saying on the televised *McLaughlin Group* that "there are only two groups that are beating the drums for war in the Middle East—the Israeli Defense Ministry and its amen corner in the United

States. . . . The Israelis want this war desperately because they want the United States to destroy the Iraqi war machine. They want to finish them off. They don't care about our relations with the Arab world."[74]

Buchanan was labeled anti-Semitic for the former line by Abe Rosenthal of the *New York Times*. Charles Krauthammer, a neoconservative newspaper columnist, concurred. Joshua Muravchik, a former socialist, published a detailed analysis of Buchanan and his anti-Semitism in the January 1991 issue of *Commentary*. Entitled "Patrick Buchanan and the Jews," Muravchik alluded to every anti-Semitic statement made in his writing career by Buchanan and found much of it credible as anti-Semitism.[75] David Frum wrote in *The American Spectator* in September 1991 essentially the same thing. Fred Barnes, then of *The New Republic*, followed up with an analysis of Buchanan's writings: "If your definition [of anti-Semitism] is someone who is personally bigoted against Jews, doesn't want them in the country club, I don't think Pat is that. If your definition is someone who thinks Israel and its supporters are playing a bad role in the world, Pat may qualify."[76]

Once again the floodgates had broken as a dispute between those who should have been working together on the vast problems facing the nation were now accusing each other of sordid motives and behavior. As Jeffrey Hart wrote in *National Review* after the Philadelphia Society meeting in 1986, "one had the sense that it is past time certain Old Right conservatives stopped griping about the neos. Yes, yes, Hayek and [Eric] Voegelin were there first, and yes, many battles were fought long ago, and yes, the old Rightists sacrificed career and status while future neocons were still basking in the establishment's approval, and yes, the Old Right may not have received as many federal posts as it would like, and yes, some neocons behave as if they have invented the wheel. But many foolish things are being said in anger."[77]

Does Hart minimize the extent of the divide? Maybe, but he seemed to recognize something neither side in the debate was recognizing; conservatism had shifted ground before and it was shifting again. The neoconservatives proved immensely helpful when it came to policy issues—welfare reform, for instance, was a neoconservative proposal first broached in Irving Kristol's *The Public Interest* in the late 1960s. The paleoconservatives were also immensely helpful, reminding conservatives about first principles. Both sides could be acutely oversensitive, as any actors in ideologically based struggles are wont to be. Both sides could be quite nasty. Allegations of anti-Semitism thrown routinely by neocons against their ideological enemies suggest a sort of residual political correctness on their part, a holdover from ideological battles more fitting of the internecine warfare between Trotskyites and Stalinists than conservatives. The countercharge that conservatism was Roman and Anglo-Catholic was also unfair and inaccurate, as many of the leading intellectual figures in conservatism were not communicants or worshippers at any church or synagogue.

Even with the often vaporous clouds hanging over conservatism in the Reagan years, there were reasons to be optimistic about the future. As Daniel Oliver put it at the 1992 meeting of the Philadelphia Society, "what an exhilarating prospect: freed of the communist threat we can spend our time debating first things. Thanks Mr. Reagan!"[78] Conservatives spent the rest of the century debating first principles and enacting new policies based on those principles. They found they had a lot of work to do in both the political and policy realm and set out to more deeply enmesh conservative principles into American politics and culture. The Reagan revolution had left many conservatives unfulfilled—could they make another one?

NOTES

1. Lee Edwards, *History of the Philadelphia Society* (Jerome, Mich.: Philadelphia Society, 2004), published by the Philadelphia Society to commemorate its 40th anniversary, copy in author's possession.

2. Cited in William F. Buckley Jr., *Miles Gone By: A Literary Autobiography* (Washington, D.C.: Regnery, 2004), 514–15.

3. See Paul Gottfried and Thomas Fleming, *The Conservative Movement* (Boston: Twayne, 1988), 72.

4. David Frum, *What's Right: The New Conservative Majority and the Remaking of America* (New York: Basic, 1996), 62.

5. See Stephen Tonsor, "Why I (Too) Am Not a Neoconservative," *National Review* (June 20, 1986): 54, reprinted in Schneider, ed., *Equality, Decadence, and Modernity: The Collected Essays of Stephen J. Tonsor* (Wilmington, Del.: Intercollegiate Studies Institute, 2005), 303–8.

6. R. Emmett Tyrrell Jr., *The Conservative Crack-Up* (New York: Summit, 1992), 235–36.

7. Russell Kirk, *Prospects for Conservatives* (Washington, D.C.: Regnery, 1989), 258.

8. John W. Sloan, *The Reagan Effect: Economics and Presidential Leadership* (Lawrence: University Press of Kansas, 1999), 77.

9. Lee Edwards, *The Conservative Revolution: The Movement that Remade America* (New York: Free Press, 1999), 241; Sloan, *The Reagan Effect*, 54.

10. Lou Cannon, *Governor Reagan: His Rise to Power* (New York: PublicAffairs, 2003).

11. Adrianna Bosch, *Ronald Reagan: An American Story* (New York: TV Books, 2000), 145–46.

12. Thomas W. Evans, *The Education of Ronald Reagan: The General Electric Years and the Untold Story of His Conversion to Conservatism* (New York: Columbia University Press, 2006).

13. Ronald Reagan, *An American Life: The Autobiography* (New York: Simon & Schuster, 1990), 232.

14. William A. Niskanen, *Reaganomics: An Insider's Account of the Policies and the People* (New York: Oxford University Press, 1988), explores the increase in government spending that occurred on Reagan's watch.

15. Daniel Patrick Moynihan, "Reagan's Bankrupt Budget," *The New Republic* (December 31, 1983): 18.

16. Paul Craig Roberts, *The Supply-Side Revolution: An Insider's Account of Policymaking in Washington* (Cambridge, Mass.: Harvard University Press, 1984).

17. William Greider, "The Education of David Stockman," *The Atlantic Monthly* (December 1981); see David Stockman, *The Triumph of Politics: Inside the Reagan Revolution* (New York: Avon, 1987).

18. James Lofton, "Dear Mr. President," *Conservative Digest* (February 1981): 1–4.

19. *New York Times* (December 12, 1980): 1A.

20. Robert D. Novak, "Reagan's Great Opportunity: The Test of a Presidential-Elect," *National Review* (November 28, 1980): 1444–45.

21. *National Review* (December 31, 1980), 6.

22. Stephen M. Teles, *The Rise of the Conservative Legal Movement: The Battle for the Control of the Law* (Princeton: Princeton University Press, 2008), 133–80, provides a good examination of the Federalist Society as a "counter-ABA."

23. *New Right Report* (July 27, 1981): 1.

24. Schlafly in *Human Events* editorial cited by *Conservative Digest* (August 1981): 9.

25. Schlafly in *Human Events*.

26. William Martin, *With God on Our Side: The Rise of the Religious Right in America* (New York: Broadway, 1996), 228–29.

27. Martin, *With God on Our Side*.

28. Richard Viguerie, *The Establishment vs. the People: Is a New Populist Revolt on the Way?* (Chicago: Regnery Gateway, 1983).

29. Speech before Conservative Political Action Conference, February 1981, *Public Papers of the Presidents: Ronald Reagan: 1981* (Washington, D.C.: U.S. Government Printing Office, 1982), 278.

30. Donald T. Critchlow, "Mobilizing Women: The Social Issues," in W. Elliott Brownlee and Hugh Davis Graham, eds., *The Reagan Presidency: Pragmatic Conservatism and Its Legacies* (Lawrence: University Press of Kansas, 2003), 302.

31. Critchlow, "Mobilizing Women," 303.

32. *National Review* (February 5, 1982): 91–93.

33. John Patrick Diggins, *Ronald Reagan: Fate, Freedom, and the Making of History* (New York: Norton, 2007), 1.

34. Reagan, Address at the University of Notre Dame, May 17, 1981, *Public Papers of the Presidents: Reagan: 1981*, 434; Address to Members of British Parliament, London, June 8, 1982, *Public Papers of the Presidents: Ronald Reagan: 1982* (Washington, D.C.: U.S. Government Printing Office, 1983), 744–47; and Speech to the National Association of Evangelicals, Orlando, Florida, March 8, 1983, *Public Papers of the Presidents: Ronald Reagan: 1983* (Washington, D.C.: U.S. Government Printing Office, 1984), 364.

35. John Lewis Gaddis, *Strategies of Containment: A Critical Reappraisal of American National Security Policy during the Cold War*, rev. exp. ed. (New York: Ox-

ford University Press, 2005), 342–79; Peter Schweizer, *Reagan's War: The Epic Story of His Forty-Year Struggle and Final Triumph over Communism* (New York: Double-day, 2002), 178–219; and Paul Kengor, *The Crusader: Ronald Reagan and the Fall of Communism* (New York: Harper Perennial, 2007).

36. Paul A. Lettow, *Ronald Reagan and His Quest to Abolish Nuclear Weapons* (New York: Random House, 2005), ix.

37. Don Oberdorfer, *From the Cold War to a New Era: The United States and the Soviet Union, 1983–1991* (Baltimore: Johns Hopkins University Press, 1998 ed.); George P. Shultz, *Turmoil and Triumph: My Years as Secretary of State* (New York: Scribner, 1993), makes a similar argument.

38. Norman Podhoretz, "Reagan's Road to Détente," *Foreign Affairs: America and the World, 1984* (Winter 1985): 463.

39. John O'Sullivan, *The President, the Pope, and the Prime Minister: Three Who Changed the World* (Washington, D.C.: Regnery, 2006).

40. John Lewis Gaddis, "Hanging Tough Paid Off," *Bulletin of the Atomic Scientists* (January/February 1989): 11–14.

41. George F. Will, "The 1980s, the Suicide of Socialism, and Other Pleasures," and "5000 Reasons to Vote for George Bush," in *Suddenly: The American Ideal at Home and Abroad, 1986–1990* (New York: Free Press, 1990), 44, 293.

42. For a sample of the irreverent nature of the *Dartmouth Review*, see James Panero and Stefan Beck, *The* Dartmouth Review *Pleads Innocent: Twenty-Five Years of Being Threatened, Impugned, Vandalized, Sued, Suspended, and Bitten at the Ivy League's Most Controversial Conservative Newspaper* (Wilmington, Del.: Intercollegiate Studies Institute, 2006).

43. Nina Easton, *Gang of Five: Leaders at the Center of the Conservative Ascendancy* (New York: Simon & Schuster, 2000), 162–63.

44. Sidney Blumenthal, "Reagan Doctrine's Passionate Advocate," *Washington Post* (December 17, 1986): A1. The author can remember seeing the Adopt a Contra poster on a dorm room wall during his undergraduate years at Drake University in the 1980s.

45. Easton, *Gang of Five*, 159.

46. Sidney Blumenthal, *The Rise of the Counter-establishment: The Conservative Ascent to Political Power* (New York: Union Square, 2008).

47. Clyde Wilson, "The Conservative Identity," *The Intercollegiate Review* 21, no. 3 (Spring 1986): 6–7.

48. Gerhart Niemeyer, "Is There a Conservative Mission?" *The Intercollegiate Review* 21, no. 3 (Spring 1986): 9; and Paul Gottfried, "A View of Contemporary Conservatism," *The Intercollegiate Review* 21, no. 3 (Spring 1986): 19–20.

49. Gottfried, "View of Contemporary Conservatism," 19.

50. Paul Gottfried and Thomas Fleming, *The Conservative Movement* (Boston: Twayne, 1988), xiii.

51. Dan Himmelfarb, "Conservative Splits," *Commentary* (May 1988), reprinted in Schneider, ed., *Conservatism in America: Since 1930: A Reader* (New York: New York University Press, 2003), 383–93.

52. Irving Kristol, "What Is a Liberal? Who Is a Conservative? *Commentary* (September 1976), 74–75.

53. Reagan, "Inaugural Address, January 20, 1981," *Public Papers of the Presidents: Reagan: 1981*, reprinted in Schneider, *Conservatism in America*, 341–46.

54. Tonsor, "Why I (Too)," 54.

55. Jeffrey Hart, *The Making of the American Conservative Mind: National Review and Its Times* (Wilmington, Del.: Intercollegiate Studies Institute, 2006), 318–19.

56. William F. Buckley Jr., "In Search of Anti-Semitism," *National Review* (December 30, 1991): 20–62.

57. Joseph Sobran, "How I Was Fired by Bill Buckley," available online at www.mecfilms.com/universe/articles/fired.htm (accessed March 27, 2007).

58. Sobran, "How I Was Fired by Bill Buckley."

59. David Frum, *Dead Right* (New York: Basic, 1994), 134.

60. Sobran, "How I Was Fired by Bill Buckley."

61. "On Culture: A Conservative Manifesto," Box 19, Folder 2, Leopold Tyrmand Papers, Hoover Institution, Stanford University.

62. See E. Christian Kopff, "*Chronicles*," in Frohnen et al., eds., *American Conservatism: An Encyclopedia* (Wilmington, Del.: Intercollegiate Studies Institute, 2006), 147–49.

63. Samuel T. Francis, "Beautiful Losers: The Failure of American Conservatism," *Chronicles* (May 1991): 14–17.

64. James Burnham, *National Review* (May 12, 1972), cited in Francis, "Beautiful Losers."

65. Francis, "Beautiful Losers," 14.

66. Ronald Reagan, Diary entry from January 28, 1982, in Brinkley, ed., *The Reagan Diaries* (New York: HarperCollins, 2007), 65.

67. Francis, "Beautiful Losers," 17.

68. Francis, "Beautiful Losers," 17.

69. Patrick J. Buchanan, *A Republic, Not an Empire* (Washington, D.C.: Regnery, 1999).

70. See Kenneth J. Heineman, *God Is a Conservative: Religion, Politics, and Morality in Contemporary America* (New York: New York University Press, 1998), 166–68.

71. Heineman, *God Is a Conservative*, 177.

72. On the Bush presidency, see John Robert Greene, *The Presidency of George H. W. Bush* (Lawrence: University Press of Kansas, 1999). For a humorous take on the Bush White House from a neoconservative perspective, see John Podhoretz, *Hell of a Ride: Backstage at the White House Follies, 1989–1993* (New York: Simon & Schuster, 1993).

73. Russell Kirk, "The Neoconservatives: An Endangered Species," Heritage Lecture # 178 (December 18, 1988), available online at www.heritage.org/Research/PoliticalPhilosophy/HL178.ctm (accessed March 31, 2007).

74. Buchanan's comments cited in David Frum, "Unpatriotic Conservatives: A War Against America," *National Review* (April 7, 2003), available at www.nationalreview.com/frum/frum031903.htm (accessed Jan 1, 2007).

75. Joshua Muravchik, "Buchanan and the Jews," *Commentary* (January 1991): 29–37.

76. Fred Barnes, quoted in Howard Kurtz, "Pat Buchanan and the Jewish Question," *Washington Post* (September 20, 1991), style section. Barnes was Buchanan's colleague on the television program *The McLaughlin Group* and has since become a leading advocate of neoconservative positions regarding the Iraq War and a champion of "big government conservatism."

77. Jeffrey Hart, "Gang Warfare in Chicago," *National Review* (June 6, 1986): 33.

78. Tim W. Ferguson, "Free to Do What?—Meeting of the Philadelphia Society and the Future of Conservatism," *National Review* (July 20, 1992).

Chapter Seven

Between Principles and Politics

My friends, this election is about more than who gets what. It is about who we are. It is about what we believe. It is about what we stand for as Americans. There is a religious war going on in this country for the soul of America. It is a cultural war as critical to the kind of nation we shall be as the Cold War itself.

—Patrick Buchanan, 1992 Republican National Committee

Robert Bork was frustrated. A well-qualified legal scholar and judge with an impressive academic record, he was nominated by Ronald Reagan to a Supreme Court vacancy in 1987. After a contentious fight in Senate Judiciary Committee hearings concerning his views of "original understanding" of the Constitution, Bork was rejected by the Senate. Bork left his Washington Court of Appeals judgeship a year later and joined the American Enterprise Institute in Washington; there, he wrote a blistering attack on the judicial nomination process, *The Tempting of America* (1990). He described how judges should interpret the Constitution based on a law's meaning at the time of its enactment. Any additional changes in statute law must be made by legislators, not by judges. Bork wrote, "A judge who announces a decision must be able to demonstrate that he began from recognized legal principles and reasoned in an intellectually coherent and politically neutral way. . . . Those who would politicize the law offer the public, and the judiciary, the temptation of results without regard to democratic legitimacy."[1]

The issue of judicial activism and judicial restraint festered throughout the 1990s. Reagan had made significant conservative appointments to the federal courts, yet the courts remained havens of activism, with justices routinely legislating from the bench. One 1996 Supreme Court case, *Romer v. Evans*, stood out for many conservatives as an example of the High Court's conduct in this regard. In *Romer* the Court decided that a Colorado referendum—passed in 1993 by a majority of Colorado's citizens—was unconstitutional. The referendum in question involved homosexuality and the denial of preferential rights for homosexuals under the state's Constitution (homosexuals were not discriminated against under Colorado law—the intention of the referendum was to deny them rights as a protected class under federal civil rights law). The Court struck down the referendum, ruling that the issue in question "make[s] them [homosexuals] unequal to everyone else" even though the wording in the referendum clearly recognized no discriminatory intent.[2]

Justice Antonin Scalia wrote in dissent, "The Court had mistaken a Kulturkampf for a fit of spite. The constitutional amendment before us here is not the manifestation of a 'desire to harm homosexuals' . . . but is rather a modest attempt by seemingly tolerant Coloradans to preserve traditional sexual mores against the efforts of a politically powerful minority to revise those mores through the use of laws. That objective, and the means chosen to achieve it, are not only unimpeachable under any constitutional doctrine hitherto pronounced; . . . They have been specifically approved by the Congress of the United States and by this Court in an earlier decision." (*Bowers v. Hardwick*, 1986). In a later opinion echoing his frustration with his colleagues Scalia wrote, "day by day, case by case, [the Court] is busy designing a Constitution for a country I do not recognize."[3]

The conservative journal *First Things* ran a symposium on the question of judicial activism in its November 1996 issue. Edited by Richard John Neuhaus, a former liberal Lutheran minister turned Catholic priest, *First Things* was formed in March 1990, dedicated to a vigorous discussion of "religion and public life." "At the heart of culture is religion," Neuhaus wrote; the journal's editors sought to take back the "naked public square."[4]

Neuhaus was a civil rights leader in his Brooklyn pastorate in the Bedford-Stuyvesant neighborhood during the 1960s and had been equally active in the anti–Vietnam War movement. Neuhaus moved to the Right by the 1980s over the issue of religion—he helped form the Institute on Religion and Democracy, which kept watch on the liberal National Council of Churches. In 1984 Neuhaus became the director of the Center on Religion and Society. Headquartered in New York, Neuhaus received his funding from the Rockford Institute and published a newsletter and quarterly journal, *This World*. In 1989 Neuhaus had a falling out with Rockford directors over their views on immigration, leading to a purported "raid" on Neuhaus's office in New York and the padlocking of the door. A year later, with funding secured from other foundations, Neuhaus formed the Institute on Religion and Public Life and began publication of *First Things*.[5]

In the introduction to the "End of Democracy?" symposium, Neuhaus addressed "whether we have reached or are reaching the point where conscientious citizens can no longer give moral assent to the existing regime." He started the discussion with the amazingly radical proposition that "the government of the United States of America no longer governs by the consent of the governed. With respect to the American people, the judiciary has in effect declared that the most important questions about how we ought to order our life together are outside the purview of 'things of their knowledge.'" "What is happening now is the displacement of a constitutional order by a regime that does not have, will not obtain, and cannot command the consent of the people," he concluded.[6]

For conservatives to speak in an idiom employing terms like "regime" and "moral assent" sparked concern about whether the participants endorsed the views of radical antiabortionists who advocated—in a truly John Brown–like manner—violence against abortion providers and the bombing of clinics to highlight the immorality of abortion. Norman Podhoretz raised this point, calling the symposium "dangerous extremism" and telling the editors that "I did not become a conservative in order to become a radical, let alone to support the preaching of revolution against this country." Podhoretz also pointedly criticized Neuhaus for raising similar questions once raised by the Left during the Vietnam era: if the war was illegitimate, as terrorist groups like the Weathermen once claimed, then only revolution and violence could stop it. Was this what Neuhaus was advocating? Podhoretz was shocked: "Fast approaching the age of seventy," he wrote, "I was too old to find a new political home."[7]

Podhoretz did not have to worry. The symposium failed to impact the debate in Washington over these issues. Even though many conservatives felt similarly that the judicial branch was out of control, there was little to be done since Democrat Bill Clinton was president. Conservatives were deeply pessimistic about the culture and believed that civilization was collapsing around them. Who was to blame? For many conservatives it was the fault of the American people, who could no longer tell right from wrong, who were conditioned to believe that the quest for materialist values trumped the quest for spiritual ones. Recapturing the empty public square for religious values— especially Christian ones—became the task of a network of conservative activists, politicians, and intellectuals, dubbed theoconservatives by journalists like Andrew Sullivan. They have impacted conservatism by the end of the century, but it turned out that like the Moral Majority and Christian Coalition before them, theocons could not provide the emperor's naked public square with new religious clothes.

MASS MEDIA AND THE GINGRICH REVOLUTION

One of the most unheralded accomplishments of the Reagan years was the decision made in 1987 by the Federal Communications Commission (FCC), established by the New Deal in the 1930s, to abolish the fairness doctrine. The Supreme Court had ruled that the doctrine—which stipulated that broadcasters provide "equal time" during coverage of political events or discussion—was not a law, but rather a regulation, freeing the FCC to get rid of it. Equal time provisions meant that anytime media was used to propagate what was seen as political speech, the other side had a chance to respond. The doctrine itself was sloppy and bifurcated political speech—weren't there more than two sides to an issue? With the equal time provision ended, talk radio helped catapult conservatives to the forefront of control over the nation's AM airwaves.

A year after that decision Rush Limbaugh, a former disc jockey and college dropout born in 1951 in Cape Girardeau, Missouri, began a national radio talk show that quickly came to dominate the ratings in the low-rated afternoon AM radio time slot. Limbaugh quickly became a dominant force not only in propagating a conservative message over the airwaves, but also a huge figure in radio as a whole. According to the ratings group Arbitron, in 2005 the Rush Limbaugh radio show drew over 13.5 million listeners, making it the highest rated daytime radio program in the country. Limbaugh's program was on for three hours a day. He discussed a conservatism that was unabashedly free market, traditionalist, and muscular when it came to using American military power. Limbaugh later defined his conservatism in a *Wall Street Journal* editorial: "we [conservatives] believe in individual liberty, limited government, capitalism, the rule of law, faith, a color-blind society, and national security."[8]

Limbaugh articulated a conservative Republican philosophy that had become a dominant part of American politics by the 1990s. Scornful of liberals and Democrats, Limbaugh castigated his opponents cleverly and wittily, defending conservatives and Republicans. His program helped make the careers of conservative politicians like Newt Gingrich, who praised Limbaugh by saying that "Rush has made it significantly more expensive to be liberal and significantly easier to be conservative. . . . He does for conservatives what National Public Radio does for liberals."[9] It was hard to argue with such a statement and the talk radio revolution that Limbaugh helped engender. Bill Clinton later said it best in frustration: "after I get off the radio with you today, Rush Limbaugh will have three hours to say whatever he wants, and I won't have an opportunity to respond, and there's no truth detector."[10] If a president could complain so vehemently that he had less rhetorical power than a radio talk show host, his complaint went a long way toward showcasing the power of Limbaugh's program and the impact it had on American politics.

One of the beneficiaries of the shift in American politics was Newt Gingrich. He became the leader of a new breed of Republican politicians more combative than an earlier generation and more interested in taking and holding onto power. Gingrich, a history professor with a PhD in Modern European history from Tulane, had taught at the University of West Georgia. Not in a tenure-track position, he looked for a way out of academia and found his niche in politics, finally winning election to Congress from his suburban Atlanta district in 1978 (he had tried two years earlier and had been unsuccessful). Gingrich was representative of the new breed of Southern Republicans coming into power and influence during the 1980s and 1990s. A Republican since he was nine years old, he helped form a Young Republicans chapter at Emory University in the 1960s and was always opposed to the "forces of corruption, racism and one-party rule" that had defined segregationist Democratic Southern politics. He supported New York Governor Nelson Rockefeller in the 1968 GOP primaries and was active supporting him until the mid-1970s, when he disavowed his liberal Republican views and moved to the Right.[11]

Gingrich was ambitious and he sought to make the Republican Party a majority party by organizing a takeover of Congress. "The Congress in the long run can change the country more dramatically than the president," he said, a statement the historian in Gingrich should have been more careful in making given the course of twentieth-century American history.[12] Gingrich persevered and formed the Conservative Opportunity Society in 1982, a political organization designed to enhance his role in the party and to propagate for conservative ideas, especially ideas having to do with the reform of the welfare state and taxes.

Throughout the 1980s Gingrich used televised coverage of Congress—C-Span, founded in 1979 and broadcast into every cable television subscriber's home—to attack the Democratic leadership. Democrats had controlled the House of Representatives since 1954 and had become an obstacle to Reagan's foreign and domestic policies. Seizing on the opportunity televised coverage of Congress provided, Gingrich accused House Democrats of appeasement over their lack of support for Reagan's foreign policy. He accused the Democrats of having a "pessimistic, defeatist and skeptical view toward the American role in the world" and challenged them to make a response. A few days later House Speaker Thomas "Tip" O'Neill, an old liberal from Massachusetts, broke House rules on personal attacks when he responded: "you deliberately stood in the well before an empty House and challenged these people and you challenged their Americanism! It's un-American! It's the lowest thing I've heard in my 32 years here!" When Gingrich spoke no one was in the room, but as Lee Edwards concluded, his "target had always been the living room, not the House floor."[13]

Gingrich received encouragement from the Reagan White House and from other like-minded Republicans. Congressmen Vin Weber (Minn.), Dick Cheney (Wyo.) and Jack Kemp (N.Y.), as well as Senator Trent Lott (Miss.), encouraged Gingrich in his actions. A few years later Pete DuPont turned over control of his defunct political action committee, GOPAC, to Gingrich, allowing the young congressman to build cadres of activists, to select candidates to run for office, and to travel throughout the country on their behalf. By the 1994 Republican takeover of Congress GOPAC had spent $8 million on mobilizing conservatives to challenge the entrenched Democratic Congress. GOPAC was, as Gingrich himself later argued, "the Bell Labs of GOP politics."[14]

Gingrich was a baby boomer, a generation that was more confrontational in its politics than their predecessors in Congress. Republicans of an earlier generation, such as House Minority Leader Robert Michel (Ill.) and Senate Minority Leader Bob Dole (Kans.) were men of compromise who worked with Democrats to secure the best deal possible on legislation. Gingrich and his younger cohorts often refused to play ball. Politics for them was "blood sport," more confrontational and contentious—no different than the manner in which leading baby boomer liberals saw the game. But it struck the older generation as ineffective and contributed to a growing divide and paralysis in Congress over political ideology.

1992: PRELUDE

Before Gingrich could bring about his political revolution, he would need to deal with the Democrat baby boomer elected to the presidency in 1992, Arkansas Governor Bill Clinton. Clinton's election was owed to rising dissatisfaction in American politics, both with the Democratic Congress—embroiled in scandal after forty years of control over the House—and the failure of the Bush White House to deal effectively with a minor recession.

Bush had squandered huge popular support in the year after the defeat of Iraq's armies in the Gulf War, neglecting domestic policy in favor of a continued focus on foreign policy. While liberals assaulted Bush for his callousness toward the jobless in what was one of the most minor and short-lived recessions of the post–World War II era, conservatives, on the other hand, roundly condemned him for being too active. To deal with mounting budget deficits compounded by the federal bailout of collapsed deregulated savings and loans, Bush agreed to a tax increase after promising at the 1988 GOP convention that he would not raise taxes. "Read my lips," he told the nation, "no new taxes." The increased taxes worked against economic recovery. He also agreed to new regulations like the Americans with Disabilities Act, forcing businesses and government to spend billions of dollars to provide equal accommodations and access to public and private facilities for disabled Americans.[15]

An equal part of dissatisfaction in 1992 was due to a lingering sense that America had become a sick society, victimized by drugs, crime, homicide, poverty, disease, and racism. Crime had accelerated during the 1980s, the climax of a thirty-year upward trend in violent crimes; especially vulnerable were the primarily minority residents of the inner cities as the crack cocaine epidemic reached its apex. The AIDS crisis, which had claimed close to 200,000 lives by 1990, as well as the perception that the Reagan administration had ignored it due to its victims being predominantly gay males, caused political problems for conservatives. Jerry Falwell commented on the immoral lifestyles of gay males: "AIDS and syphilis and all sexually transmitted diseases are God's judgment upon the total society for embracing what God has condemned: sex outside of marriage." Pat Buchanan mocked "the poor homosexuals. They have declared war on nature and now nature is exalting an awful retribution."[16]

Few conservatives were that extreme in their rhetoric, including Ronald Reagan. Critics claimed Reagan was indifferent to AIDS. They blamed him for not using the bully pulpit of the presidency to speak out about the disease until 1987; in fact, he spoke about it in 1985 when responding to a question about AIDS research. According to the nonpartisan Congressional Research Service the Reagan administration spent more than $5 billion on AIDS research during his presidency.[17] Activist groups such as ACT-UP and Queer Nation believed it wasn't enough money and blamed Reagan for his hostility toward the homosexual community. As former Reagan speechwriter Peter Robinson said, "of course, people will say that it wasn't enough. But, of course, that's the kind of argument that takes place over every item in the federal budget." Former Reagan aide Martin Anderson defused the other notion, that Reagan was hostile to homosexuals: "I remember Reagan telling us that in Hollywood he knew a lot of gays, and he never had any problem with them."[18] But the perception lingered that conservatives were indifferent to the human cost of AIDS, even after prominent conservatives, such as Terry Dolan, the head of the National Conservative Political Action Committee, succumbed to the disease. AIDS knew no ideological boundaries.

When responding to problems like AIDS conservatives continued to emphasize individual responsibility. In part that was Buchanan's point, harshly expressed. But conservative Christians continued to fight against the teaching of sex education in schools, opposed distributing latex condoms at schools— instead they preached abstinence and a growing number of teenagers began to take up the pledge to abstain from sex before marriage. Throughout the 1990s Christian conservatives became more important than ever before within the GOP coalition. Pat Robertson's run for the presidency in 1988 had sparked an increased political activism on the part of Christians. The Christian Coalition, formed by Robertson after the election and headed up by Ralph Reed, became an important political action committee. Equally important was James Dobson's Focus on the Family, an organization founded by the Christian psychiatrist-minister in the 1980s but now with added clout due to the establishment of the Family Research Council, a pro-family organization headquartered in Washington. Throughout the 1990s Republican politicians were responsive to the growing concerns of Christians, so much so that they became an indispensible part of the Republican coalition.

Conservatives preached individual responsibility in the solution of many other social problems. Libertarian author Charles Murray, for instance, had argued in *Losing Ground: American Social Policy, 1950–1980* (1984) about the negative impact of welfare and government programs on the plight of the urban poor. Murray discussed how government intervention had made the problem of poverty worse, an argument conservatives had long advanced. The ideal of equality of result rather than equality of opportunity had been the great contribution of liberalism and the evidence existed that such a philosophy did not work. "Billions for equal opportunity, not one cent for equal outcomes," Murray wrote. "Some people are better than others. They deserve more of society's rewards, of which money is only one small part. . . . Government cannot identify the worthy, but it can protect a society in which the worthy can identify themselves."[19]

Returning the poor to being rational actors in a competitive system, rather than dependents in a system concocted by government bureaucrats was Murray's main point. "The first effect of the new rules was to make it profitable for the poor to behave in the short term in ways that were destructive in the long term," Murray wrote. "We tried to provide more for the poor and produced more poor instead. We tried to remove the barriers to escape from poverty, and inadvertently built a trap."[20]

A decade later Murray went further in his argument about poverty and its causes. In *The Bell Curve* (1994), coauthored with Harvard social scientist Richard Herrnstein (who died soon after the book's publication) the authors claimed that intelligence quotient (IQ) scores were directly related to who got ahead in American life and to who did not. More often than not, the authors claimed, those scores were genetically and racially determined. Their main argument was that a growing divide threatened American life in the future. Those groups and individuals with higher IQs would have tremendous advantages in life while those without would not. They also specified that specific racial groups had higher IQs (such as Ashkenazi Jews and East Asians) while other racial groups had lower IQs (such as many European whites and African Americans). In a *New York Times* article Murray sounded like nineteenth-century social Darwinist Herbert Spencer when he questioned whether teaching some of the mentally disadvantaged would be a net loss to society: "for many people, there is nothing they can learn that will repay the cost of teaching."[21]

Reaction from the political Left was harsh. Murray wrote about it in an article published in *Commentary* in October 1995 entitled "The Bell Curve and Its Critics." Murray and Herrnstein were depicted as racists for raising the issue of measuring the psychometric characteristics of racial groups. They were against the egalitarian nature of society by even raising the idea that some groups can't be taught. But they also raised a completely egalitarian principle as well: was America becoming a society where a small oligarchy of intelligent and powerful people dominated at the expense of the unintelligent? Murray argued that they wanted a society where individuals—in spite of their intelligence (or lack of it)—could play certain roles. In essence the authors of *The Bell Curve* were challenging the very unequal society preferred by elites who controlled social policy. They raised important issues about IQ that continue to be debated today.[22]

Conservatives offered other policy proposals designed to help fix a host of social problems. They recommended tougher prosecutions of crime, including stiffer sentences for drug users. In the early 1980s James Q. Wilson promoted the theory of "broken windows," an idea that recommended that if cities let property decay, then respect for property, and property crimes, worsened. Since the 1960s conservatives associated with the journal *The Public Interest* had diagnosed the problems associated with Aid to Families with Dependent Children (AFDC) and had urged experiments to promote programs designed to move dependent women and children from poverty to opportunity. Murray's diagnosis sped up the process. In 1993 conservative Wisconsin Governor Tommy Thompson experimented with welfare reform ideas that became a model for the federal program—signed by Bill Clinton into law in 1996—to end the AFDC system and to encourage welfare recipients to return to work.[23]

Economist Milton Friedman recommended school vouchers for parents of children living in failed school districts (allowing the parents money for their children to attend private schools—even parochial and religious schools—and opting out of the public school system). Vouchers were unpopular with educational interest groups and teachers' unions, yet libertarian activist Clint Bolick prevailed on city officials in Milwaukee to start a program in the early 1990s. Homeschooling, illegal in the 1980s, blossomed as well. Many parents removed their children from public education altogether. The homeschool movement was driven by evangelical Christian parents who opted out of the system and formed their own homeschool networks of parents and churches.[24]

Conservative legislators, at both the state and federal level, relied on prominent think tanks to make their case for reform. Various state think tanks developed during the 1990s as the federalist system promoted such experimentation at the state level. One of the most successful state think tanks was Michigan's Mackinac Center for Public Policy, which started in 1987 as a one-man operation located behind a pizza shop in Midland, Michigan.

Founded by the indefatigably optimistic Lawrence Reed—known as the "Johnny Appleseed" of libertarianism—the former academic-turned-think-tank-executive helped turn Mackinac into the most prominent state think tank in the country, with a budget of $4 million and a staff of thirty-two policy scholars in 2006. Reed promoted school choice, privatization of government services (like garbage collection), and tax reform, earning him enemies like organized labor in heavily unionized Michigan. One of his most important contributions was helping educate other individuals and groups on how to establish their own think tanks and policy institutes. By the end of the century there were forty-eight state-based conservative or libertarian think tanks in the country, and many of them sent representatives to biannual weekend workshops at Mackinac educating the participants on how to run a think tank. State-level think tanks have a network of support from various foundations and a coordinated council—the State Policy Network—which keeps the focus on the activities and supplies grants to coordinate activities. Liberal and radical groups lacked comparable organizations.[25]

Nevertheless, despite the argument that conservatives wanted to help the poor escape the confines of government dependency, whether in substandard inner-city public school districts or in the confines of female dependence on welfare, a plethora of arguments were employed against those who recommended ending such programs. If welfare were ended, for instance, "there would be a rise in homelessness, a lot more hunger and a lot more despair," said Washington-based advocate Robert Greenstein.[26] The argument about vouchers and school choice was greeted with hostility from the National Education Association and from education administrators who were threatened by such reforms. A politics of racial grievance rocked American culture, as many of the reforms advocated by conservative policy experts were aimed at the problems faced by inner-city African Americans. African American leaders attacked the conservatives as seeking to undermine the civil rights gains in America and reverse the progress made since the 1960s. It was difficult for conservatives to challenge these views.

The politics of grievance and racial resentment boiled over in 1992. The beating by the Los Angeles police of drug-addicted motorist Rodney King in March 1991—the incident was taped and broadcast widely—and the consequent acquittal of those police officers by a white jury in suburban Simi Valley, led to four days of riots in Los Angeles in April 1992, as predominantly black and Hispanic youths attacked Korean-owned businesses and assaulted whites in broad daylight, doing millions of dollars of property damage and leading to the deaths of fifty-two people. Republican Governor Pete Wilson was forced to request federal help to put down the riots.

While an investigation into the riots followed and much of the blame was again placed on poverty and the hopelessness of urban young people—mimicking investigations into the causes of "civic disorder" after riots in the 1960s—many Americans refused to accept such conclusions. The riots were televised live on CNN; Korean store owners who were targeted were not part of the white power structure, but rather immigrants—typically well-educated immigrants—trying to achieve the American dream. While a massive infusion of money and assistance into inner-city Los Angeles followed after the riots, the behavior of thousands of rioting young people was now viewed in criminal terms, not as an excuse for poverty.

CLINTON AND CONSERVATIVES

Clinton tapped into this growing dissatisfaction far better than any other candidate that year. He ran in the Democratic primaries as a political moderate, castigating his opponents for appeasing Left-wing cultural radicals who had moved the party so far away from its roots in the postwar era. Clinton had plenty of skeletons in his closet that dogged him through primary season, particularly womanizing, draft dodging, and smoking marijuana. But he successfully dodged the allegations and benefited from being the leader of the Democratic Leadership Council (DLC). The DLC was formed in 1985 to deal with the declining electoral fortunes of the party and to restore the moderate Democratic label to prominence within the party. It was composed of mainly Southern Democrats (Jesse Jackson mocked it as "Democrats for the Leisure Class"). The long search for one of their own to lead the party back toward the center culminated with Clinton's nomination.[27]

Clinton spoke "values talk," discussing the importance of a two-parent family—one of the reasons he supported time limitations for welfare recipients. He discussed religion as an important factor in society. Most importantly, Clinton was unafraid to speak out against those, such as Jesse Jackson, who excused individual misbehavior and blamed all the ills of America on race. After the LA riots female rap star Sistah Souljah was quoted as saying, "if black people kill black people every day, why not have a week and kill white people?" Clinton responded at Jackson's Rainbow Coalition convention when he stated, "if you took the words 'white' and 'black' and reversed them, you might think David Duke was giving that speech." Jackson was not happy but later came to be one of Clinton's biggest supporters and defenders.

Clinton also tapped into dissatisfaction over the economy and blamed it on a "decade of greed," arguing that he would contribute to a rejuvenation of the middle class in America. He turned a minor recession in his rhetoric into the Great Depression and put Bush on the defensive the entire campaign. "It's the Economy, Stupid," was the refrain from Clinton's "War Room," political advisors James Carville, George Stephanopolous, Dee Dee Meyers, and Paul Begala, who made (too) much of the recession and equally slow recovery. To help, he promised a mishmash of policies such as a middle-class tax cut (which he reneged on once in office) and job training programs.[28]

Clinton's targeting of the economy and of the Reagan years pushed *National Review* to dedicate an entire issue in August 1992 to "The Real Reagan Record." *NR*'s economics analyst Ed Rubinstein wrote, "Ronald Reagan inherited an economy that was in the midst of its worst crisis since the Great Depression. In January 1981 the unemployment rate stood at 7.4 percent, on its way up to 10 percent. . . . Two years into Ronald Reagan's Presidency the economy began to recover. By most conventional indices the recovery was strong and sustained, outlasting Mr. Reagan's Presidency by nearly two years." *National Review* assembled strong data to showcase the rise in real incomes that occurred, home ownership rates, and lower taxes. It did little to assuage the voters.[29] Using the economy as his main issue, Clinton defeated Bush and independent candidate H. Ross Perot to win the presidency.

Despite Clinton's interest in values talk, his first year in the White House followed the prototypical liberal script. There were problems in his desire to secure a Cabinet that "looked just like America." He nominated three women to be attorney general before the third, Janet Reno, was confirmed by the Senate (the first two had problems with not paying their foreign nannies Social Security). There was a flap over gays serving in the military, which Clinton raised early in his first year after saying in the campaign he did not condone gays serving in the military. The compromise position, "Don't Ask, Don't Tell" pleased no one. Clinton raised personal income taxes as well, using the budget deficits of the Reagan-Bush years as an excuse to do so (after having promised a middle-class tax cut during the campaign). Finally, there was the effort to create a huge new governmental health care plan that would create a single-payer system modeled on those of Europe and Canada. "Hillary Care," as it was called, after his wife Hillary Rodham Clinton, who headed up the effort, floundered and never reached the Democratic Congress or even a congressional committee for a vote. Part of the reaction against Hillary Care was fueled by the conservative media, including Limbaugh, as well as the think tanks and other institutions conservatives had created over the previous twenty years.[30]

GINGRICH REVOLUTION

The result was the Gingrich revolution, the Republican takeover of Congress in the 1994 midterm elections. The GOP had won control of both houses of Congress for the first time in forty years. As Clinton pollsters Mark Penn and Douglas Schoen explained, "the 1994 midterm election was a complete rejection of what the Democratic Party had come to represent—bigger government, more taxes, higher spending, more bureaucracy."[31] Gingrich had turned what were essentially local election contests for Congress into referenda on the Democratic Party and Bill Clinton. Gingrich created the Contract with America, a brilliant political strategy—tested in focus groups and polls by Republican pollster Frank Luntz—to link the fortunes of Republicans running in local races to a national program. The Contract was focused on congressional reform after "forty years of one-party rule." Signers pledged themselves on the first day of the 104th Congress to cut the number of House committees and staff, make laws passed by Congress binding on Congress, conduct an audit of Congress, have a three-fifths rule to pass tax increases, and to require public openness for committee meetings. It also committed those who signed to support tax reform, a balanced budget, welfare reform, Social Security reforms, and other pro-family initiatives.[32] It was a centrist conservative document, not straying too far from the margins of debate and recapturing for the GOP the leadership ideals associated with Reagan by the American public.

It worked splendidly. The Republicans gained fifty-four seats in the House (seventy-three freshmen were elected that year) and did extremely well with white male voters and those disaffected by Clinton. Evangelical Christians also strongly supported the GOP, with Clinton's scandals being a prime cause of their dissatisfaction with the Southern Baptist president. House Speaker Thomas Foley was defeated for reelection, as was the powerful chairman of the House Ways and Means Committee Illinois Congressman Dan Rostenkowski. In the Senate the GOP picked up eight seats, to take control of that body for the first time since 1986. With Gingrich in charge as speaker of the House, the Republicans claimed a revolution and used the first hundred days of the new Congress to pass their Contract with America.

In the first year of the new Congress the Republican revolutionaries acted with a political fervency not seen in Washington in some time. Not only did they follow through with the passage of every aspect of the Contract with America, but they set out to constrain spending, battling with Clinton over a budget proposed by the Congress that would have slashed $1 trillion in federal spending and balanced the budget in seven years. The Democrats and many Republicans were convinced the budget would affect the poor and hurt the elderly (most of spending reductions came from eliminating fraud and waste in Medicare). Clinton refused to sign the budget and then refused to sign continuing resolutions that would keep the federal government open for business. The impasse led to two government shutdowns in November and December of 1995.

Gingrich and the GOP leadership in the House and Senate blinked first. The freshmen who believed they were elected to fulfill the promise of reform made to voters intended to play hardball, without worrying about the consequences politically. South Carolina Representative Lindsey Graham said, "if we don't hold the line here Clinton's back in the ball game. This is critically important. Don't give in now." Representative Tom Coburn from Oklahoma told Gingrich it was like negotiating with a labor union official: "you never give an indication of what you might do and you never ever back down."[33] But Gingrich, pressured by moderate Republicans like Bob Dole, did back down. The Republican leadership caved in to Clinton and the government reopened. Representative Steve Largent, a conservative from Oklahoma and former NFL star wide receiver, recalled how the Gingrich revolution ended: "the shutdown revealed the weakness in our armor. Clinton never failed to exploit that weakness."[34]

Revolutions rarely succeed in accomplishing everything the revolutionaries want to accomplish, but it was clear from the failure to control spending that the Republican freshmen of 1994—many of whom promised to limit their terms in office—met their match in both Clinton and in the typical "career congressman." The GOP leadership never again made budget fights a priority, engaging in an orgy of discretionary spending since 1996 unbefitting limited-government conservatives. While Congress still accomplished some major initiatives, ending welfare with Clinton's signing of the Personal Responsibility Act of 1996 and eventually achieving a balanced budget, Clinton—improbably—won reelection, moving to the center and triangulating the Republicans by taking away their initiatives. Republican presidential candidate Bob Dole had little chance to defeat Clinton, who won reelection with only 49 percent of the popular vote.

The resulting developments in Clinton's second term were not favorable to conservatism as it had developed politically since the days of Barry Goldwater. In political terms conservatism reached a high point by the mid-1990s. But it was a conservatism more connected to the mainstream of the Republican Party than at any other point in its history. And not all Republicans accepted conservative principles when it came to limiting government and lowering taxes. Conservative Republicans shaped policies like never before but they were also captives of Washington special interests and indifferent to continuing the revolution.[35]

Gingrich was one of them. Reelected narrowly as speaker, and nearly ousted as speaker in a coup led by Tom DeLay, he made a deal with Clinton to secure a balanced budget that increased spending significantly, in return for a $500 child tax credit. By 1998 he had been outwitted and outfoxed by Clinton; not even Clinton's impeachment could prevent Gingrich from giving up office first—he resigned from Congress in November 1998 owing to an ethics probe into a book deal he had signed; ironically it was the same issue that Gingrich had employed successfully to oust Democrat Speaker Jim Wright seven years earlier.

Conservatives were caught between principles and politics unlike at any time in the century. Most conservatives supported the efforts to investigate Clinton's conduct before he became president—the Whitewater land scandal—and were driven to undermine the president through investigations into corruption within the Clinton presidency. *The American Spectator* played the largest role in these investigations, sending reporter David Brock to Arkansas to investigate Clinton, whom editor R. Emmett Tyrrell referred to as the "boy president." Brock subsequently recanted his role in the "Arkansas Project" in a memoir entitled *Blinded by the Right* (2001), recounting how he made up information in his articles and was pressured to do so by the editors of the magazine. None of his charges have ever been corroborated and the magazine did expose several important facts: that, as governor Clinton had used Arkansas state troopers to solicit women for him and that one of these women—whom the magazine inadvertently outed, named "Paula"—was a victim of sexual harassment when the president exposed himself to her in a hotel room. The woman, Paula Jones, later successfully sued the president. It was from his deposition in this criminal case—and his lies to the grand jury investigating it—that the roots of the Monica Lewinsky scandal arose.[36]

Discovered by *Newsweek* in early 1998—resulting from inside information from federal employee Linda Tripp and her friend Lucianne Goldberg—the Lewinsky scandal was investigated by Whitewater Special Prosecutor Kenneth Starr, including depositions of the president, a DNA test of Clinton to see if it matched a semen stain on Lewinsky's blue dress, and a circus style atmosphere of who slept with whom and when. Starr released a highly detailed report of the shenanigans to the public in the fall of 1998, which was lurid in its details and caused the public to feel sympathetic toward the president. With public opinion on Clinton's side, the GOP Congress nevertheless impeached Clinton on four counts, including perjury and suborning perjury; Clinton was tried by the Senate in November 1998 and acquitted. The Clinton political team, including the First Lady, called the investigation the result of a "vast right-wing conspiracy." Delays in Starr's investigation, especially a deposition of Lewinsky, hurt his case and allowed the Clinton political team to use the media effectively to turn the investigation against the investigators.[37] There were willing co-conspirators, such as feminists, who decided that a president who supported abortion rights trumped one who sexually harassed an intern, a far cry from their position only seven years earlier when Bush Supreme Court nominee Clarence Thomas was grilled in Senate hearings for alleged—and far less serious—improprieties against a staff member, Anita Hill.[38]

The American people may have been upset by the behavior of Clinton but were more alarmed by the misbehavior of Republicans in the impeachment of the president. Impeaching Clinton never had the support of the public and the GOP leadership defied public opinion when they impeached and tried the president. This prompted William Bennett to write, in *The Death of Outrage* (1999), how Americans had become completely bamboozled by Clinton's lack of remorse for his behavior and what this meant for American democracy. "It is said that private character has virtually no impact on governing character. . . . These arguments define us down; they assume a lower common denominator of behavior and leadership than we Americans ought to accept."[39] Bennett did not explore the roots of this decline—he had already done this in a 1992 memoir, *The De-valuing of America*, and a 1993 Heritage Foundation report, *The Index of Leading Cultural Indicators*, which reported on the high rates of out-of-wedlock births, high numbers of divorces, and growing drug and criminal problems.[40] Many Americans seemed to share the dysfunction of the president and could relate to it, a postmodern condition where instead of wanting the best from our leaders, people seemed to think they should be more like us, human and flawed in every way, a diagnosis of the sclerosis of democracy and leadership Irving Babbitt had made in the 1920s. Bennett should not have been surprised by the culture's indifference to the sexual affairs of the president (indeed, his own brother served as Clinton's attorney).

ALL PUNDITS, ALL THE TIME

The Gingrich revolution and the impeachment of Clinton allowed for the development of a new punditry on the Right linking conservatism in the public mind with individuals who were brash and controversial. Ann Coulter, a tall intelligent blond lawyer who comedian Bill Maher called "conservatism's diva," moved into the top ranks of conservative punditry with wicked assaults on liberalism. Her first book, *High Crimes and Misdemeanors* (1999), was a best seller and wittily covered the lies of Clinton (and her role in uncovering them) during impeachment. Her syndicated column and appearances on Fox News and other media outlets made her uniquely positioned to give a conservative gloss to the typical news reports about contemporary events. Gifted in her talent for bromidic verbal ripostes, Coulter shocked many audiences when she labeled liberals as traitors in one book and assaulted (often righteously, to young conservatives raised on a steady diet of political correctness) the hypocrisy of liberal policy makers and pundits.

Coulter and many other pundits owed quite a bit of their growing celebrity and recognition to the Fox News Channel, a cable television channel founded by Australian media mogul Rupert Murdoch in 1996. Fox was headed up by Roger Ailes, a conservative speechwriter for Bush who had worked on many political campaigns. It quickly displaced CNN as the most watched political news station and it made the careers of many ostensibly conservative news reporters and television personalities, such as Sean Hannity and Bill O'Reilly. But Fox followed a script featuring mainstream GOP positions on conservative issues ranging from abortion to impeachment to foreign policy to immigration. Further, it featured conservative politicians and pundits and not conservative intellectuals. Increasingly, it was also driven by a younger generation of neoconservative commentators who were given air time because of the links with Murdoch's other ventures in media, the journal of opinion *The Weekly Standard*.

The Weekly Standard soon became the bellwether for neoconservative journalism. It was a tightly edited and well-written publication specializing in reporting on policy and politics from inside the GOP revolution. Founded in October 1995 it was edited by William Kristol, the son of Irving Kristol and prominent historian Gertrude Himmelfarb. Kristol held a PhD in political theory from Harvard and taught at the Kennedy School of Government before entering public service as assistant secretary of education under William Bennett. He then served as a chief of staff to Vice President Dan Quayle. In 1993 he received $1.3 million in grants to establish the Committee for the Republican Future, becoming the "faxer-in-chief" of the Gingrich revolution. Along with cohorts such as David Tell, Kristol bombarded the GOP with memos outlining a victory strategy for elections. With the Gingrich revolution secured, he used his connections with Rupert Murdoch to get him to fund the *Standard*.[41]

The Weekly Standard influenced the direction of conservatism in a more substantive way than any publication since Buckley's *National Review* in the mid-1950s. Like Buckley's magazine it saw its role as promoting a new conservatism, one combining an expanded role for American power in the world, cultural modernism, an elite view of politics (it disdained conservative populism), and, by the beginning of the new century, the creation of a "national greatness conservatism" that had more in common with the conservatism of Theodore Roosevelt than with that of Ronald Reagan or Barry Goldwater. Kristol brought Fred Barnes over from rival *The New Republic*; David Brooks, John Podhoretz, and David Tell also served as editors of the magazine.

NEOCONS VERSUS PALEOCONS

Kristol was influenced during his graduate school career by the writings of Leo Strauss. Strauss has become a controversial figure on the American Right. A brilliant political theorist and teacher at the University of Chicago until his death in 1973, the German born Jewish Strauss—who fled the Nazis to come to America in the 1930s—became a popular professor at the South Side Chicago school. "Strauss didn't have students," Milton Himmelfarb wrote, "he had disciples."[42] Strauss's most important contribution to political theory was *Natural Right and History* (1950), which described the dualism between the classical philosophical conception of nature and modernity's replacement of nature with history. Strauss was in many respects a conservative in that he opposed the "modern project" and sought a return to the classical philosophical world.[43]

Students could attain knowledge about this lost world if they closely studied texts that revealed—somewhere between the lines of what was written—the true intentions of what authors wanted to say. Only a few highly educated individuals, a "democratic aristocracy," as journalist Nina Easton called it, should be allowed to participate in the discovery.[44] Historian Shadia Drury described this tendency as "radical elitism," that only a few highly cultivated intellects could ever know the truth.[45] "What Strauss imparted to his students," Francis Fukuyama wrote, "was not a set of public policy directives but rather a desire to take seriously and understand the western philosophical tradition."[46]

Kristol never studied with Strauss. Rather, he worked with Harvey Mansfield, a leading Straussian scholar and a gifted political theorist. There were other second-generation neoconservatives, such as Paul Wolfowitz and Richard Perle, influenced by Strauss and his University of Chicago protégé, Allan Bloom. Bloom wrote a bestselling book published in 1987, *The Closing of the American Mind*, an attack on cultural decadence and how universities and colleges were failing in their mission to cultivate the intellect. In his gloomy book, Bloom attacked the cultural relativism then prevalent on elite college campuses like Chicago, arguing instead for the inculcation of virtue based on the study of a great books tradition, "the only serious solution" to the crisis facing higher education. He recommended the great books tradition at the very university that had implemented such a tradition decades earlier under the presidency of Robert Maynard Hutchins.[47]

Bloom saw the idea of Western civilization as a universal force in human history. His interests were philosophical and modernist, not religious. His views were rooted in the Enlightenment secularist worldview—which many neoconservatives accepted—and not in the Christian religious foundation emphasized by traditionalist conservatives like Russell Kirk. Since the publication of his book, conservatives have continued to lament the steep decline in programs in Western civilization at the college level. They have also attacked the reigning relativism and postmodernism existing at many campuses. Bloom fought against an elitist university culture that had abandoned the principles and civilization upon which it was based. Historian Stephen Tonsor expressed this near his retirement from teaching when he wrote Henry Regnery, "I am very fearful of a collapse of the Humanities on a national scale. It is though there was some intellectual equivalent of the AIDS virus which got inside the minds of faculty and administrators under fifty. I don't know what the answer to this problem is. These people are all in place and will control the universities and colleges for at least another twenty years. It is rather like the takeover of the German universities by the Nazis."[48]

Neoconservatives influenced by Strauss and Bloom gained far more attention for their roles in public life than for their academic influence. After the Cold War's sudden denouement many older neoconservatives found themselves adrift. The communist movement had been their whole world—both in joining it and in leaving it—and they suddenly found their country without a serious ideological threat and themselves without a role in the post–Cold War world. But many relished this. It was time to rethink American foreign policy. Jeane Kirkpatrick wrote, "the time when Americans should bear such unusual burdens (as the Cold War) is past. With a return to 'normal' times, we can again become a normal nation—and take care of pressing problems of education, family, technology and industry."[49]

Francis Fukuyama, a second-generation neoconservative and a classmate of Kristol's at Harvard, concurred with Kilpatrick in his influential essay "The End of History," published in the summer 1989 issue of the neoconservative journal *The National Interest*. In the article, later expanded into book form and published as *The End of History and the Last Man* (1992), Fukuyama seemed to suggest that the end of the Cold War brought with it the triumph of liberal democracy. "The century that began full of self-confidence in the ultimate triumph of Western liberal democracy seems at its close to be returning full circle to where it started . . . to an unabashed victory of economic and political liberalism," Fukuyama wrote. "What we may be witnessing is not just the end of the Cold War, or the passing of a particular period of post-war history, but the end of history as such: that is, the end point of mankind's ideological evolution and the universalization of Western liberal democracy as the final form of human government."[50]

Fukuyama's article and subsequent book were criticized for their brash interpretation, both in his philosophical arguments about an end of history (which comes from Karl Marx and Georg Wilhelm Friedrich Hegel) and also for his insistence that Western liberal democracy had triumphed. Any historian—and not a political theorist—would have warned against such overt triumphalism.

And it was the historically minded conservatives who objected the loudest to Fukuyama's (and other neoconservatives') understanding of post–Cold War world affairs. In a review of Fukuyama's book in *Chronicles*, Hungarian émigré historian John Lukacs labeled Fukuyama a "fool." "Fukuyama's mind is philosophical, whence his troubles arise," Lukacs wrote. "Like his mentor Leo Strauss he knows (or thinks he knows) plenty of philosophy, while his ignorance of history is lamentable and abysmal." Lukacs described how Fukuyama envisioned a world where people in Cambodia, Ghana, Rwanda, and Bosnia all lived happy liberal democratic lives, reading Adam Smith and Gladstone now that the Cold War was over. "Clap and trap," he concluded.[51]

Pat Buchanan, who had opposed even the Gulf War, now became the leading voice for those critical of an expanded post–Cold War role for America in world affairs. Buchanan argued for a return to protectionism as America's manufacturing sector faced increased competition from low wage–paying manufacturing interests in China and Mexico. He argued vociferously for an assertive conservative nationalism in trade policy, an end to open-border immigration and a foreign policy that avoided wars except when national interests were directly threatened. In these positions he had the support of paleoconservatives affiliated with the Rockford Institute who emphasized similar views. He also gained support from conservatives who viewed immigration's impact as especially threatening to American democracy and to American identity.[52]

In 1992 Buchanan challenged George H. W. Bush for the Republican nomination and while he did not win one primary or caucus, his outsider candidacy helped spark a conservative populism that culminated in the Perot candidacy. At the GOP convention in Houston that year Buchanan attacked the Clintons in prime time, speaking of a divided nation and a culture war between conservative Christian-minded Americans and secular liberals. He was not invited to speak again by the party, which accepted the journalistic conclusion that Buchanan's speech went too far. "Wall to wall ugly," one commentator called the mood at the convention.

In 1996 Buchanan campaigned against Bob Dole and won the New Hampshire primary before fading against the moderate Kansas Republican. He continued in his role as a television pundit and syndicated columnist, writing books warning against globalization's impact, *The Great Betrayal* (1994); a foreign policy based on empire, *A Republic, Not an Empire* (1999); and the decline of Western values, *The Death of the West* (2001). In 2000 he was the presidential candidate of the Reform Party and failed to even win a percentage point of the popular vote. While Buchanan was very popular with a conservative populist base and his books were best sellers, his foreign policy views never caught fire with the wider electorate, who, in the comfort of the "peace dividend" and booming economy of the 1990s seemed to retreat from foreign policy concerns altogether. If anybody's vision for a post–Cold War world seemed to dominate in the 1990s, it was Fukuyama's, not Buchanan's.

Second-generation neoconservatives took up the call for an expanded role for American power after the Gulf War; during the first Bush administration they were positioned to shape such a vision. Undersecretary of Defense for Policy Paul Wolfowitz drafted an important memorandum for then-Secretary of Defense Dick Cheney outlining American military strategy in the 1990s. Wolfowitz argued for the continuation of a powerful military force: "it took us only five short years to go from having the strongest military establishment in the world with no challengers, to having a force that was barely able to hang on to the Korean peninsula against the attack of a fourth-rate country."[53] Pressure to demobilize the armed forces existed then as it existed after the Cold War, but new dangers existed in the Middle East and in North Korea. Wolfowitz continued to see Saddam Hussein as a dangerous figure, in spite of the ease with which American forces dispatched his armies in 1991. Wolfowitz also cautioned against Iran's growing influence in the region.

The Wolfowitz memorandum embarrassed the Bush administration when it leaked to the press; it was eventually downgraded and rewritten. But key elements came to define the foreign policy of George W. Bush after the September 11, 2001, terrorist attacks on the United States. Wolfowitz argued for a new world order based on American military supremacy, downgrading the status of the United Nations (and even regional alliances such as NATO). He even discussed the doctrine of preemption, especially with America facing the threat of weapons of mass destruction in the hands of rogue states. Ten years after Wolfowitz's original memorandum, George W. Bush resurrected its central arguments in his West Point address in 2002, outlining what came to be called the Bush Doctrine.[54]

Historian John Ehrman claims that neoconservatives were adrift in the 1990s. Some sought Clinton's ear, like former social democrat Joshua Muravchik, who published "Conservatives for Clinton" in the November 1992 issue of *Commentary*. "To my surprise," Muravchik wrote, "I'm supporting Bill Clinton for president." Muravchik's support for Clinton was based on the Democrat's insistence that democracy trump every other value. "When Chinese students demonstrated for democracy in China, Bush was inert. When communist regimes fell, Bush did not rush in to shore up new democracies," Muravchik wrote.[55] What could Bush have done? What would Reagan have done differently? Bush never went far enough for the neoconservatives in Iraq, refusing to violate United Nations resolutions and remove Hussein from power. By not intervening in China after the crushing of pro-democracy demonstrators, Bush signified his lack of concern about democracy. Bush was prudent in his foreign policy decisions. Neoconservatives expected much more.

What neoconservatives wanted was a return to an idealistic foreign policy based on the expansion of democracy and the principles of what Ben Wattenberg referred to as "the first universal nation" and what other neoconservatives like Max Boot have labeled "Wilsonianism on steroids."[56] They believed that no rival power could threaten America's military hegemony and that America was unchallengeable in world affairs—it had become a "unipolar nation" in the words of columnist Charles Krauthammer.[57] William Kristol and Robert Kagan argued in a 1996 *Foreign Affairs* article for "a neo-Reaganite foreign policy" based on a "benevolent hegemony" of American power. The authors argued for a foreign policy that "resist[ed], and where possible, undermin[ed] rising dictators and hostile ideologies" and "provid[ed] assistance to those struggling against the more extreme manifestations of human evil." They argued for regime change when necessary, to alter foreign policy in a manner favorable to American national interests.[58]

What was neo-Reaganite about such a policy? Reagan had not used American military power to change regimes—save for the 1983 invasion of Grenada, which posed a threat to its neighbors as well as a strategic threat to American interests in the Caribbean. Reagan had refused to use military power to break up the Soviet empire in eastern Europe and had refused to extend American power beyond its means elsewhere in the world. While he had labeled the Soviet Union the "evil empire," this was not done in a manner inconsistent with efforts to solve problems between the two rivals. Reagan was open to negotiations with the Soviets on terms favorable to American interests.

The second-generation neoconservatives went far beyond Reagan in their foreign policy doctrine. In 1997 they formed Project for the New American

Century (PNAC). Its founders included, among others, Kristol, Fukuyama, Kagan, Krauthammer, Perle, Donald Rumsfeld, Norman Podhoretz, William Bennett, Jeb Bush, Gary Bauer, and Steve Forbes. It was an organization that aimed to "make the case and rally support for American global leadership."[59] A number of their studies appeared in *The Weekly Standard* and there was cross-fertilization between the think tank and the magazine on a number of foreign policy issues. In January 1998 PNAC sent a letter to Clinton advocating regime change in Iraq after Hussein had refused further UN inspections of weapons of mass destruction and had hindered efforts to continue sanctions applied on Iraq after its invasion of Kuwait. "The only acceptable strategy is one that eliminates the possibility that Iraq will be able to use or threaten to use weapons of mass destruction. In the near term, this means a willingness to undertake military action as diplomacy is clearly failing. In the long term, it means removing Saddam Hussein and his regime from power. That now needs to become the aim of American foreign policy," the authors wrote.[60] Five years later PNAC had its wish and had its war—and it didn't have to change one argument, as if U.S. policy in Iraq had not changed at all in the intervening years.

CONSERVATISM TRANSFORMED

But the second-generation neoconservatives also sought to transform conservatism in other ways. David Brooks of *The Weekly Standard* argued in favor of a return to "national greatness" (an odd choice of terms in that it hearkened back to early twentieth-century German nationalism). In March 1997 Brooks discussed the late nineteenth-century culture of Gilded Age America, employing the Jefferson Building of the Library of Congress as his departure point. "At their best," Brooks wrote, "[Gilded Age Americans] asked big questions: how can America produce a culture it can be proud of?" American politicians a century later "don't dare to make great plans or issue large challenges to themselves and their country. At a moment of world supremacy unlike any other, Americans are not asking big questions about their civilization," Brooks glumly concluded.[61]

Brooks blamed this indifference to "big questions" on the inward turn in American culture that occurred in the post–World War II era. The personal is political trumped the national good; individualism trumped the communal order and populism trumped elitism. Conservatives had been arguing about such issues for most of the twentieth century. Brooks sought something different, a return to a nationalist ideal more befitting of Washington, D.C., in the New Deal years than the nation's capital under Reagan. "It is primarily the fault of conservatives that America has lost a sense of national mission and national greatness," Brooks wrote, blaming them for turning their antistatist and populist concerns into a generalized hostility toward nationalism and elitism. "In their passion for devolution, conservatives have neglected the need for a strong national government," he scolded. Unlike the late nineteenth-century Americans, "today's congressional conservatives couldn't conceivably sponsor a daring statement of American greatness like the Jefferson Building. . . . Few conservatives could even conceive of a federal arts program that would reflect glory on America."[62]

Brooks failed to discuss the impediments to the national greatness ideal. Who would pay for it? Who would be put in charge of deciding what the nation was and what should be honored in the first place? Brooks longed for a national greatness when the very definition of nation was under challenge from postmodern intellectuals (nations are, after all "imagined communities"), multiculturalists, and diversity scolds. Brooks seemed to write in a vacuum—how would any conservative propose to honor national greatness in an era when the very definition of *nation* and *greatness* would be contested by innumerable committees and interest groups, when the very idea of national history was no longer taught in schools? When Ronald Reagan was honored with a building in Washington, it proved to be the largest federal office building in the capital, housing government bureaucrats, a cruel joke for conservatives and Reaganites.

The idea Brooks raised went further. It emphasized a return to the ideals of Teddy Roosevelt and the New Nationalism of the early twentieth century. It sought to thoroughly transform conservatism from a doctrine of limited government to one embracing the power of nationalism, and the state's role in making a nation great. Such a policy not only meant an expansion of government's role—for which Brooks drew condemnation from many conservatives—but also a more imperialist conception of American foreign policy—Washington as the new Rome or London.

If adopted by a conservative politician, such an ideal would go a long way toward reshaping what conservatism represented in American culture and in American ideas. One of those politicians was waiting in the wings and after an initial flirtation with John McCain in the 2000 GOP presidential primaries, the neoconservatives embraced Texas Governor George W. Bush as the candidate who could bring about the type of conservatism they sought.

NOTES

1. Robert H. Bork, *The Tempting of America: The Political Seduction of the Law* (New York: Free Press, 1990), 2.

2. *Romer v. Evans*, U.S. Supreme Court 517 U.S. 620 (decided May 20, 1996).

3. Antonin Scalia, dissent in *Romer v. Evans*.

4. "Editorial: Putting First Things First," *First Things* (March 1990), available online at www.firstthings.com/article.php3?id_article=5300 (accessed April 22, 2007).

5. Background on Neuhaus from Damon Linker, *The Theocons: Secular America under Siege* (New York: Anchor, 2007 ed.). Linker was a former editor at *First Things* and eventually turned against the "doctrinaire" religious views expressed at the journal. See Gary Dorrien, *The Neoconservative Mind: Politics, War, and the Culture of Ideology* (Philadelphia: Temple University Press, 1993), 345–48.

6. Richard John Neuhaus, "The End of Democracy? Introduction," *First Things* (November 1996), available online at www.firstthings.com/article.php3?id_article=3950 (accessed April 24, 2007).

7. Norman Podhoretz, *My Love Affair with America: The Cautionary Tale of a Cheerful Conservative* (New York: Free Press, 2000), 205–10.

8. Information on Limbaugh ratings and program from Richard Viguerie and David Franke, *America's Right Turn: How Conservatives Used New and Alternative Media to Take Power* (Chicago: Bonus Books, 2004), 195–97; Rush Limbaugh, "Holding Court," *Wall Street Journal* (October 17, 2005).

9. Viguerie and Franke, *America's Right Turn*, 187.

10. Viguerie and Franke, *America's Right Turn*, 188.

11. Background on Gingrich from Lee Edwards, *The Conservative Revolution: The Movement that Remade America* (New York: Free Press, 1999), 268–84; and Donald T. Critchlow, *The Conservative Ascendancy: How the GOP Right Made Political History* (Cambridge, Mass.: Harvard University Press, 2007), 243–45.

12. Edwards, *The Conservative Revolution*, 277.

13. Edwards, *The Conservative Revolution*, 282.

14. Edwards, *The Conservative Revolution*, 282.

15. See Greene, *The Presidency of George H. W. Bush* (Lawrence: University Press of Kansas, 1999); see, for an insider's guide, John Podhoretz, *Hell of a Ride: Backstage at the White House Follies, 1989–1993* (New York: Simon & Schuster, 1993).

16. Kenneth J. Heineman, *God Is a Conservative: Religion, Politics, and Morality in Contemporary America* (New York: New York University Press, 1998), 143.

17. See Robert M. Collins, *Transforming America: Politics and Culture during the Reagan Years* (New York: Columbia University Press, 2006), 134–39; and Critchlow, *Conservative Ascendancy*, 216–19. Compare Collins's and Critchlow's treatments of AIDS and Reagan, based on documentary evidence, with Sean Wilentz, *The Age of Reagan: A History, 1974–2008* (New York: Harper, 2008), 185–86, who argues that Reagan appealed to political groups and his conservative base to do nothing about AIDS. Wilentz relies on Lou Cannon's treatment and not the primary evidence in the Reagan Library.

18. On Reagan and AIDS, see Deroy Murdock, "Anti-Gay Gipper? A Lie About Reagan," *National Review Online* (December 3, 2003), available at www.nationalreview.com/murdock/murdock200312030913.asp (accessed May 22, 2007).

19. Charles Murray, *Losing Ground: American Social Policy, 1950–1980* (New York: Basic, 1984), 233–34.

20. Murray, *Losing Ground*, 233.

21. Jason DeParle, "Daring Research or Social Science Pornography?: Charles Murray," *New York Times* (October 9, 1994): 1, 3, 4.

22. Charles Murray, *"The Bell Curve* and Its Critics," *Commentary* (May 1995): 23–31.

23. Jason DeParle, *American Dream: Three Women, Ten Kids, and a Nation's Drive to End Welfare* (New York: Viking, 2004), is an astute journalistic analysis of the history of welfare reform and its impact in Milwaukee, Wisconsin.

24. Clint Bolick, *Voucher Wars: Waging the Legal Battle over School Choice* (Washington, D.C.: Cato Institute, 2003).

25. For a good profile of Lawrence Reed see Jason DeParle, "Right-of-Center Guru Goes with Gospel of Small Government," *New York Times* (November 17, 2006): 1.

26. Greenstein in DeParle, "Daring Research," 4.

27. On the DLC see Kenneth S. Baer, *Reinventing Democrats: The Politics of Liberalism from Reagan to Clinton* (Lawrence: University Press of Kansas, 2000).

28. On the 1992 campaign from the Clinton perspective see George Stephanopolous, *All Too Human: A Political Education* (New York: Back Bay, 2000).

29. "The Real Reagan Record," *National Review* (August 31, 1992): 25–62.

30. Rich Lowry, *Legacy: Paying the Price for the Clinton Years* (Washington, D.C.: Regnery, 2003), is a highly readable conservative overview of the Clinton era.

31. Baer, *Reinventing Democrats*, 233.

32. See "Contract with America" in Schneider, ed., *Conservatism in America since 1930: A Reader* (New York, 2003), 424–27.

33. Tom A. Coburn, with John Hart, *Breach of Trust: How Washington Turns Outsiders into Insiders* (Nashville, Tenn.: Thomas Nelson, 2003), 55–56.

34. Coburn, *Breach of Trust*, 61.

35. Matthew Continetti, *The K Street Gang: The Rise and Fall of the Republican Machine* (New York: Doubleday, 2006), tells this story quite effectively.

36. See David Brock, *Blinded by the Right: The Conscience of an Ex-Conservative* (New York: Three Rivers, 2003).

37. Michael Isikoff, *Uncovering Clinton: A Reporter's Story* (New York: Crown, 1999), provides a lively account by one of the journalists who broke the story.

38. A charge especially made by conservative columnist Ann Coulter, *High Crimes and Misdemeanors: The Case against Bill Clinton* (Washington, D.C.: Regnery, 2002).

39. William Bennett, *The Death of Outrage: Bill Clinton and the Assault on American Ideals* (New York: Free Press, 1998).

40. William J. Bennett, *The Index of Leading Cultural Indicators* (Washington, D.C.: Touchstone, 1994).

41. Background on Kristol from Nina Easton, *Gang of Five: Leaders at the Center of the Conservative Ascendancy* (New York: Simon & Schuster, 2000), 34–38, 41–47, 266–89.

42. Easton, *Gang of Five*, 38.

43. See a discussion of Strauss's ideas in George H. Nash, *The Conservative Intellectual Movement in America: Since 1945*, 3rd ed. (Wilmington, Del.: Intercollegiate Studies Institute, 2006), 347–50; and Alfred S. Regnery, *Upstream: The Ascendance of American Conservatism* (New York: Threshold, 2008), 259–61. A very useful analysis of antimodern thought in American conservatism is Ted V. McAllister, *Revolt against Modernity: Leo Strauss, Eric Voegelin, and the Search for a Postliberal Order* (Lawrence: University Press of Kansas, 1996).

44. Easton, *Gang of Five*, 41.

45. Easton, *Gang of Five*, 41.

46. Francis Fukuyama, *America at the Crossroads: Democracy, Power, and the Neoconservative Legacy* (New Haven, Conn.: Yale University Press, 2006), 22–23.

47. Allan Bloom, *The Closing of the American Mind* (New York: Simon & Schuster, 1988).

48. Letter from Stephen Tonsor to Henry Regnery, June 17, 1991, Box 121 (Tonsor Corr.), Regnery Papers, Hoover Institution, Stanford University.

49. Jeane J. Kirkpatrick, "A Normal Country in a Normal Time," *National Interest* (Fall 1990): 40–44. She expanded on this theme in her last book, *Making War to Keep Peace* (New York: Harper, 2007).

50. Francis Fukuyama, *The End of History and the Last Man* (New York: Free Press, 1992), 64–65.

51. John Lukacs, "Francis Fukuyama and Graham Fuller," in Lukacs, *Remembered Past: John Lukacs on History, Historians, and Historical Knowledge: A Reader*, ed. Malvasi and Nelson (Wilmington, Del.: Intercollegiate Studies Institute, 2005), 353–55.

52. Patrick J. Buchanan, *The Great Betrayal: How American Sovereignty and Social Justice Are Being Sacrificed to the Goals of the Global Economy* (New York: Little, Brown, 1998); *The Death of the West: How Dying Populations and Immigrant Invasion Imperil Our Country and Civilization* (New York: St. Martin's Griffin, 2002); and *State of Emergency: The Third World Invasion and Conquest of America* (New York: Thomas Dunne, 2006).

53. James Mann, *Rise of the Vulcans: The History of Bush's War Cabinet* (New York: Penguin, 2004), 198–200; and Stefan Halper and Jonathan Clarke, *America Alone: The Neo-conservatives and the Global Order* (New York: Cambridge University Press, 2004), 145–46.

54. See John Lewis Gaddis, *Surprise, Security, and the American Experience* (Cambridge, Mass.: Harvard University Press, 2004), 83–91.

55. Joshua Muravchik, "Conservatives for Clinton," *Commentary* (November 1992); see, also, John Ehrman, *The Rise of Neoconservatism: Intellectuals and Foreign Affairs, 1945–1994* (New Haven, Conn.: Yale University Press, 1995).

56. See Ben Wattenberg, *The First Universal Nation: Leading Indicators and Ideas about the Surge of America in the 1990s* (New York: Free Press, 1991); Max Boot quoted in Jeffrey Hart "Why I Am a Conservative: Symposium," *Modern Age* (Summer 2007), 25.

57. Charles Krauthammer, "The Unipolar Moment," *Foreign Affairs: America and the World 1990/91* (Winter 1991): 23–33.

58. William Kristol and Robert Kagan, "Toward a Neo-Reaganite Foreign Policy," *Foreign Affairs* 75: 4 (1996): 18–32.

59. "Statement of Principles," Project for a New American Century available online at www.newamericancentury.org/statementofprinciples.htm (accessed May 17, 2007).

60. Letter to William Jefferson Clinton, January 26, 1998, PNAC Web site available online at www.newamericancentury.org/statementofprinciples.htm (accessed May 17, 2007).

61. David Brooks, "A Return to National Greatness: A Manifesto for a Lost Creed," *The Weekly Standard* (March 3, 1997), available at www.weeklystandard .com/Content/Protected/Articles/000/000/0008/333pjkmj.asp (accessed May 25, 2007).

62. Brooks, "A Return to National Greatness."

Postscript

Scratch the American conservative and you'll often find a radical of sorts.

—John Lukacs

"For better or for worse," the editors of *Policy Review* wrote, "modern ideological conservatism constitutes a completed body of thought." Such sentiments were published in the last year of what turned out to be the conservative century, an era that saw the rise and demise of ideological movements, like communism and fascism, first prophesied by the Romantic revolutionaries of the previous century. It was an era that saw modern liberalism dominate politically and then falter, replaced by a political conservatism that remained dominant into the first decade of the twenty-first century. "The principal activity of ideological conservatism at century's end takes place not in the realm of ideas, but in the world of politics."[1]

And so it seemed in 1999. What the editors of *Policy Review*—then published by the Heritage Foundation—could not foresee or predict was how fleeting the politicized conservatism of Barry Goldwater–Ronald Reagan–Newt Gingrich could be when devoid of the basic ideas that made such a politics possible in the first place. What constituted and defined American conservatism for decades was so altered by two decades of conservative political power that what passed for conservatism in the new century was profoundly divorced from the original political fusionist ideas developed by Frank Meyer in the 1950s. But that conservatism, it is important to remember, was also divorced from its earliest predecessors in the first half of the century. Conservatism remained remarkably protean, in spite of the best wishes of those who saw it as a completed body of thought.

The election of George W. Bush in the disputed 2000 presidential election gave hope to political conservatives that their ideas and power were in the ascendant after eight years of Bill Clinton. Bush, like his father, was not a movement conservative but he did express through the campaign that he was a Reaganite and he emphasized enough of the central elements of conservatism, emphasizing tax cuts, hostility toward abortion, and "a foreign policy which reflects American character," to gain support from conservative magazines and think tanks. He emphasized that he was a "compassionate conservative," a term created by academic Marvin Olasky, saying frequently that "it is compassionate to help our citizens in need. It is conservative to insist on accountability and results."[2]

The first eight months of Bush's presidency were uneventful. He delighted social conservatives when he prohibited the further use of stem cells procured from aborted fetuses for research into cures for diseases—instead, stem cell lines already in use would be the only ones allowed in government-funded research. He also spoke forcefully against abortion and against gay marriage, an issue rising in importance in states like Hawaii and Massachusetts. He was unapologetic about his support for a pro-life position. He also delighted conservatives when he signed a tax cut in June 2001, an across-the-board cut lasting ten years. He had taken conservative positions on most issues, but his overall popularity with the American public was low.[3]

There was a strong sense, even with these accomplishments, that Bush would be a one-term president. By the end of his first summer in office the administration was adrift. Then, on the morning of September 11, 2001, two hijacked passenger airliners were flown into New York's World Trade Center Twin Towers. After several hours, the towers collapsed from the intense heat produced by the jet fuel. Another hijacked passenger plane flew into the Pentagon; a fourth, commandeered by passengers, crashed in a field near Shanksville, Pennsylvania, likely intended for the White House.

September 11th and the deaths of close to three thousand people that day changed the Bush presidency and changed Bush's conservatism as well. Bush's presidency now had a purpose. He rallied the American people in the wake of the shocking attacks to go to war against the terrorist culprits responsible for the carnage, the al-Qaeda movement led by Osama bin Laden. Bin Laden and his terrorist movement had been responsible for several attacks on American interests around the world during the Clinton administration, including the bombing of the warship USS *Cole*, the destruction of two American embassies in Africa, and the bombing of the Khobar Towers apartment complex in Saudi Arabia. Bin Laden was the son of a billionaire from Saudi Arabia who was influenced by radical Islam to make jihad against the Soviet invasion of Afghanistan. After the Afghan war, bin Laden urged the overthrow of the Saudi royal family, particularly after they had let American troops occupy the Muslim holy land during the Gulf War.[4]

Using the failed state of Afghanistan as a base area, al-Qaeda spread its influence and recruited members throughout the world to conduct operations against America. In the fall of 2001, Bush gained NATO's support to remove the Taliban government from Afghanistan. The western European countries and the United States were united in their determination to deny al-Qaeda an operating base in Afghanistan. Bush addressed Congress and declared: "Our war on terror begins with al Qaeda but it does not end there. It will not end until every terrorist group of global reach has been found, stopped, and defeated." He then uttered some amazing words signifying a major shift in his thinking and the increasing prominence of neoconservatives in the making of his foreign policy. Bush said, "Every nation, every region now has a decision to make. Either you are with us, or you are with the terrorists. From this day forward, any nation that continues to harbor or support terrorism will be regarded by the United States as a hostile regime."[5]

In January 2002 Bush's State of the Union address named North Korea, Iraq, and Iran as an "axis of evil." The phrase was followed with a warning: "I will not wait on events, while dangers gather. I will not stand by, as peril draws closer and closer. The United States of America will not permit the world's most dangerous regimes to threaten us with the world's most destructive weapons."[6] The "axis of evil" phrase with its clear allusions to Reagan's evil empire speech was drafted by David Frum, a Canadian-born journalist who had written for *The Wall Street Journal* and had been a fellow at the Manhattan Institute in New York before joining the Bush White House as a speechwriter. Frum had written two perceptive books on conservatism, *Dead Right* (1994) and *What's Right* (1996).

Bush sought nothing less than the remaking of American foreign policy. At West Point in 2002 Bush raised the right of nations to defend themselves from "weapons of mass destruction" delivered by "unbalanced dictators" and said that the United States would not sit idly by and be attacked. Rather, Bush reserved the right to preempt an attack by going on the offensive against threatening states. This became the basis for the "most thorough reassessment of American national security strategy in fifty years" historian John Lewis Gaddis wrote.[7] Bush was not only going to preempt threats by using American military power to attack tyrants who he believed threatened American interests, but he wanted to secure the right to do so from the international community. Failing that, Bush was willing to act without such approval. This is exactly the point Wolfowitz had made in 1992 and it was exactly the sort of thinking embraced by pundits like Charles Krauthammer when he discussed America as a unipolar nation, or William Kristol when he described America as a "benevolent hegemon." The administration turned most of its attention to Iraq, which became the proving ground for the Bush Doctrine.

On March 17, 2003, after failing to secure a UN Security Council resolution to remove Saddam Hussein from power—instead the Security Council voted for further weapons inspections—Bush and British ally Tony Blair, joined by dozens of other nations in what Bush called a "coalition of the willing," invaded Iraq and within three weeks had defeated Iraqi forces and marched into Baghdad. The aftermath of victory and the occupation of Iraq proved more problematic. Inadequate preparations for the occupation, inadequate forces, and inadequate management by the Americans as well as the beginnings of an insurgency, led by Sunni Arabs loyal to Hussein, Shia Arabs loyal to Iran, and al-Qaeda, forced the Americans into insurgent warfare, which the military had never been very good at fighting. Yet, improbably, after five years of fighting and the development of a new strategy that involved counterinsurgency and a "surge" of additional American troops, there has been tremendous progress in Iraq and even hope that some form of democratic government and stability will develop there when the Americans leave. In spite of progress the Iraq War remains unpopular with large majorities of the American people and contributed to a weakened Bush presidency and the Republican loss of Congress in 2006.

The Iraq War has also split conservatives, although the nature of the split reflected the continued hostility between neoconservatives and paleoconservatives. In 2002, Pat Buchanan, Taki Theodoracopulos (a Greek playboy who had written for *National Review*), and Scott McConnell, founded a new publication entitled *The American Conservative*. Buchanan wrote in the first issue, "what comes after all the celebratory gunfire when wicked Saddam is dead?" He then described how Arabic people had removed imperial powers before, warning, "we have started up the road to empire and over the next hill we shall meet those who went before. The only lesson we learn from history is that we do not learn from history."[8] *The American Conservative* would be both paleoconservative in its focus on the decline of American manufacturing and on issues like immigration, and antiwar, especially when it featured positive articles on Bush critics Norman Mailer and Gore Vidal.

Antiwar conservatives sought to expose who would benefit from the war itself. Buchanan, Joe Sobran, and Samuel Francis believed the blame fell on those who espoused close relations with Israel. Buchanan wrote in "Whose War?" in the March 2003 issue of *The American Conservative*, "we charge that a cabal of polemicists and public officials seeks to ensnare our country in a series of wars that are not in America's interests. We charge them with colluding with Israel to ignite those wars. . . . We charge them with deliberately damaging U.S. relations with every state in the Arab world that defies Israel or supports the Palestinian people's right to a homeland of their own. We charge that they have alienated friends and allies all over the Islamic and Western world through their arrogance, hubris and bellicosity."[9] In December 2002 Samuel Francis wrote in *Chronicles* that "the Bush administration should not only ignore the advice of such characters as Michael Ledeen and Norman Podhoretz but consider placing them under surveillance as possible agents of a foreign power."[10] If the neoconservative cabal was indeed a cabal working on behalf of a foreign power, it was amazingly open about its intentions, and as historian Gaddis wrote, "quite candid" in what it wanted to accomplish.[11]

Analyzing such sentiments, David Frum unleashed a vitriolic attack on what he called "Unpatriotic Conservatives" in the April 7, 2003, issue of *National Review*. Frum wrote that the antiwar conservatives "are relatively few in number, but their ambitions are large. They aspire to reinvent conservative ideology: to junk the 50-year-old conservative commitment to defend American interests and values throughout the world—the commitment that inspired the founding of this magazine—in favor of a fearful policy of ignoring threats and appeasing enemies."[12] He named Buchanan and longtime conservative columnist Robert Novak as the most famous of these antiwar conservatives and charged that it was Novak who first raised the connection between the terrorist attacks on America and American support for Israel. He concluded his piece by writing that the unpatriotic conservatives "began by hating neoconservatives. They came to hate their party and this president. They have finished by hating their country. War is a great clarifier. It forces people to take sides. The paleoconservatives have chosen—and the rest of us must choose too. In a time of danger, they have turned their backs on their country. Now we turn our backs on them."[13]

The response was immediate. Sam Francis was unapologetic for holding his paleoconservative views, writing in his syndicated column that "Frum imagines that he and his neocon Likudniks are the real conservatives. . . . The point is that it's Mr. Frum and his phony neocon cronies who have perverted, misrepresented, and abandoned the real conservative tradition. It's the paleos who guard it."[14] Much of the problem centered on the piece appearing in *National Review* that William F. Buckley Jr. still oversaw as editor in chief. While Rich Lowry, a young conservative in his thirties was the new editor of the magazine, Buckley could still approve or disapprove content. And he did nothing to stop the attack on the paleoconservatives. In 2004 however, the paleoconservatives received some vindication when Buckley told the *New York Times*, "with the benefit of minute hindsight, Saddam Hussein wasn't the kind of extra-territorial menace that was assumed by the administration one year ago. If I knew then what I know now about what kind of situation we would be in, I would have opposed the war."[15]

The neoconservatives who helped push the case for war against Iraq
proved to be rather fickle themselves. With the occupation not going the way
they intended, many neoconservative supporters of the war, including
Richard Perle, Kenneth Adelman, and David Frum, blamed the president for
failures in Iraq. In *Vanity Fair* magazine in January 2007, Perle blamed "dysfunction" in the Bush White House: "the decisions did not get made that
should have been. . . . At the end of the day, you have to hold the president
responsible." He then went on to say that "I think if I had been Delphic, and
had seen where we are today, and people had said, 'Should we go into Iraq?'
I think now I probably would have said, 'No, let's consider other strategies
for dealing with the thing that concerns us most, which is Saddam supplying
weapons of mass destruction to the terrorists.'" Kenneth Adelman argued that
"the idea of a tough foreign policy on behalf of morality, the idea of using our
power for moral good in the world . . . is not going to sell." Frum blamed the
president as well, saying that "while the president said the words, he just did
not absorb the ideas."[16] Other neoconservative outlets like *The Weekly Standard* remained committed to the war and to the transformation of Iraq into a
democratic nation.

Iraq was not the only divide within conservatism. The Republican failure
to reduce government spending and the growth of government bureaucracy
also caused dissension. In his first term as president Bush failed to veto one
bill from Congress. Bush endorsed the Ted Kennedy–authored No Child Left
Behind Act, giving the federal government greater powers over education in
the country. The GOP Congress passed a Medicare Prescription Drug Act in
2005, a new entitlement for senior citizens on Medicare. The GOP embraced
earmarks in spending bills and by 2004 the Congress had increased nondis-
cretionary spending by 18.4 percent in the years 2002–2004. Columnist
George Will wrote that "the conservatism that defined itself in reaction
against the New Deal—minimal government conservatism—is dead."[17] Bush
and the GOP Congress added more red ink and more new spending programs
to government than any Congress since the days of Lyndon Johnson.

Some conservatives applauded the shift. Fred Barnes of *The Weekly Standard* described Bush as a "big government conservative." "To gain free-
market reforms," Barnes wrote, "he's willing to broaden programs and increase spending." Barnes discussed how Bush favored expansion of the
prescription drug benefit in Medicare if it led to reforms to push more sen-
iors into private insurance. He supported No Child Left Behind because it
gave him a chance to reform the education department. Big government
conservatives "simply believe in using what would normally be seen as liberal means—activist government—for conservative ends. And they're willing to spend more and increase the size of government in the process."[18]

Barnes applauded this technique, but it has moved conservatism in the public mind far away from its original small government principles. On the majority of issues it is hard to see Bush as a conservative, yet the equation of Bush with conservatism echoes in the public's mind and will hasten the speed at which the Reagan conservatism crumbles.

Conservatives continue to face difficulties over what their ideas stand for and what their legacy is in the new century. Conservatism continues to be remarkably protean and conservatives have altered their ideas, changed their perspectives, and altered their movement's history over the course of the twentieth century. Yet the current conservative identity crisis is a severe one and is testing the will of both politicized conservatives to stay the course in pursuit of smaller government and low taxes, as well as conservative intellectuals to have faith in a restoration of the primacy of Western culture in an increasingly fragmented and multicultural society. What emerges from this identity crisis will, for all practical purposes, bear little resemblance (on most levels) to the conservatism that preceded it. But if history should teach us anything it is that conservatives have been at this point before—repeatedly—in what turned out to be the conservative century.

NOTES

1. "Conservatism at the End of the Century: A Prospectus," *Policy Review* (December 1999 and January 2000), 3–9.

2. Marvin Olasky, *Compassionate Conservatism: What It Is, What It Does, and How It Can Transform America* (New York: Simon and Schuster, 2000).

3. A point made by Sean Wilentz, *The Age of Reagan: A History, 1974–2008* (New York: Harper, 2008), 439.

4. See Lawrence Wright, *The Looming Tower: Al-Qaeda and the Road to 9/11* (New York: Knopf, 2006).

5. George W. Bush, Address to a Joint Session of Congress and the American People, November 2001, available at www.whitehouse.gov/news/releases/2001/09/20010920-8 .html (accessed January 21, 2008).

6. Stefan Halper and Jonathan Clarke, *America Alone: The Neo-conservatives and the Global Order* (New York: Cambridge University Press, 2004), 139–41.

7. John Lewis Gaddis, *Surprise, Secrecy, and the American Experience* (Cambridge, Mass.: Harvard University Press, 2004), 81.

8. Patrick J. Buchanan, *Where the Right Went Wrong: How Neoconservatives Subverted the Reagan Revolution and Hijacked the Bush Presidency* (New York: St. Martin's Griffin, 2005), 29.

9. Patrick J. Buchanan, "Whose War?" *The American Conservative* (March 24, 2003): 4–9.

10. Samuel Francis, "Principalities and Power: World War IV," *Chronicles* (December 2002), available online at www.samfrancis.net/pdf/all2002.pdf (accessed January 27, 2008).

11. Gaddis, *Surprise, Secrecy,* 83.

12. David Frum, "Unpatriotic Conservatives," *National Review* (April 7, 2003), available online at www.nationalreview.com/frum/frum031903.htm (accessed January 27, 2008).

13. Frum, "Unpatriotic Conservatives."

14. Samuel Francis, "Good Riddance to *National Review*," syndicated column (March 27, 2003), available online at www.vdare.com/francis/frum.htm (accessed January 27, 2008).

15. *New York Times* (July 3, 2004).

16. David Rose, "Neo Culpa," *Vanity Fair* (November 2006), available at www.vanityfair.com/politics/features/2006/12/neocons200612 (accessed January 12, 2008).

17. George Will, "Big Government Conservatism is Reagan's Legacy," syndicated column, *Topeka Capital-Journal* (February 12, 2007).

18. Fred Barnes, "Big-Government Conservatism," *Wall Street Journal* (August 15, 2003), available online at www.weeklystandard.com/Content/Public/Articles/000/000/003/017wgfhc.asp

Bibliography

MANUSCRIPT SOURCES

Chicago Historical Society, Chicago, Ill.
  Sterling Morton Papers
  Clarence Manion Papers
Hagley Library and Museum, Wilmington, Del.
  J. Howard Pew Papers
  Jaspar Crane Papers
  Joseph N. Pew Papers
  National Association of Manufacturers Papers
Herbert Hoover Presidential Library, West Branch, Iowa
  Herbert Hoover Post-presidential Papers
  Felix Morley Papers
  Rose Wilder Lane Papers
  Robert Wood Papers
Hoover Institution on War, Revolution, and Peace, Stanford University
  America First Papers
  Henry Regnery Papers
  Stephen Tonsor Papers
  Patrick Dowd Papers
  James Burnham Papers
  Frank Meyer Papers
  Leopold Tyrmand Papers
  Marvin Liebman Papers
Johns Hopkins University Special Collections, Baltimore, Md.
  William Lalley Papers

Library of Congress, Washington, D.C.
    Robert A. Taft Papers
    William A. Rusher Papers
University of Oregon Library, Eugene, Ore.
    John T. Flynn Papers
    T. Coleman Andrews Papers
University of Virginia Department of Special Collections, Charlottesville, Va.
    James Jackson Kilpatrick Papers
    Harry Byrd Papers
Vanderbilt University, Heard Library, Nashville, Tenn.
    Richard Weaver Papers
    Donald Davidson Papers
Yale University, Beinecke Rare Book and Manuscript Library, New Haven, Conn.
    Seward Collins Papers
Yale University, Sterling Library, New Haven, Conn.
    Albert Jay Nock Papers
    William F. Buckley Jr. Papers

PERIODICALS

Articles from the following publications are cited in endnotes.

The American Conservative
American Review
American Spectator
analysis
Appeal to Reason
Atlantic Monthly
The Bookman
Bulletin of the Atomic Scientists
Chronicles
Commentary
Conservative
Conservative Digest
Constitutional Review
First Things
The Freeman
Human Events

The Intercollegiate Review
Left and Right
Libertarian Forum
Libertarian Review
Modern Age
The National Interest
National Review
New Criterion
New Guard
New Republic
New Right Report
Newsweek
New York Times
New York Times Book Review
Policy Review
The Public Interest
Reason
Triumph
The Wall Street Journal
Washington Post
The Weekly Foreign Letter
The Weekly Standard
Wired

BOOKS AND JOURNAL ARTICLES

Agar, Herbert, and Allen Tate, eds. *Who Owns America? A New Declaration of Independence.* Wilmington, Del.: ISI Books, 1999. First published 1936.

Allitt, Patrick. *Catholic Intellectuals and Conservative Politics in America, 1950–1985.* Ithaca, N.Y.: Cornell University Press, 1993.

Anderson, Martin. *Revolution: The Reagan Legacy.* Exp. upd. edition. Stanford, Calif.: Hoover Institution Press, 1990.

Andrew, John A. *The Other Side of the Sixties: Young Americans for Freedom and the Rise of Conservative Politics.* New Brunswick, N.J.: Rutgers University Press, 1997.

———. *Power to Destroy: The Political Uses of the IRS from Kennedy to Nixon.* Chicago: Ivan R. Dee, 2002.

Babbitt, Irving. *Democracy and Leadership.* Indianapolis: Liberty Fund, 1979.

———. *Rousseau and Romanticism.* New Brunswick, N.J.: Transaction, 2004.

Bachrack, Stanley D. *The Committee of One Million: "China Lobby" Politics, 1953–1971.* New York: Columbia University Press, 1976.

Baer, Kenneth S. *Reinventing Democrats: The Politics of Liberalism from Reagan to Clinton.* Lawrence: University Press of Kansas, 2000.

Bartley, Robert L. *The Seven Fat Years and How to Do It Again.* New York: Free Press, 1995.

Bastiat, Frederic. *The Law.* Translated by Dean Russell. Irvington-on-Hudson, N.Y.: Foundation for Economic Education, 1998. First published in 1850.

Beito, David T., and Linda Royster Beito. "Gold Democrats and the Decline of Classical Liberalism, 1896–1900." *The Independent Review* (Spring 2000): 555–75.

Bell, Daniel., ed. *The Radical Right.* Garden City, N.Y.: Doubleday, 1964.

Belloc, Hilaire. *The Servile State.* Indianapolis, Ind.: Liberty Fund, 1977. First published 1913.

Bennett, William J. *The Death of Outrage: Bill Clinton and the Assault on American Ideals.* New York: Free Press, 1998.

——. *The De-valuing of America: The Fight for Our Country and Our Children.* New York: Simon & Schuster, 1994.

——. *The Index of Leading Cultural Indicators.* Washington, D.C.: Touchstone, 1994.

Benowitz, June Melby. *Days of Discontent: American Women and Right-Wing Politics, 1933–1945.* DeKalb: Northern Illinois University Press, 2002.

Berg, A. Scott. *Lindbergh.* New York: Berkley Books, 1998.

Berman, William C. *America's Right Turn: From Nixon to Bush.* Baltimore: Johns Hopkins University Press, 1994.

Billingsley, Kenneth Lloyd. *Hollywood Party: How Communism Seduced the American Film Industry in the 1930s and 1940s.* Rocklin, Calif.: Prima Lifestyles, 1998.

Bjerre-Poulsen, Niels. *Right Face: Organizing the American Conservative Movement, 1945–1965.* Copenhagen: Museum Tusculanum, 2003.

Black, Earl, and Merle Black. *The Rise of Southern Republicans.* Cambridge: Belknap Press, 2003.

Bloom, Allan. *The Closing of the American Mind.* New York: Simon & Schuster, 1988.

Blumenthal, Sidney. *The Rise of the Counter-establishment: The Conservative Ascent to Political Power.* New York: Union Square, 2008.

Bolick, Clint. *Voucher Wars: Waging the Legal Battle over School Choice.* Washington, D.C.: Cato Institute, 2003.

Bork, Robert H. *Slouching Towards Gomorrah: Modern Liberalism and American Decline.* New York: HarperCollins, 1996.

——. *The Tempting of America: The Political Seduction of the Law.* New York: Free Press, 1990.

Bosch, Adriana. *Reagan: An American Story.* New York: TV Books, 2000.

Bozell, L. Brent. *The Warren Revolution: Reflections on the Consensus Society.* Chicago: Crown, 1966.

Brennan, Mary C. *Turning Right in the Sixties: The Conservative Capture of the GOP.* Chapel Hill: University of North Carolina Press, 1995.

——. *Wives, Mothers, and the Red Menace: Conservative Women and the Crusade Against Communism.* Boulder: University Press of Colorado, 2008.

Brinkley, Alan. *The End of Reform: New Deal Liberalism in Recession and War.* New York: Knopf, 1995.

  221

——. "The Problem of American Conservatism." *American Historical Review* (April 1994): 409–29.

Brock, David. *Blinded by the Right: The Conscience of an Ex-Conservative.* New York: Three Rivers, 2003.

Brownlee, W. Elliott, and Hugh Davis Graham, eds. *The Reagan Presidency: Pragmatic Conservatism and Its Legacies.* Lawrence: University Press of Kansas, 2003.

Buchanan, Patrick J. *The Death of the West: How Dying Populations and Immigrant Invasions Imperil Our Country and Civilization.* New York: St. Martin's Griffin, 2002.

——. *The Great Betrayal: How American Sovereignty and Social Justice Are Being Sacrificed to the Gods of the Global Economy.* New York: Little, Brown, 1998.

——. *A Republic, Not an Empire: Reclaiming America's Destiny.* Washington, D.C.: Regnery, 1999.

——. *Right From the Beginning.* Washington, D.C.: Regnery Gateway, 1990.

——. *State of Emergency: The Third World Invasion and Conquest of America.* New York: Thomas Dunne, 2006.

——. *Where the Right Went Wrong: How Neoconservatives Subverted the Reagan Revolution and Hijacked the Bush Presidency.* New York: St. Martin's Griffin, 2005.

Buckley, William F. Jr. *The Jeweler's Eye: A Book of Irresistible Political Reflections.* New York: Putnam, 1968.

——. *Miles Gone By: A Literary Autobiography.* Washington, D.C.: Regnery, 2004.

——, ed. *Odyssey of a Friend: The Correspondence of Whittaker Chambers and William F. Buckley Jr., 1954–1961.* New York: Putnam Publishing, 1969.

——. *Up From Liberalism.* New York: McDowell Obolensky, 1959.

Burnham, James. *Containment or Liberation?* New York: John Day, 1953.

——. *The Managerial Revolution: What Is Happening in the World.* New York: The John Day Company, 1941.

Busch, Andrew E. *Reagan's Victory: The Presidential Election of 1980 and the Rise of the Right.* Lawrence: University Press of Kansas, 2005.

Cannon, Lou. *Governor Reagan: His Rise to Power.* New York: PublicAffairs, 2003.

——. *Reagan.* New York: Putnam, 1985.

Carlson, Allan. *The New Agrarian Mind: The Movement Toward Decentralist Thought in Twentieth-Century America.* New Brunswick, N.J.: Transaction, 2000.

Carter, Dan T. *The Politics of Rage: George Wallace, the Origins of the New Conservatism, and the Transformation of American Politics.* New York: Simon & Schuster, 1995.

Chafe, William H., ed. *The Achievement of American Liberalism: The New Deal and Its Legacies.* New York: Columbia University Press, 2003.

Chamberlain, John. *Farewell to Reform: The Rise, Life, and Decay of the Progressive Mind in America.* Chicago: Quadrangle, 1965 ed.

Chamberlin, William Henry. *America's Second Crusade.* Chicago: Regnery Publishing, 1950.

——. *Confessions of an Individualist.* New York: Macmillan, 1940.

Chambers, Whittaker. *Witness.* Washington, D.C.: Regnery, 1980. First published 1954.

Chang, Gordon H. *Friends and Enemies: The United States, China, and the Soviet Union, 1948–1972.* Stanford: Stanford University Press, 1990.

Chodorov, Frank. *Fugitive Essays: Selected Writings of Frank Chodorov.* Edited by Charles H. Hamilton. Indianapolis: Liberty Fund, 1980.

———. *Out of Step: The Autobiography of an Individualist.* New York: Devin-Adair, 1962.

Clymer, Adam. *Drawing the Line at the Big Ditch: The Panama Canal Treaties and the Rise of the Right.* Lawrence: University Press of Kansas, 2008.

Coburn, Tom A., with John Hart. *Breach of Trust: How Washington Turns Outsiders into Insiders.* Nashville, Tenn.: Thomas Nelson, 2003.

Collins, Robert M. *The Business Response to Keynes, 1929–1964.* New York: Columbia University Press, 1982.

———. *More: The Politics of Economic Growth in Postwar America.* New York: Oxford University Press, 2000.

———. *Transforming America: Politics and Culture during the Reagan Years.* New York: Columbia University Press, 2006.

Continetti, Matthew. *The K Street Gang: The Rise and Fall of the Republican Machine.* New York: Doubleday, 2006.

Coulter, Ann. *High Crimes and Misdemeanors: The Case against Bill Clinton.* Washington, D.C.: Regnery, 2002.

———. *Slander: Liberal Lies About the American Right.* New York: Three Rivers Press, 2002.

———. *Treason: Liberal Treachery from the Cold War to the War on Terrorism.* New York: Crown Forum, 2003.

Courtois, Stéphane, Nicolas Werth, Jean-Louis Panné, Andrzej Paczkowski, Karel Bartosek, and Jean-Louis Margolin, eds. *The Black Book of Communism: Crimes, Terror, Repression.* Cambridge, Mass.: Harvard University Press, 1999.

Cram, Ralph Adams. *My Life in Architecture.* New York: Little, Brown, 1937.

———. *The Nemesis of Mediocrity.* Boston: Marshall Jones Co., 1917.

Crespino, Joseph. *In Search of Another Country: Mississippi and the Conservative Counterrevolution.* Princeton: Princeton University Press, 2007.

Critchlow, Donald T. *The Conservative Ascendancy: How the GOP Right Made Political History.* Cambridge, Mass.: Harvard University Press, 2007.

———. *Intended Consequences: Birth Control, Abortion, and the Federal Government in Modern America.* New York: Oxford University Press, 1999.

———. *Phyllis Schlafly and Grassroots Conservatism: A Woman's Crusade.* Princeton: Princeton University Press, 2005.

Critchlow, Donald T., and Agnieszka Critchlow, eds. *Enemies of the State: Personal Stories from the Gulag.* Chicago: Ivan R. Dee, 2002.

Crocker, George N. *Roosevelt's Road to Russia.* Chicago: Regnery Publishing, 1959.

Crunden, Robert M., ed. *The Superfluous Men: Conservative Critics of American Culture, 1900–1945.* 2nd ed. Wilmington, Del.: Intercollegiate Studies Institute, 1999.

Curtis, George M. III, and James J. Thompson Jr., eds. *The Southern Essays of Richard M. Weaver.* Indianapolis: Liberty Fund, 1987.

Dallek, Matthew W. *The Right Moment: Ronald Reagan's First Victory and the Decisive Turning Point in American Politics*. New York: Free Press, 2000.

Dallek, Robert. *Franklin D. Roosevelt and American Foreign Policy*. New York: Oxford University Press, 1972.

Davidson, Eugene. "Richard Malcolm Weaver—Conservative." *Modern Age* (Summer 1963): 226–30.

Davies, Gareth. *From Opportunity to Entitlement: The Transformation and Decline of Great Society Liberalism*. Lawrence: University Press of Kansas, 1996.

Dawley, Alan. *Changing the World: American Progressives in War and Revolution*. Princeton: Princeton University Press, 2003.

Dennis, Lawrence. *The Coming American Fascism*. New York: Harper, 1936.

Dennis, Lawrence, and Maximillian St. George. *The Trial on Trial*. New York: National Civil Rights Committee, 1946.

DeParle, Jason. *American Dream: Three Women, Ten Kids, and a Nation's Drive to End Welfare*. New York: Viking, 2004.

Diggins, John Patrick. *Ronald Reagan: Fate, Freedom, and the Making of History*. New York: Norton, 2007.

———. *Up from Communism: Conservative Odysseys in American Intellectual Development*. New York: Columbia University Press, 1994 ed.

Doenecke, Justus D., ed. *In Danger Undaunted: The Anti-Interventionist Movement of 1940–1941 as Revealed in the Papers of the America First Committee*. Stanford, Calif.: Hoover Institution Press, 1990.

———. *Not to the Swift: The Old Isolationists in the Cold War Era*. Cranbury, N.J.: Associated University Presses, 1979.

———. *Storm on the Horizon: The Challenge to American Intervention, 1939–1941*. Lanham, Md.: Rowman & Littlefield, 2000.

Doherty, Brian. *Radicals for Capitalism: A Freewheeling History of the Modern American Libertarian Movement*. New York: PublicAffairs, 2007.

Dorrien, Gary. *The Neoconservative Mind: Politics, Culture, and the War of Ideology*. Philadelphia: Temple University Press, 1993.

Dunn, Charles W. *The Future of Conservatism: Conflict and Consensus in the Post-Reagan Era*. Wilmington, Del.: Intercollegiate Studies Institute, 2007.

Durr, Kenneth D. *Behind the Backlash: White Working-Class Politics in Baltimore, 1940–1980*. Chapel Hill: University of North Carolina Press, 2003.

Easton, Nina J. *Gang of Five: Leaders at the Center of the Conservative Ascendancy*. New York: Simon & Schuster, 2000.

Ebenstein, Alan. *Friedrich Hayek: A Biography*. New York: Palgrave Macmillan, 2001.

Edwards, Lee. *The Conservative Revolution: The Movement that Remade America*. New York: Free Press, 1999.

———. *Educating for Liberty: The First Half-Century of the Intercollegiate Studies Institute*. Washington, D.C.: Regnery Publishing, 2003.

———. *The Essential Ronald Reagan: A Profile in Courage, Justice, and Wisdom*. Lanham, Md.: Rowman & Littlefield, 2005.

———. *Goldwater: The Man Who Made a Revolution*. Washington, D.C.: Regnery, 1995.

——. *History of the Philadelphia Society*. Jerome, Mich.: Philadelphia Society, 2004. Published by the Philadelphia Society to commemorate its 40th anniversary, copy in author's possession.

——. *The Power of Ideas: The Heritage Foundation at 25 Years*. Ottawa, Ill.: Jameson, 1997.

Ehrman, John. *The Eighties: America in the Age of Reagan*. New Haven, Conn.: Yale University Press, 2005.

——. *The Rise of Neoconservatism: Intellectuals and Foreign Affairs, 1945–1994*. New Haven, Conn.: Yale University Press, 1995.

Eow, Gregory. "Fighting A New Deal: Classical Liberal Thought in the Depression Years." PhD dissertation, Rice University, 2007.

Evans, M. Stanton. *Blacklisted by History: The Untold Story of Senator Joe McCarthy and His Fight Against America's Enemies*. New York: Crown Forum, 2007.

——. *The Liberal Establishment*. New York: Devin-Adair, 1965.

Evans, Thomas W. *The Education of Ronald Reagan: The General Electric Years and the Untold Story of His Conversion to Conservatism*. New York: Columbia University Press, 2006.

Everitt, David. *A Shadow of Red: Communism and the Blacklist in Radio and Television*. Chicago: Ivan R. Dee, 2007.

Farber, David. *Chicago '68*. Chicago: University of Chicago Press, 1994.

——, ed. *The Sixties: From Memory to History*. Chapel Hill: University of North Carolina Press, 1994.

——. *Taken Hostage: The Iran Hostage Crisis and America's First Encounter with Radical Islam*. Princeton: Princeton University Press, 2006.

Federici, Michael. *The Challenge of Populism: The Rise of Right-Wing Democratism in Postwar America*. Westport, Conn.: Praeger, 1991.

Feulner, Edwin J. Jr. *Intellectual Pilgrims: The Fiftieth Anniversary of the Mont Pelerin Society*. Washington, D.C.: self-published, 1999.

Fine, Sidney. *Laissez-Faire and the General Welfare State: A Study of Conflict in American Thought, 1865–1910*. Ann Arbor: University of Michigan Press, 1956.

Flamm, Michael W. *Law and Order: Street Crime, Civil Unrest, and the Crisis of Liberalism in the 1960s*. New York: Columbia University Press, 2005.

Fleming, Thomas. *The Illusion of Victory: America in World War I*. New York: Basic, 2003.

——. *The New Dealers' War: F. D. R. and the War within World War II*. New York: Basic, 2001.

Flynn, John T. *The Road Ahead: America's Creeping Revolution*. New York: Devin-Adair, 1949.

——. *While You Slept: Our Tragedy in Asia and Who Made It*. New York: Devin-Adair, 1951.

Fones-Wolf, Elizabeth A. *Selling Free Enterprise: The Business Assault on Labor and Liberalism, 1945–1960*. Urbana: University of Illinois Press, 1995.

Francis, Sam. *Shots Fired: Sam Francis on America's Culture War*. Edited by Peter Gemma. Vienna, Va.: FGF Books, 2006.

Francis, Samuel. *Beautiful Losers: Essays on the Failure of American Conservatism.* Columbia: University of Missouri Press, 1993.

Fried, Richard M. *Nightmare in Red: The McCarthy Era in Perspective.* New York: Oxford University Press, 1990.

———. *The Russians Are Coming! The Russians Are Coming! Pageantry and Patriotism in Cold-War America.* New York: Oxford University Press, 1998.

Friedberg, Aaron L. *In the Shadow of the Garrison State: America's Anti-Statism and Its Cold War Grand Strategy.* Princeton: Princeton University Press, 2000.

Friedman, Milton. *Capitalism and Freedom.* Chicag: University of Chicago Press, 1962.

Friedman, Milton, and Rose D. Friedman. *Two Lucky People: Memoirs.* Chicago: University of Chicago Press, 1999.

Friedman, Murray. *The Neoconservative Revolution: Jewish Intellectuals and the Shaping of Public Policy.* Cambridge: Cambridge University Press, 2005.

Frohnen, Bruce, Jeremy Beer, and Jeffrey O. Nelson, eds. *American Conservatism: An Encyclopedia.* Wilmington, Del.: Intercollegiate Studies Institute, 2006.

Frum, David. *Dead Right.* New York: Basic, 1994.

———. *What's Right: The New Conservative Majority and the Remaking of America.* New York: Basic, 1996.

Fukuyama, Francis. *America at the Crossroads: Democracy, Power, and the Neoconservative Legacy.* New Haven, Conn.: Yale University Press, 2006.

———. *The End of History and the Last Man.* New York: Free Press, 1992.

Gaddis, John Lewis. *The Cold War: A New History.* New York: Penguin, 2006.

———. *Strategies of Containment: A Critical Appraisal of American National Security Policy during the Cold War.* Rev. exp. ed. New York: Oxford University Press, 2005.

———. *Surprise, Security, and the American Experience.* Cambridge, Mass.: Harvard University Press, 2004.

———. *The United States and the End of the Cold War: Implications, Reconsiderations, Provocations.* New York: Oxford University Press, 1992.

———. *The United States and the Origins of the Cold War, 1941–1947.* New York: Columbia University Press, 1972.

Garfinkle, Adam. *Telltale Hearts: The Origins and Impact of the Vietnam Anti-War Movement.* New York: Palgrave Macmillan, 1997.

Garrett, Garet. *Defend America First: The Antiwar Editorials of the Saturday Evening Post, 1939–1942.* Edited by Bruce Ramsey. Caldwell, Idaho: Caxton, 2003.

———. *The People's Pottage.* Caldwell, Idaho: Caxton, 1953.

———. *Salvos Against the New Deal: Selections from the Saturday Evening Post, 1933–1940.* Caldwell, Idaho: Caxton, 2002.

Garrow, David. *The FBI and Martin Luther King.* New York: Norton, 1981.

Garthoff, Raymond. *From Détente to Confrontation: American-Soviet Relations from Nixon to Reagan.* Rev. ed. Washington, D.C.: Brookings Institution, 1994.

Gay, Peter. *Modernism: The Lure of Heresy: From Baudelaire to Beckett and Beyond.* New York: Norton, 2008.

Gellman, Irwin. *The Contender: Richard Nixon: the Congress Years, 1946–1952.* New York: Free Press, 2007 ed.

Girdler, Thomas. *Bootstraps*. New York: C. Scribner's and Sons, 1943.

Goldberg, Robert Alan. *Barry Goldwater*. New Haven, Conn.: Yale University Press, 1995.

Goldwater, Barry M. *The Conscience of a Conservative*. Shepherdsville, Ky.: Victor, 1960.

——. *With No Apologies: The Personal and Political Memoirs of Barry Goldwater*. New York: William Morrow, 1979.

Goldwater, Barry M., with Jack Casserly. *Goldwater*. New York: Doubleday, 1988.

Goodman, Walter. *The Committee: The Extraordinary Career of the House Committee on Un-American Activities*. New York: Farrar, Straus & Giroux, 1968.

Gottfried, Paul Edward. *After Liberalism: Mass Democracy and the Managerial State*. Princeton: Princeton University Press, 2001.

——. *Conservatism in America: Making Sense of the American Right*. New York: Palgrave Macmillan, 2007.

——. *Multiculturalism and the Politics of Guilt: Toward a Secular Theocracy*. Columbia: University of Missouri Press, 2002.

——. *The Search for Historical Meaning: Hegel and the Postwar American Right*. DeKalb: Northern Illinois University Press, 1986.

Gottfried, Paul, and Thomas Fleming. *The Conservative Movement*. Boston: Twayne, 1988.

Greene, John Robert. *The Presidency of George H. W. Bush*. Lawrence: University Press of Kansas, 1999.

——. *The Presidency of Gerald Ford*. Lawrence: University Press of Kansas, 1993.

Halper, Stefan, and Jonathan Clarke. *America Alone: The Neo-conservatives and the Global Order*. New York: Cambridge University Press, 2004.

Hamby, Alonzo L. *Beyond the New Deal: Harry Truman and American Liberalism*. New York: Columbia University Press, 1973.

——. *For the Survival of Democracy: Franklin Roosevelt and the World Crisis of the 1930s*. New York: Free Press, 2004.

Hart, Jeffrey. *The Making of the American Conservative Mind: National Review and Its Times*. Wilmington, Del.: Intercollegiate Studies Institute, 2006.

Hartwell, Max. *A History of the Mont Pelerin Society*. Indianapolis: Liberty Fund, 1995.

Hartz, Louis. *The Liberal Tradition in America*. New York: Harcourt, 1955.

Hayek, Friedrich A. *The Constitution of Liberty*. Chicago: University of Chicago Press, 1960.

——. *The Road to Serfdom*. Chicago: University of Chicago Press, 1994. First published 1944.

Haynes, John E. *Red Scare or Red Menace? American Communism and Anticommunism in the Cold War Era*. Chicago: Ivan R. Dee, 1996.

Haynes, John Earl, and Harvey Klehr. *In Denial: Historians, Communism, and Espionage*. San Francisco: Encounter, 2003.

——. *Venona: Decoding Soviet Espionage in America*. New Haven, Conn.: Yale University Press, 1999.

Hayward, Steven F. *The Age of Reagan: The Fall of the Old Liberal Order, 1964–1980*. New York: Prima Lifestyles, 2001.

Heale, M.J. *American Anticommunism: Combating the Enemy Within, 1830–1970.* Baltimore: Johns Hopkins University Press, 1990.

Heineman, Kenneth J. *Campus Wars: The Peace Movement at American State Universities in the Vietnam Era.* New York: New York University Press, 1994.

——. *God Is a Conservative: Religion, Politics, and Morality in Contemporary America.* New York: New York University Press, 1998.

Herman, Arthur. *Joseph McCarthy: Reexamining the Life and Legacy of America's Most Hated Senator.* New York: Free Press, 1999.

Herrnstein, Richard J., and Charles Murray. *The Bell Curve: Intelligence and Class Structure in American Life.* New York: Free Press, 1996.

Himmelstein, Jerome L. *To the Right: The Transformation of American Conservatism.* Berkeley: University of California Press, 1989.

Hodgson, Godfrey. *The World Turned Right Side Up: A History of the Conservative Ascendancy in America.* New York: Houghton Mifflin, 1996.

Hoeveler, J. David Jr. *The New Humanism: A Critique of Modern America, 1900–1940.* Charlottesville: University Press of Virginia, 1977.

——. *Watch on the Right: Conservative Intellectuals in the Reagan Era.* Madison: University of Wisconsin Press, 1991.

Hofstadter, Richard. *The Age of Reform.* New York: Vintage, 1960.

Holtz, William. *Ghost in the Little House: A Biography of Rose Wilder Lane.* Columbia: University of Missouri Press, 1995.

Horowitz, David A. *Beyond Left and Right: Insurgency and the Establishment.* Urbana: University of Illinois Press, 1997.

Isikoff, Michael. *Uncovering Clinton: A Reporter's Story.* New York: Crown, 1999.

Jeansonne, Glen. *Women of the Far Right: The Mothers' Movement and World War II.* Chicago: University of Chicago Press, 1996.

Judis, John B. *William F. Buckley, Jr.: Patron Saint of the Conservatives.* New York: Simon and Schuster, 1990.

Kaufman, Burton I. *The Presidency of James Earl Carter, Jr.* Lawrence: University Press of Kansas, 1993.

Kaufman, Robert G. *Henry M. Jackson: A Life in Politics.* Seattle: University of Washington Press, 2000.

Kazin, Michael. *The Populist Persuasion: An American History.* Ithaca, N.Y.: Cornell University Press, 1998.

Kennedy, David M. *Freedom From Fear: The American People in Depression and War, 1929–1945.* New York: Oxford University Press, 2001.

——. *Over Here: The First World War and American Society.* New York: Oxford University Press, 1980.

Kern, Stephen. *The Culture of Time and Space, 1880–1918.* DeKalb: Northern Illinois University Press, 1986.

Kilpatrick, James Jackson. *The Sovereign States.* Chicago: Regnery Publishing, 1957.

Kimball, Warren. *The Juggler: Franklin Roosevelt as Wartime Statesman.* Princeton: Princeton University Press, 1994.

Kirk, Russell. *The Conservative Mind: From Burke to Santayana.* Chicago: Regnery, 1953.

———. *The Politics of Prudence.* Bryn Mawr, Pa.: Intercollegiate Studies Institute Books, 1996.

———. *Prospects for Conservatives.* Washington, D.C.: Regnery, 1989.

———. *Redeeming the Time.* Wilmington, Del.: Intercollegiate Studies Institute Books, 1996.

———. *The Sword of Imagination: Memoirs of a Half-Century of Literary Conflict.* Grand Rapids, Mich.: Eerdmans, 1995.

Kirkpatrick, Jeane J. *Making War to Keep Peace.* New York: Harper, 2007.

Keller, Morton. *In Defense of Yesterday: James M. Beck and the Politics of Conservatism, 1861–1936.* New York: Coward-McCann, 1958.

Kelley, John L. *Bringing the Market Back In: The Political Revitalization of Market Liberalism.* New York: New York University Press, 1997.

Kelly, Daniel. *James Burnham and the Struggle for the World: A Life.* Wilmington, Del.: Intercollegiate Studies Institute, 2002.

Kengor, Paul. *The Crusader: Ronald Reagan and the Fall of Communism.* New York: Harper Perennial, 2007.

Kengor, Paul, and Peter Schweizer, eds. *The Reagan Presidency: Assessing the Man and His Legacy.* Lanham, Md.: Rowman & Littlefield, 2005.

Klehr, Harvey, John Earl Haynes, and Fridrikh Igorevich Firsov. *The Secret World of American Communism.* New Haven, Conn.: Yale University Press, 1995.

Kristol, Irving. *Neoconservatism: The Autobiography of an Idea: Selected Essays, 1949–1995.* New York: Free Press, 1995.

Kruse, Kevin M. *White Flight: Atlanta and the Making of Modern Conservatism.* Princeton: Princeton University Press, 2005.

Lacey, Michael, ed. *The Truman Presidency.* Cambridge: Cambridge University Press, 1991.

Larson, Edward J. *Summer for the Gods: The Scopes Trial and America's Continuing Debate over Science and Religion.* New York: Basic, 2006.

Lasch, Christopher. *The True and Only Heaven: Progress and Its Critics.* New York: Norton, 1991.

Lassiter, Matthew D. *The Silent Majority: Suburban Politics in the Sunbelt South.* Princeton: Princeton University Press, 2005.

Layman, Geoffrey. *The Great Divide: Religious and Cultural Conflict in American Party Politics.* New York: Columbia University Press, 2001.

Leffler, Melvyn. *A Preponderance of Power: National Security, the Truman Administration, and the Cold War.* Stanford, Calif.: Stanford University Press, 1993.

Lettow, Paul. *Ronald Reagan and His Quest to Abolish Nuclear Weapons.* New York: Random House, 2005.

Liebman, Marvin. *Coming Out Conservative: An Autobiography.* San Francisco: Chronicle, 1992.

Link, William A. *Righteous Warrior: Jesse Helms and the Rise of Modern Conservatism.* New York: St. Martin's, 2008.

Linker, Damon. *The Theocons: Secular America under Siege.* New York: Anchor, 2007 ed.

Lloyd, Gordon, ed. *The Two Faces of Liberalism: How the Hoover–Roosevelt Debate Shapes the 21st Century.* Salem, Mass.: M & M Scrivener, 2007.

Lora, Ronald, and William Henry Longton, eds. *The Conservative Press in Twentieth-Century America.* Westport, Conn.: Greenwood, 1999.

Lowry, Rich. *Legacy: Paying the Price for the Clinton Years.* Washington, D.C.: Regnery, 2003.

Lukacs, John. *Remembered Past: John Lukacs on History, Historians, and Historical Knowledge.* Edited by Mark G. Malvasi and Jeffrey O. Nelson. Wilmington, Del.: Intercollegiate Studies Institute, 2005.

McAllister, Ted V. *Revolt against Modernity: Leo Strauss, Eric Voegelin, and the Search for a Postliberal Order.* Lawrence: University Press of Kansas, 1996.

McCloskey, Robert Green. *American Conservatism in the Age of Enterprise, 1865–1910.* Cambridge, Mass.: Harvard University Press, 1951.

McDonald, W. Wesley. *Russell Kirk and the Age of Ideology.* Columbia: University of Missouri Press, 2004.

McGerr, Michael. *A Fierce Discontent: The Rise and Fall of the Progressive Movement in America, 1870–1920.* New York: Free Press, 2003.

McGirr, Lisa. *Suburban Warriors: The Origins of the New American Right.* Princeton: Princeton University Press, 2001.

Mann, James. *Rise of the Vulcans: The History of Bush's War Cabinet.* New York: Penguin, 2004.

Marlin, George J. *The American Catholic Voter: 200 Years of Political Impact.* South Bend, Ind.: St. Augustine's, 2004.

Martin, William. *With God on Our Side: The Rise of the Religious Right in America.* New York: Broadway, 1996.

Matusow, Allen J. *The Unraveling of America: A History of Liberalism in the 1960s.* New York: Perennial, 1985.

Mencken, H. L. *A Mencken Chrestomathy.* New York: Vintage, 1982 ed.

———. *Notes On Democracy.* New York: Knopf, 1926.

Meyer, Frank S. *In Defense of Freedom: A Conservative Credo.* Washington, D.C.: Regnery, 1962.

———. *In Defense of Freedom and Related Essays.* Indianapolis: Liberty Fund, 1996.

———, ed. *What Is Conservatism?* Chicago: Regnery Publishing, 1964.

Micklethwait, John, and Adrian Wooldridge. *The Right Nation: Conservative Power in America.* New York: Penguin, 2004.

Middendorf, J. William II. *A Glorious Disaster: Barry Goldwater's Presidential Campaign and the Origins of the Conservative Movement.* New York: Basic, 2006.

Miles, Michael. *The Odyssey of the American Right.* New York: Oxford University Press, 1980.

Miscamble, Wilson. *From Roosevelt to Truman: Potsdam, Hiroshima, and the Cold War.* Cambridge: Cambridge University Press, 2006.

Moley, Raymond. *After Seven Years.* New York: Harper, 1939.

Morgan, Dan. *Rising in the West: The True Story of an Okie Family from the Great Depression through the Reagan Years.* New York: Knopf, 1992.

Morley, Felix. *For the Record.* Washington, D.C.: Regnery, 1979.

Moser, John E. *Right Turn: John T. Flynn and the Transformation of American Liberalism.* New York: New York University Press, 2005.

Murphy, Paul V. *The Rebuke of History: The Southern Agrarians and American Conservative Thought.* Chapel Hill: University of North Carolina Press, 2001.

Murray, Charles. *Losing Ground: American Social Policy, 1950–1980.* New York: Basic, 1984.

Nasaw, David. *Andrew Carnegie.* New York: Penguin, 2006.

Nash, George H. *The Conservative Intellectual Movement in America: Since 1945.* 2nd ed. Wilmington, Del.: Intercollegiate Studies Institute, 1996.

———. *The Conservative Intellectual Movement in America: Since 1945.* 3rd ed. Wilmington, Del.: Intercollegiate Studies Institute, 2006.

Niskanen, William A. *Reaganomics: An Insider's Account of the Policies and the People.* New York: Oxford University Press, 1988.

Nock, Albert Jay. *Memoirs of a Superfluous Man.* Tampa, Fla.: Hallberg Publishing, 1994 ed.

———. *Our Enemy the State.* San Francisco: Fox and Wilkes Books, 1994. First published 1935.

———. *The State of the Union: Essays in Social Criticism.* Edited by Charles H. Hamilton. Indianapolis: Liberty Fund, 1991.

Oberdorfer, Don. *From the Cold War to a New Era: The United States and the Soviet Union, 1983–1991.* Baltimore: Johns Hopkins University Press, 1998 ed.

Olasky, Marvin. *Compassionate Conservatism: What It Is, What It Does, and How It Can Transform America.* New York: Simon and Schuster, 2000.

O'Reilly, Kenneth. *"Racial Matters": The FBI's Secret War on Black America, 1960–1972.* New York: Free Press, 1991.

Ortega, Jose y Gasset. *The Revolt of the Masses.* New York: Norton, 1932.

Oshinsky, David. *A Conspiracy So Immense: The World of Joe McCarthy.* New York: Oxford University Press, 2005 ed.

O'Sullivan, John. *The President, the Pope, and the Prime Minister: Three Who Changed the World.* Washington, D.C.: Regnery, 2006.

Panero, James, and Stefan Beck. *The* Dartmouth Review *Pleads Innocent: Twenty-Five Years of Being Threatened, Impugned, Vandalized, Sued, Suspended, and Bitten at the Ivy League's Most Controversial Conservative Newspaper.* Wilmington, Del.: Intercollegiate Studies Institute, 2006.

Panichas, George. *The Critical Legacy of Irving Babbitt.* Wilmington, Del.: Intercollegiate Studies Institute, 1999.

———, ed. *The Essential Russell Kirk: Selected Essays.* Wilmington, Del.: Intercollegiate Studies Institute, 2006.

Patterson, James T. *Congressional Conservatism and the New Deal: The Growth of the Conservative Coalition in Congress, 1933–1939.* Lexington: University of Kentucky Press, 1967.

———. *Mr. Republican: A Biography of Robert A. Taft.* Boston: Houghton Mifflin, 1972.

Perlstein, Rick. *Before the Storm: Barry Goldwater and the Unmaking of the American Consensus.* New York: Hill and Wang, 2001.

———. *Nixonland: The Rise of a President and the Fracturing of America.* New York: Scribner, 2008.

Person, James E., Jr. *Russell Kirk: A Critical Biography of a Conservative Mind.* Lanham, Md.: Madison Books, 1999.

Phillips, Kevin P. *The Emerging Republican Majority.* New Rochelle, N.Y.: Arlington House, 1969.

Piereson, James. *Camelot and the Cultural Revolution: How the Assassination of John F. Kennedy Shattered American Liberalism.* San Francisco: Encounter, 2007.

Podhoretz, John. *Hell of a Ride: Backstage at the White House Follies, 1989–1993.* New York: Simon & Schuster, 1993.

Podhoretz, Norman. *Breaking Ranks: A Political Memoir.* New York: Harper & Row, 1979.

———. *Making It.* New York: Random House, 1967.

———. *My Love Affair with America: The Cautionary Tale of a Cheerful Conservative.* New York: Free Press, 2000.

———. "Reagan's Road to Détente." *Foreign Affairs: America and the World, 1984* (Winter 1985): 446–64.

Powell, Jim. *FDR's Folly: How Roosevelt and His New Deal Prolonged the Great Depression.* New York: Crown Forum, 2003.

Powers, Richard Gid. *Not Without Honor: The History of American Anticommunism.* New York: Free Press, 1996.

Radosh, Ronald. *Prophets on the Right: Profiles of Conservative Critics of American Globalism.* New York: Simon & Schuster, 1975.

Radosh, Ronald, and Allis Radosh. *Red Star over Hollywood: The Film Colony's Long Romance with the Left.* San Francisco: Encounter, 2003.

Raimando, Justin. *An Enemy of the State: The Life of Murray N. Rothbard.* Amherst, N.Y.: Prometheus, 2000.

———. *Reclaiming the American Right: The Lost Legacy of the Conservative Movement.* Burlingame, Calif.: Center for Libertarian Studies, 1993.

Rand, Ayn. *Atlas Shrugged.* New York: Random House, 1957.

Reagan, Ronald. *An American Life: The Autobiography.* New York: Simon & Schuster, 1990.

———. *The Reagan Diaries.* Edited by Douglas Brinkley. New York: HarperCollins, 2007.

Regnery, Alfred S. *Upstream: The Ascendance of American Conservatism.* New York: Threshold, 2008.

Regnery, Henry. *A Few Reasonable Words: Selected Writings.* Wilmington, Del.: Intercollegiate Studies Institute, 1996.

———. *Memoirs of a Dissident Publisher.* Chicago: Regnery Publishing, 1985.

———. *Perfect Sowing: Reflections of a Bookman.* Wilmington, Del.: Intercollegiate Studies Institute, 1999.

Ribuffo, Leo P. *The Old Christian Right: The Protestant Far Right from the Great Depression to the Cold War.* Philadelphia: Temple University Press, 1983.

Roberts, Paul Craig. *The Supply-Side Revolution: An Insider's Account of Policymaking in Washington.* Cambridge, Mass.: Harvard University Press, 1984.

Rodgers, Marion Elizabeth. *Mencken: The American Iconoclast.* New York: Oxford University Press, 2005.

Romerstein, Herbert, and Eric Breindel. *The Venona Secrets: Exposing Soviet Espionage and America's Traitors.* Washington, D.C.: Regnery, 2000.

Rorabaugh, William. *Berkeley at War: The 1960s.* New York: Oxford University Press, 1990.

Rossiter, Clinton. *Conservatism in America.* 2nd ed. Cambridge, Mass.: Harvard University Press, 1962.

Rothbard, Murray N. *For a New Liberty: The Libertarian Manifesto.* New York: Collier, 1978 ed.

Rusher, William A. *The Making of a New Majority Party.* Ottawa, Ill.: Sheed & Ward 1975.

———. *The Rise of the Right.* New York: Morrow, 1984.

Russello, Gerald J. *The Postmodern Imagination of Russell Kirk.* Columbia: University of Missouri Press, 2007.

Ryant, Carl. *Profit's Prophet: Garet Garrett (1878–1954).* Selingsgrove, N.Y.: Susquehanna University Press, 1989.

Rymph, Catherine E. *Republican Women: Feminism and Conservatism from Suffrage through the Rise of the New Right.* Chapel Hill: University of North Carolina Press, 2006.

Ryn, Claes G. *America the Virtuous: The Crisis of Democracy and the Quest for Empire.* New Brunswick, N.J.: Transaction, 2003.

Sandbrook, Dominic. *Eugene McCarthy and the Rise and Fall of Postwar American Liberalism.* New York: Knopf, 2004.

Schlafly, Phyllis. *A Choice Not an Echo.* Alton, Ill.: Pere Marquette, 1964.

———. *Feminist Fantasies.* Dallas: Spence, 2003.

Schneider, Gregory L. *Cadres for Conservatism: Young Americans for Freedom and the Rise of the Contemporary Right.* New York: New York University Press, 1998.

———, ed. *Conservatism in America since 1930: A Reader.* New York: New York University Press, 2003.

———, ed. *Equality, Decadence, and Modernity: The Collected Essays of Stephen J. Tonsor.* Wilmington, Del.: Intercollegiate Studies Institute, 2005.

Schoenwald, Jonathan M. *A Time For Choosing: The Rise of Modern American Conservatism.* New York: Oxford University Press, 2001.

Schulman, Bruce J. *The Seventies: The Great Shift in American Culture, Society, and Politics.* New York: Free Press, 2001.

Schulman, Bruce J., and Julian Zelizer, eds. *Rightward Bound: Making America Conservative in the 1970s.* Cambridge, Mass.: Harvard University Press, 2008.

Schuparra, Jurt. *Triumph of the Right: The Rise of the California Conservative Movement, 1945–1966.* Armonk, N.Y.: Sharpe, 1998.

Schwarz, Fred. *Beating the Unbeatable Foe: One Man's Victory over Communism, Leviathan, and the Last Enemy.* Washington, D.C.: Regnery, 1996.

Schweizer, Peter. *Reagan's War: The Epic Story of His Forty-Year Struggle and Triumph over Communism.* New York: Doubleday, 2002.

Scotchie, Joseph. *Barbarians in the Saddle: An Intellectual Biography of Richard Weaver.* New Brunswick, N.J.: Transaction, 1997.

———. *The Paleoconservatives: New Voices of the Old Right.* New Brunswick, N.J.: Transaction, 1999.

Self, Robert O. *American Babylon: Race and the Struggle for Postwar Oakland.* Princeton: Princeton University Press, 2003.

Shafer Byron E., and Richard Johnston. *The End of Southern Exceptionalism: Class, Race, and Partisan Change in the Postwar South.* Cambridge, Mass.: Harvard University Press, 2006.

Shirley, Craig. *Reagan's Revolution: The Untold Story of the Campaign that Started It All.* Nashville, Tenn.: Thomas Nelson, 2005.

Shlaes, Amity. *The Forgotten Man: A New History of the Great Depression.* New York: HarperCollins, 2007.

Shogan, Robert. *Backlash: The Killing of the New Deal.* Chicago: Ivan R. Dee, 2006.

Shultz, George P. *Turmoil and Triumph: My Years as Secretary of State.* New York: Scribner, 1993.

Simonelli, Frederick J. *American Fuehrer: George Lincoln Rockwell and the American Nazi Party.* Urbana: University of Illinois Press, 1999.

Skinner, Kiron K., Annelise Anderson, and Martin Anderson, eds. *Reagan in His Own Hand: The Writings of Ronald Reagan that Reveal His Revolutionary Vision for America.* New York: Free Press, 2001.

Sloan, John W. *The Reagan Effect: Economics and Presidential Leadership.* Lawrence: University Press of Kansas, 1999.

Small, Mevin. *The Presidency of Richard M. Nixon.* Lawrence: University Press of Kansas, 2003.

Smant, Kevin J. *Principles and Heresies: Frank S. Meyer and the Shaping of the American Conservative Movement.* Wilmington, Del.: Intercollegiate Studies Institute, 2002.

Smith, James Allen. *The Idea Brokers: Think Tanks and the Rise of the New Policy Elite.* New York: Free Press, 1990.

Smith, Mark A. *The Right Talk: How Conservatives Transformed the Great Society into the Economic Society.* Princeton: Princeton University Press, 2007.

Smith, Richard Norton. *The Colonel: The Life and Legend of Robert R. McCormick, 1880–1955.* New York: Houghton Mifflin, 1997.

Smith, Ted III. *In Defense of Tradition: Collected Short Writings of Richard M. Weaver, 1929–1963.* Indianapolis: Liberty Fund, 2000.

———, ed. *Steps Towards Restoration: The Consequences of Richard Weaver's Ideas.* Wilmington, Del.: Intercollegiate Studies Institute, 1998.

Spencer, Herbert. *The Man Versus the State.* Indianapolis: Liberty Fund, 1982 ed.

Steinfels, Peter. *The Neoconservatives: The Men Who Are Changing America's Politics.* New York: Touchstone, 1980.

Stephanopolous, George. *All Too Human: A Political Education.* New York: Back Bay, 2000.

Stockman, David A. *The Triumph of Politics: The Inside Story of the Reagan Revolution.* New York: Avon, 1987.

Stone, Albert R., Jr. "Seward Collins and the *American Review*: Experiment in Profascism, 1933–1937." *American Quarterly* 12, no. 1 (Spring 1960): 3–19.

Strausz-Hupe, Robert, William R. Kinter, and Stefan T. Possony. *A Forward Strategy for America*. New York: Harper, 1961.

Sugrue, Thomas. *The Origins of the Urban Crisis: Race and Inequality in Postwar Detroit*. Princeton: Princeton University Press, 1994.

Sumner, William Graham. *On Liberty, Society, and Politics: The Essential Essays of William Graham Sumner*. Edited by Robert C. Bannister. Indianapolis: Liberty Fund, 1992.

Suri, Jeremi. *Power and Protest: Global Revolution and the Rise of Détente*. Cambridge, Mass.: Harvard University Press, 2003.

Taft, Robert A. *A Foreign Policy for Americans*. New York: Doubleday, 1951.

Tanenhaus, Sam. *Whittaker Chambers: A Biography*. New York: Random House, 1997.

Teachout, Terry. *The Skeptic: A Life of H. L. Mencken*. New York: HarperCollins, 2002.

Teles, Steven M. *The Rise of the Conservative Legal Movement: The Battle for the Control of the Law*. Princeton: Princeton University Press, 2008.

Thomas, Clarence. *My Grandfather's Son: A Memoir*. New York: Harper, 2007.

Toplin, Robert Brent. *Radical Conservatism: The Right's Political Religion*. Lawrence: University Press of Kansas, 2006.

Trilling, Lionel. *The Liberal Imagination: Essays on Literature and Society*. New York: Viking, 1950.

Tuccille, Jerome. *It Usually Begins with Ayn Rand*. New York: Stein and Day, 1971.

Twelve Southerners. *I'll Take My Stand: The South and the Agrarian Tradition*. Baton Rouge: Louisiana State University Press, 1977. First published 1930.

Tyrrell, Jr., R. Emmett. *The Conservative Crack-Up*. New York: Summit, 1992.

Van Mises, Ludwig, *Liberalism: The Classical Tradition*. Indianapolis: Liberty Fund, 2005.

Viguerie, Richard A. *The Establishment vs. the People: Is a New Populist Revolt on the Way?* Chicago: Regnery Gateway, 1983.

——. *The New Right: We're Ready to Lead*. Falls Church, Va.: Viguerie 1980.

Viguerie, Richard A., and David Franke. *America's Right Turn: How Conservatives Used New and Alternative Media to Take Power*. Chicago: Bonus Books, 2004.

Waddell, Brian. *The War Against the New Deal: World War II and American Democracy*. DeKalb: Northern Illinois University Press, 2001.

Wattenberg, Ben. *The First Universal Nation: Leading Indicators and Ideas about the Surge of America in the 1990s*. New York: Free Press, 1991.

Weaver, Richard M. *Ideas Have Consequences*. Chicago: University of Chicago Press, 1948.

——. *The Southern Tradition at Bay: A History of Postbellum Thought*. New Rochelle, N.Y.: Arlington House, 1968.

——. "Up From Liberalism." *Modern Age* (Winter 1958–1959): 21–32.

Weinstein, Allen. *Perjury: The Hiss-Chambers Case*. New York: Vintage Books, 1979.

Weinstein, Allen, and Alexander Vassiliev. *The Haunted Wood: Soviet Espionage in America—The Stalin Era*. New York: Random House, 1998.

Welch, Robert. *The Blue Book of the John Birch Society.* Belmont, Mass: Western Island Publishers, 1959.

——. *The Politician.* Belmont, Mass.: Western Island Publishers, 1963.

Wells, Tom. *The War Within: America's Battle over Vietnam.* Berkeley: University of California Press, 1994.

Whitaker, Robert W., ed. *The New Right Papers.* New York: St. Martin's, 1982.

White, F. Clifton, with William J. Gill. *Suite 3505: The Story of the Draft Goldwater Movement.* New Rochelle, N.Y.: Arlington House, 1967.

White, Theodore H. *The Making of the President: 1964.* New York: Atheneum, 1965.

Wilentz, Sean. *The Age of Reagan: A History, 1974–2008.* New York: Harper, 2008.

Will, George F. *Suddenly: The American Ideal at Home and Abroad, 1986–1990.* New York: Free Press, 1990.

Wilson, Clyde N., ed. *A Defender of Southern Conservatism: M. E. Bradford and His Achievements.* Columbia: University of Missouri Press, 1999.

Wiltz, John E. *From Isolation to War, 1931–1941.* New York: Thomas Y. Crowell, 1968.

Witcover, Jules. *Strange Bedfellows: The Short and Unhappy Marriage of Richard Nixon and Spiro Agnew.* New York: PublicAffairs, 2007.

Wolfskill, George. *Revolt of the Conservatives: The American Liberty League, 1934–1937.* New York: Houghton Mifflin, 1962.

Woods, Jeff. *Black Struggle and Red Scare: Segregation and Anti-Communism in the South, 1948–1968.* Baton Rouge: Louisiana State University Press, 2003.

Wright, Lawrence. *The Looming Tower: Al-Qaeda and the Road to 9/11.* New York: Knopf, 2006.

Wriston, Henry M. *Challenge to Freedom.* New York: Harper, 1943.

Yergin, Daniel, and Joseph Stanislaw. *The Commanding Heights: The Battle for the World Economy.* New York: Free Press, 2002.

Young, Fred D. *Richard M. Weaver, 1910–1963: A Life of the Mind.* Columbia: University of Missouri Press, 1995.

Index

About the Author

Gregory L. Schneider is an associate professor of American history at Emporia State University. He is the author or editor of three books and serves as a senior fellow with the Flint Hills Center for Public Policy.